CONSTRUCTING SOCIAL THEORIES

Constructing
Social
Theories

Arthur L. Stinchcombe

The University of Chicago Press

Chicago and London

The University of Chicago Press, Chicago 60637
The University of Chicago Press, Ltd., London

© 1968 by Arthur L. Stinchcombe
All rights reserved. Published 1968
University of Chicago Press edition 1987
Printed in the United States of America

96 95 94 93 92 91   5 4 3

Library of Congress Cataloging in Publication Data
Stinchcombe, Arthur L.
   Constructing social theories.

   Reprint. Originally published: New York: Harcourt,
Brace & World, c1968.
   Includes bibliographical references and index.
   1. Sociology—Methodology.   I. Title.
HM24.S76   1987   301'.01   87-5080
ISBN 0-226-77484-8 (pbk.)

Preface

In my first year of graduate-school, I turned in a paper to Reinhard Bendix called "Rhetorical Opportunities in Some Theories of Social Change." After some discussion of the substance of the paper, he made a comment that has shaped my attitude toward "theory." He said, "You know, a little bit of theory goes a long way." He went on to say I ought to decide what phenomena I wanted to explain.

A second graduate-school conversation, with Philip Selznick, shaped my attitude toward what theory is for. He remarked that one felt satisfied that he understood something when he could summarize in a sentence the guts of a phenomenon. He gave the illustration that he felt satisfied when he realized that the achievement of the Bolshevik parties was "to turn a voluntary association into an administrative apparatus." To use, as a criterion of judgment, the guts of the phenomenon—what is going on—is better than to use any logical or formal criterion.

If nevertheless I have decided to write a book on the logic of theory construction, it is because people sometimes do worse empirical work than they might because they are confused by logical and philosophical difficulties. People do actually fail to do the sensible thing because they think it implies some "assumption" that they are unwilling to make, or because they think a particular form of argument is associated logically with some unacceptable general world view. There is a good deal of nonsense talked in the social sciences about "assumptions," "approaches," "*sui generis*," "operational definition," and the like. Mostly this nonsense does not interfere with the work of the discipline, but this is because exceptional men trust their intuition rather than their logical and philosophical prejudices.

If, as Abraham Flexner once commented, the greatness of a research enterprise depends on the use it makes of its mediocre men, then explicit analysis of the logical form of the intuition of exceptional men may decrease our dependence on genius. The purpose of this book is similar to that of a calculus text: to enable sophomores to do what once strained Newton's powers.

Talcott Parsons maintained in his *Structure of Social Action* that his was an "inductive" work, in which he tried to identify the common features of the work of great sociological theorists so that the rest of us could go and do likewise. This book is "inductive" in the same sense, though it is more concerned with the logical form of argument than with the substantive conclusions, and with the details of particular explanations than with overall theoretical structures. But "induction" in the domain of theory depends on the selection of materials to analyze. Knowing how the man on the street theorizes about social phenomena is sociologically important in explaining his behavior, but it is not useful in training people to become theorists. My main debts are to those theorists I have known, either through their writing or close up, whom I thought sufficiently worth imitating to try to figure out what made them so great.

I have had the good fortune of watching two great contemporary theorists at work from close up, James S. Coleman and Otis Dudley Duncan. Both do empirical work and are mathematically competent, which disqualifies them from playing that social role in the discipline which is called "theorist." But the proportion of new explanations of social phenomena due to these two men is very large, and this creativity definition of what a theorist is, is preferable to defining him by his incompetence at empirical work.

When I talk about Coleman and Duncan's "new" explanations, I naturally define the newness in terms of my own intellectual biography. I consider what I learned in graduate school as "what we already knew." Surprisingly few people already knew it. Although subjectively it seems queer to me to acknowledge that I learned "new" things in school, I evidently learned a good deal that was new to people not at Berkeley. Knowing that real people wrote such books as Philip Selznick's *Organizational Weapon,* Reinhard Bendix's *Work and Authority in Industry,* and S. M. Lipset, Martin Trow, and James S. Coleman's *Union Democracy* has decisively shaped my conception of what kind of thinking is worth imitating. It has shaped my judgment of what good argument is and hence provided me with criteria to tell when my job of explicating logic was done. There are many explications of the logic of social theorizing which analyze arguments no serious student of society would bother to make.

Finally, my ideals of what explanations are worth analyzing are shaped by my tastes in classical theorists. I have preferred Max Weber to all others, with Emile Durkheim, Karl Marx, and Leon Trotsky behind Weber at an equal distance. One of the chief disappointments of my intellectual life is never having been able to sell Trotsky as anything but a lesser Marxist. Robert K. Merton was another classical writer who ranked with Durkheim, Marx, and Trotsky in my earlier intellectual life. I have been a bit bewildered by his becoming a contemporary as I grow older.

My wife, unlike most wives who appear in prefaces, has been alternately a hindrance and a help, impatient and patient, destructive and supportive of the enterprise. I would not have married the Griselda that most authors evidently marry.

ARTHUR L. STINCHCOMBE

Contents

CHAPTER FIVE
THE CONCEPTUALIZATION OF ENVIRONMENTAL EFFECTS   201

CHAPTER SIX
CONCEPTS ABOUT THE STRUCTURE OF ACTIVITIES   233

CONSTRUCTING SOCIAL THEORIES

CHAPTER ONE

Introduction

This book is based on a conception of the scientific tasks of theory in social explanation. Theory ought to create the *capacity to invent explanations*. During the course of research in a particular substantive area, a sociologist is ordinarily confronted with phenomena for which there are no theories. His job (at least at the current stage of development of sociology) is primarily to invent theories, and only secondarily to test them. But theories ought not to be invented in the abstract by conceptual specialists; they should be adequate to the tasks of explanation posed by the data.

I believe a variety of theoretical strategies were used by those great empirical analysts whom we admire for their contributions to theory. Max Weber, Karl Marx, or Emile Durkheim did not work mainly at what we now call "theory." Instead, they worked out explanations of the growth of capitalism, or of class conflict, or of primitive religion. In doing so, they used a wide variety of theoretical methods.

The usefulness of these theorists for contemporary sociologists comes not so much from their particular explanations. Usually we can now do better than they did, because the empirical basis for their explanations has been tested and found wanting. Instead, their usefulness is in showing us how a great mind works when he wants to explain a social phenomenon.

I have tried to extract the bare logical form of a variety of theoretical strategies. Sometimes one of these strategies works, sometimes another. Constructing theories of social phenomena is done best by those who have a variety of theoretical strategies to try out.

Thus I conceive of the purpose of this book to be that of providing alternative strategies in constructing theories of social phenomena. The crucial question to ask of a strategy is not whether it is true, but whether it is sometimes useful. I have a firm conviction that some things are to be explained one way, some another. Trying to explain a phenomenon by a strategy inappropriate to the empirical terrain, because one thinks that a strategy is a "theory" which must be either true or false, leads into ambushes. Some things are to be explained by personality dynamics, some things by their consequences, and some things by ecological causes. Some personality theories are true, some functional theories are true, and some ecological theories are true. Which kind is true of a particular phenomenon is a matter for investigation, not for debate among "theorists."

Thus the point of view of this book is deliberately eclectic. The reader will find no cases of one "approach" contradicting or conflicting with another "approach." If one approach does not work for explaining a particular phenomenon, the theorist should try another. He ought to be trained to be so good at the various approaches that he is never at a loss for alternative explanations.

The Status of Explanations Proposed

The main task this book sets itself is to lay out the underlying logical structure of various theoretical strategies which are commonly useful in explaining social phenomena. In each case I have tried to give sufficient examples of explanations using a given logical structure to show its working applicability. In many cases, these examples are ones I have invented for the purpose. There are two reasons for this.

One is that an argument about practical methods for constructing social theories is a pretty poor show if it cannot construct any. If the logical strategies outlined are useful in constructing social explanations, then I as well as the reader ought to be able to use them.

The second reason is the excitement that comes from a new view of things. What makes explaining a social phenomenon worthwhile for me is not that it can be reduced to some general logical skeleton, but that the skeleton carries beautiful empirical flesh. Social theories are applied logical forms. The form has its own beauty, which is why mathematics is esthetically gratifying. But I chose to be a sociologist rather than a mathematician for good and sufficient motives. In short, many of the examples are mine because I like them, and I hope the reader will, too.

Given the basic purpose of the book, to teach logical strategies in theory construction, the truth of particular explanations is a secondary consideration. So as not to confuse and offend the reader, and to convince him of the usefulness of the strategies, I have generally preferred explanations that I thought basically sound. No doubt many of them, if they stimulate empirical work, will turn out not to have been sound.

Occasionally I have used explanations that I believe to be defective. For instance, I think Marx's theory of the social causes of parliamentary democracy outlined in Chapter Three is on the wrong track, though there is an element of truth in it. I have used such explanations because they exemplify particularly well a certain theoretical strategy.

Empirical Derivations from Explanations

The reason for having theories of social phenomena is to explain the pattern in observations of the world. I believe it incumbent on a book on social theory that it show how to derive empirical results from theories. If the concepts in a theory are so vague that it is difficult to find corresponding observations, they are unlikely to be useful in illuminating the pattern in observations. That is, a theory to be useful must be specific enough that it might be disproved.

In the course of giving examples of social explanations, I have therefore made a great many statements about the real world, about the facts. These involve both the theories and the observational statements about how the causal forces involved are manifested in the real world. If many of the theories developed here are sure to turn out to be false, even more of the empirical statements will. For there is an additional source of error in guessing that a specific theoretical concept is well represented by a particular observation.

For example, in Chapter Five there are some arguments about the military conditions under which political borders are likely to be also cultural borders. Although I think that cultural borders are mainly determined by certain characteristics of the political situation near borders, and that these aspects of the political situation are mainly determined by military considerations, there may be some other crucial determinants of cultural borders which overwhelm these effects. In that case, the military analysis might be perfectly correct, but the indicator of political effects (namely cultural borders) may be too impure to reflect the true military situation.

Given the purpose of showing how empirical derivations can be obtained from many different theories, I am inevitably drawn into making statements about the world in substantive fields in which I am massively ignorant. But for a social theorist ignorance is more excusable than vagueness. Other investigators can easily show that I am wrong if I am sufficiently precise. They will have much more difficulty showing by investigation what, precisely, I mean if I am vague. I hope not to be forced to weasel out with, "But I didn't really mean that." Social theorists should prefer to be wrong rather than misunderstood. Being misunderstood shows sloppy theoretical work.

Thus I make no apology for the false statements about the world which are sure to be found here.

The Development of the Book

Given this general purpose, the book is organized in levels of increasing intuitive difficulty. We start in Chapter Two with the simplest theoretical structures in common use in social explanation, theories of the form: "A variation in x causes a variation in y." The variables x and y are conceived to correspond directly to observations, so that a variation in an observed phenomenon corresponds to a variation in a causal force, x, and another observed variation corresponds to a variation in an effect, y. There are usually many observable variations in phenomena which correspond to variations in the supposed causal forces and effects. We will treat the numerous patterns of observations which can be derived from such a simple causal theory.

We will also use these simple theories, and their close relatives, to outline the basic logic of "testing" theories by use of observations. One tests theories comparing empirical derivations from the theories to observations. But some observational consequences of a theory are more useful than others as a test. Some consequences of a theory are also consequences of many other theories. If these are true, they increase the credibility of many theories a little. Those consequences which are very unlikely under other theories, if confirmed by observations, increase the credibility of a theory from which they can be derived by a great deal.

The formal logic of such testing, as developed by Polya,[1] will be presented and exemplified with sociological examples. In particular we will discuss the theoretical function of statistical tests.

In Chapter Three we will consider the logical structure of more complex causal structures. First, we will take up a two-component logical structure, "demographic" theories. These have two basic causal components, one which determines the *number of people* of a certain kind, and another which determines a *"proportionality factor"* which is applied to these numbers of people to obtain a measure of the total causal force. These proportionality factors include *rates* (*e.g.,* birth rates), *quantities* (*e.g.,* productivities), and *proportions* (*e.g.,* proportion Democratic in the electorate).

Then we will consider an especially important kind of three-element causal structure, "functional" theories. These involve causal connections between *structures, consequences* of those structures, and *tensions* which tend to disturb those consequences. Because of a causal loop by which consequences tend to reinforce or select structures which have favorable results, consequences play a peculiarly important role in the overall causal structure.

[1] Georgi W. Polya, *Patterns of Plausible Inference,* Vol. 2 of *Mathematics and Plausible Reasoning* (Princeton, N.J.: Princeton University Press, 1954).

After treating the basic form of functional theory, we will treat the variant Marxian form. This involves taking into account the *power* of different groups for which a structure has differential consequences.

Finally we will treat various simple forms of causal structures of an infinite character. Many social phenomena tend to be causes of themselves—once established, they tend to maintain themselves. This gives rise to an infinite self-replicating causal loop, which preserves social effects of historical causes. We will consider why functional, institutional, and resource-using phenomena tend to regenerate themselves. This analysis gives rise to predictions about which traditional patterns will tend to be preserved, and which will tend to change. In an appendix we treat a form of mathematics particularly convenient for treating functional and "historicist" explanatory structures.

In Chapters Four, Five, and Six we turn to strategies of concept formation. That is, Chapters Two and Three concern the logical form of *relations* between conceptual variables. In these earlier chapters, the conceptual variables have names like "x," "y," "structure," "homeostatic variable," "tension," and so on. But for variables to have clean and economical relations to each other, they have to be defined properly. If a conceptual variable really has eight or ten distinct causal components (as, for instance, "social class" has), then its relations to other variables will be shifting and messy. Structural variables representing a single causal force are difficult for many people to construct, because people's intuition tends to run in psychological ruts.

The first set of logical strategies for concept construction that we will consider has to do with the relation of *power* to social activities. By the power of an individual (or other decision unit) we mean the amount of difference his decision can make in some aspect of social activity. If the social activity is entirely determined by forces outside his decision, then he has no power over it. If all aspects of the social activity can be determined by his decision, he has total power over it.[2]

---

[2] This conception of power is equivalent to that of Robert A. Dahl, "The Concept of Power," *Behavioral Science*, Vol. 2 (July, 1957), pp. 201–15, except that Dahl restricts attention to the probability of obedience in a binary choice situation.

After a brief introduction to the general concept of power, we will turn to the concept of *legitimacy*. Doctrines of legitimacy both reinforce and limit power by specifying the conditions under which an exercise of power can be backed up by other centers of power. I have the power to use my house as I see fit if I can call on the government to prevent interference. As a policeman, I can exercise the power of arrest if I can call on other policemen to back me up. The doctrine of privacy which legitimates my control of my house, or the criminal law which legitimates my arresting someone, specifies when I can call on the aid of others. This illustrates the strategy of concept formation of a type in which a *chain of contingent activities* by different people determines a phenomenon. Characteristics of the chain (*e.g.*, doctrines of legitimacy specifying contingencies) influence the elements of the chain (*e.g.*, exercise of power).

A second conception of power phenomena relates power to *information* and illustrates the application of certain cybernetic notions to social phenomena. Power can be exercised over the behavior of another person only if that person can find out what the power-holder wants and only if the power-holder can find out what the person is doing. The amount of control by a power-holder can be only as great as the capacity of the two-way communications channels between him and the person. This is why *authority* (regular wielding of power) and *administration* (regular processing of information) are so closely related empirically. Variables determining the capacity of communications channels thus determine the structure of authority and its effectiveness.

Then we will treat the concept of *political access*. Many times the radicalism of a group is thought to be determined by the fact that it is "politically isolated" and cannot influence policy. We will show how this concept can be formed from a conception of a chain of communication of demands (*e.g.*, voter to congressman, congressman to congressional majority, majority to the executive branch). Political access is the product of the probabilities that a demand will pass through each of the links in the channel.

Then we will treat the concept of *institutions*. Institutions are concentrations of power in the service of some value. A correlation between power and commitment to a certain value is thus the defining characteristic of an institution and determines its causal impact on social life.

In the final section of Chapter Four, we treat the interrelation between power structures of society as a whole and the formation of organizations to carry out large-scale projects. This treatment illustrates the strategy of forming a *feasible set* of coalitions: those coalitions which could carry out the project or create the organization, as a preliminary to studying which coalitions actually do.

This series of strategies for analyzing power phenomena illustrates the eclectic nature of the book. Rather than focusing on what power "really is" and its general causes and effects, we are interested in formulating causal components of social phenomena involving power. For some power phenomena, the variable of legitimacy (whether it will be backed up if necessary) is the main causal force. For some others, the variable of whether or not the power-holder can communicate effectively with the person he is trying to influence is critical. For others, the pattern of legitimate influence on policy decisions determines political reactions of the population. For still others, the crucial question is the correlation between power and value commitments in institutions. For forming new organizations with specific purposes, the distribution of the specific powers needed to carry out the project is critical.

These various strategies of concept construction ought to be chosen on the ground of whether they fit one's conceptions of the causal forces in the observations. There is no general theoretical ground for deciding that the crucial thing about power is, for instance, its legitimacy. Perhaps that is crucial in explaining revolutions, but it is usually not a relevant variable in industrial administration, where information is a great deal more important.

In Chapter Five we turn to the problem of environmental effects on the behavior associated with an element of the social system. We will treat two main kinds of elements: individual people and points in space.

For individuals, we will treat two topics. First we will discuss the formation of concepts of the influence of group culture on an individual. Then we will treat several ways of conceptualizing the effects of *opportunities* posed by the social structure on individual behavior. In both these cases we must form concepts which have an *environmental* component (culture, number of vacancies) and a *relational* component which specifies the individual's relation to the structural force.

The final section of Chapter Five returns in a different way to a problem of power. The *military vulnerability* of a point in space depends on the environmental variable of the amount of military resources held by defenders and attackers. But it also depends on the relational variable of how far away these resources are, and how much it would cost to bring them to the point. By applying exactly the same strategy of environmental explanation as used for individuals, we can derive a number of important geopolitical concepts.

The final chapter is devoted to concepts having to do with the structure of activities. Activities have causal relations to each other, independently of who does them. These causal relations among activities create systematic patterns of the organization of activities. Many of the most useful concepts of sociology have no men in them, in the sense that different men carrying out the same set of activities will reproduce the pattern of activities. This is because many of the causal relations among activities depend very little on the characteristics of the men who carry them out. Information on the men is therefore irrelevant from a causal point of view.

A first fundamental feature of the relation between activities of two or more people is whether or not the people doing one pay attention to the other activity. The activity of writing a book on social theory has a different impact on the student's behavior if he reads it than if he does not. Particularly the cultural impact of activities on other people's minds depends on the structure of attention. Hence we will develop a number of concepts about the structure of attention in different situations. This will provide concepts measuring the probable cultural impact of behavior in different attention structures.

Another major feature of activities which determines their social impact is their *variability*. Briefly, things that do not vary do not require decisions. We do not need information on things we do not have to decide about. Consequently social structures for processing information and making decisions (especially administration and commercial institutions) are to be explained by the variability of their inputs and activities.

We will treat three concepts related to variance which are useful in explaining social patterns. One is the *information and decision burden* of a ton of goods. A car of coal is homogeneous; it usually has one origin and one destination, one seller and one buyer. A car of "less than carload lots" is heterogeneous; it has many origins and destinations, many sellers and buyers. The number of decisions that will have to be made per ton is much higher in the second case, and so the information that goes along with it must be higher.

A second variance-related concept is that of the *rate of social reconstruction* of organizations. A new organization has to be put together to build a given building, because it is different from other buildings and because of the variability of construction demand. The same organization that produced electricity last year can do it again this year. Hence the proportion of all organizational arrangements which are less than a year old will be much higher in construction. Many administrative differences flow from this.

Third, we will treat the concept of uncertainty and its relation to magic, borrowing from Malinowski.

The final section of Chapter Six treats concepts of the spatial organization of activities. Causal relations among activities usually decline with distance. Any causal relation which makes one of the activities easier will tend to cause activities to clump together. These may be called "external effects" or "externalities" of activities.

In the second half of the final section we will treat the relation of administrative activity to nodes in transportation systems. Nodes are places where many transportation lines meet. Naturally, that is the place to locate the decisions about which outgoing transportation line one is to take. Various features of flows of goods which create administrative and information activities at nodes will be outlined.

Concluding Comments

My experience in both teaching and learning strategies of theory building suggests that it is best done by attacking empirical problems oneself. The examples used here reflect my own empirical interests. Many of them have to do with power phenomena and with problems of the relation between administrative organization and society. This is not because these are the representative problems of the discipline, nor because the strategies are uniquely useful there. Instead it is because I have wondered about phenomena in these areas more often than in other areas.

Although I can, and do, recommend these phenomena to people to work on, as the ones I find difficult enough to keep me interested and important enough to be worth explaining, the reader may find some of them pretty dull. Who cares why great banks are located in ports?

But I am convinced that the logical forms of explanation and concept construction outlined here have wide applicability. I usually assign students in a theory class the following task: Choose any relation between two or more variables which you are interested in; invent at least three theories, not now known to be false, which might explain these relations; choosing appropriate indicators, derive at least three different empirical consequences from each theory, such that the factual consequences distinguish among the theories.

This I take to be the model of social theorizing as a practical scientific activity. A student who has difficulty thinking of at least three sensible explanations for any correlation that he is really interested in should probably choose another profession.

My experience with gifted analysts of empirical data suggests that eventually the student ought to be able to produce the three theories and nine derivations within an hour or two. If this is a reasonable norm, then a student should have time while reading this book to get a great deal of practice at social theorizing. And although it may reflect my dim view of the state of the discipline, I think the only way to get theories of many important phenomena is to make them up oneself.

CHAPTER TWO

The Logic of Scientific Inference

I / FUNDAMENTAL FORMS OF SCIENTIFIC INFERENCE

In order to construct theories for a science, we must have in mind the logical requirements for testing the theories against the facts. Hence our first task is to outline the fundamental logical forms of scientific inference, or of "induction," which form the common basis of the sciences.

Theoretical and Empirical Statements

Scientific inference starts with a *theoretical statement,* an element of a theory, which says that one class of phenomena will be connected in a certain way with another class of phenomena. A famous example in sociological theory would be Durkheim's theory of egoistic suicide, which might be stated as: "A higher degree of individualism in a social group causes a higher rate of suicide in that group." Here "individualism" is a variable meaning, roughly, "the degree to which all activities of the person are controlled by

15

well-defined norms enforced regularly and effectively by people in the environment, as opposed to morality determined by the individual himself by his own decisions." A person is in a more individualistic social situation, then, when fewer demands are made on him—as when he is single rather than a married man with children, or when his country is not in crisis (so he has fewer duties). He is in a more individualistic situation also when a group of which he is a member does not govern his activity in detail but leaves it to his own discretion (as when he is a Protestant rather than a Catholic), when the group which regulates his conduct is not so compact that it can surround him with others who enforce the group's prescriptions (as, in Durkheim's time in France, the Jews were more compact than other social groups).

As we can see from this example, the concepts in the theoretical statement may be at quite different levels of abstraction, with "individualism" being a property of groups which is inferred quite indirectly while the suicide rate is at a low level of abstraction and is directly observable.

From this theoretical statement we derive, by logical deduction and by operational definitions of the concepts, an *empirical statement*. The theoretical statement then *implies* logically the empirical statement. An empirical statement is one which states that: "If we make such and such observations, they will have such and such results." For instance, some of the empirical statements which Durkheim derived from his theory of egoistic suicide are: Protestants in France will have higher suicide rates than Catholics in France; Protestant regions of German provinces will have higher rates of suicide than Catholic regions; married men in France will have lower rates of suicide than single men and will have even lower rates if they have children; men who practice the free professions and generally well-educated men will have higher rates of suicide than workers or less educated people; in times of parliamentary crisis, the suicide rates will go down in France; and others. Such logical derivation from theoretical statements involves stating the meaning of the concepts in terms of observations. The statements above, that Protestants have a higher degree of individualism than Catholics, bachelors than married men with children, and populations during parliamentary crises than populations during routine politics, are essential in the derivation of empirical statements. And derivation involves straightforward logical deduction.

After this logical deduction of empirical statements from the theory, one can make the observations called for in the empirical statements to see whether or not they are true. As a practical matter, it is important to describe the observations in such a way that they can actually be made with the resources the investigator has at his disposal, but that does not affect the logic of the matter. All theories will imply some empirical statements (that is, some descriptions of possible observations) which cannot actually be tested because of lack of time, or lack of money, or technical impossibility.

Testing Theories with Observations

Once the observations are in fact made, we can compare them with the empirical statement and find out whether or not the statement is true. For simplicity in the discussion, let us call the theory A, and one of its empirical consequences B. And let us use an arrow with a double shaft $\Rightarrow$ for "implies." Then we have two logical situations:

SITUATION I	SITUATION II
$A \Rightarrow B$	$A \Rightarrow B$
B false	B true
A false	A more credible

In situation I, classical logic gives the results. If A implies B, then not-B implies not-A. If Durkheim's theory implied that Protestants ought to have a higher rate of suicide in France, and they in fact have a lower rate, then his theory is false. (The difficulty may be either in the statement that individualism causes suicide or in the statement that Protestants are more individualistic than Catholics, but one or the other must be wrong.) The deduction could be wrong for "irrelevant" reasons, as for instance because there are not enough observations to give a good estimate of the "true" suicide rate and therefore the theory should have been stated explicitly with a restriction on the sizes of the groups to which

[1] The notation here follows Georgi W. Polya, *Patterns of Plausible Inference*, Vol. 2 of *Mathematics and Plausible Reasoning* (Princeton, N.J.: Princeton University Press, 1954).

it applies (but such complexities will be dealt with later). The canons of logic demand that we reject our theory if it implies something that is false.

But classical canons of logic have nothing to say in the second case, if our observations "confirm" or "support" or "are consistent with" our theory. Yet our intuition tells us strongly that *something* has happened to our theory. We have, as we say, "tested" the theory against the facts, and it has stood the test. Intuitively it seems to us that by virtue of the test our theory has become more believable or, as we have said above, "*A* more credible." The whole edifice of scientific inference rests on the logical situation described above in situation II, on "affirming the consequent" of a theory, in the language of logic.

Intuitively we can formulate the logical incompleteness of situation II, the situation of affirming the consequent, by saying that "there are a lot of other possible explanations for *B*." For instance, the higher suicide rate of French Protestants might be explained by their occupations, by the lesser emphasis on the sin of suicide in Protestant theology, by the fact that confessors are available to every Catholic in times of trouble and distress, and so forth. Yet we still feel that if Durkheim's theory implied this fact, and if the fact turned out the way it was predicted, Durkheim's theory has been shown to be a better theory than it was before.[2]

Multiple Tests of Theories

Our problem is to analyze this intuition on which science is based in order to describe more precisely how facts can "support theories" and hence what kinds of facts and what kinds of theories we need to be oriented to. First, the list of implications given above

---

[2] Sometimes the dependence of scientific inference on situation II is formulated by saying that "the test of scientific theories is prediction." A theory may, however, be able to predict things and yet be false, as shown by the falsification of *other* "predictions." Moreover, various systematic ways of guessing the future values of some variable ("projections") are also sometimes called predictions, as in the statement, "The Protestant suicide rate in France will probably be higher than the Catholic rate next year, since it was higher last year, and experience shows a high degree of stability of suicide rates." Such projections are often administratively useful but have little to do with science.

from Durkheim's theory of egoistic suicide suggests an elaboration. For the theory implies that Protestants will have higher suicide rates than Catholics, and hence that (B_1) Protestant countries will have higher suicide rates than Catholic countries, that (B_2) Protestant regions of Germany will have higher suicide rates than Catholic regions, and that (B_3) Protestants in France will have higher suicide rates than Catholics. Durkheim makes these derivations and collects the statistics to test his theory. The logical alternatives then become:

SITUATION I	SITUATION II	SITUATION III
$A \Rightarrow B$	$A \Rightarrow B$	$A \Rightarrow B_1, B_2, B_3$
B false	B true	B_1, B_2, B_3 all true
A false	A more credible	A substantially more credible

That is, a multiple test of a theory is more convincing than a single test. Intuitively speaking, we have given the theory more chances to be disproved, and it has stood up under them all. Presumably there are fewer other possible explanations of B_1, B_2, and B_3 *taken together* than there are for B as an isolated empirical statement.

Now let us suppose that we have already derived B_1, B_2, and B_3 from Durkheim's theory and have found that indeed Protestant countries, Protestant regions in Germany, and Protestants in France have lower suicide rates. Then let us consider the credibility added to Durkheim's theory if we were to show that the various regions of Austria had higher suicide rates, the higher their proportion Protestant. Compare this with the credibility added if we show that men with children have a lower suicide rate than bachelors and men without children. That is, suppose that we can make only one more observation, given our resources, and we have to choose between an empirical statement very similar to those we have already proved and one very different. It is clear that the "surprise value" of the observation on bachelors is much greater than the surprise value of *another* observation on Protestants and Catholics. If the theory can imply such different kinds of empirical statements as one about religion and one about marital status, then we feel intuitively that the theory has been subjected to a tougher test than it has if we merely repeat observations similar to those we have already made.

SITUATION I	SITUATION II	SITUATION III	SITUATION IV
$A \Rightarrow B$	$A \Rightarrow B$	$A \Rightarrow B_1, B_2, B_3$	$A \Rightarrow B_1, B_2, B_3$
B false	B true	B_1, B_2, B_3 similar	B_1, B_2, B_3 different
A false	A more credible	A substantially more credible	A much more credible

This result is summarized in the figure above. It says both that the more different things we can derive (situation III), and the more different kinds of implications we can derive (situation IV), the stronger will be our test of the theory. If the theory stands up under a tougher test, it becomes more credible than it is if it stands up when we have subjected it only to weak tests. If it fails any of the tests, it is false, either in the underlying statement or in the specification of the observations which the concepts of the theory refer to.

The Fundamental Criterion of a Strong Test of Theory

What guides our intuition to the conclusion that multiple, different tests of the consequences of a theory are better than a single, isolated test? In order to answer this question, we must consider the *alternative theories* which might be explanations of various phenomena in the world. In general, we imagine that before our investigation there are many alternative theories that one might hold about what goes on in the world. Many of these will be theories that someone else has already thought of, and many of them will be theories that we will think of during our investigation. But many of the theories that might be true will be theories that no one has ever thought of. In other words, we have a very large class of possible theories which are consistent with past knowledge, some of which are known and some of which are not.

For any given observation which is an implication of A, say B_1, there will be *some* of the possible alternative theories which will imply not-B_1. If we then demonstrate B_1, these alternative theories are falsified. This leaves us with *fewer alternative possible theories* to our own. We can diagram this situation as follows (this is exactly comparable to situation II above, but formulated in a different way):

SITUATION II, REFORMULATED
(*Situation before testing B_1*)

A or $(C, D, E, \ldots, Q, R, S, \ldots)$
$A \Rightarrow B_1$
$(C, E, \ldots, Q, S, \ldots) \Rightarrow B_1$
$D, R \Rightarrow$ not-B_1
B_1 true
_____
D, R false (by classical logic)
A or $(C, E, \ldots, Q, S, \ldots)$
A more credible
(but also $C, E, \ldots, Q, S, \ldots$ more credible)

That is, with the test B_1 we eliminate D and R from among the possible alternatives, making *all* of those which imply B_1 more credible. Among those theories made more credible by this elimination of competitors is our own theory, A.

Now if we have several implications from our theory, but all are quite similar, we eliminate some particular and erratic alternatives to our theory. If, for instance, we test only the implication from Durkheim's theory that Protestants in France will kill themselves more often than Catholics in France, some peculiarity of the situation of Protestants in France or of their history (such as the fact that they are a very small minority, or that there was selective migration at the time of the exodus of the French Huguenots) might explain the facts, since all these particular alternative theories imply the empirical statement. If we check the other derivations about Protestant countries and about regions in Germany, these peculiar explanations or alternative theories are also eliminated. But as the number of *similar* tests to the theory increases, *the number of alternative theories each new test eliminates* becomes much smaller.

Then if we turn to a quite different implication of our original theory, for instance, that men with children should kill themselves less often (in France) than bachelors, it will eliminate quite a different set of alternative theories. Thus what we mean when we say that two implications of a theory are "quite different" is that *there is almost no overlap* between the theories that imply the one empirical statement and the theories that imply the other. For instance, the number of alternative theories which imply *both* that Protestants will have more suicide in the different regions of Germany *and* that men with children will have more than bachelors is much smaller than the number which would imply *both* that Protestant regions in Germany will have higher suicide rates *and* that Protestants in France will have higher suicide rates. This is so because all theories which involve Protestantism as a cause will imply both of the second pair, but (probably) only one of the first pair. We can represent this situation in the following figure:

$$A \text{ OR } (C, D, E, F, \ldots, Q, R, S, T, \ldots)$$
(*Situation before either test*)

SITUATION III, REFORMULATED	SITUATION IV, REFORMULATED
$A \Rightarrow B_1, B_2$	$A \Rightarrow B_1, B_n$
B_1, B_2 similar	B_1, B_n very different
$C, R \Rightarrow$ not B_1	$C, R \Rightarrow$ not B_1
$C, S \Rightarrow$ not B_2	$D, E \Rightarrow$ not B_n
B_1, B_2 true	B_1, B_n true
C, R, S false	C, R, D, E false
A or $(D, E, F, \ldots, Q, T, \ldots)$	A or $(F, \ldots, Q, S, T, \ldots)$
A substantially more credible	A much more credible

Thus, because the empirical statements B_1 and B_2 are both implied by C, either one of them is sufficient to eliminate it, and (at least in this respect) the second test, which rejected C again, was "wasted." Only S, a particular explanation for the result B_1 which could not explain B_2, was eliminated by the second test, by B_2. But when B_1 and B_n are different, there is no (or very little) overlap in the theories which might explain them. Hence more alternative theories are eliminated by checking two very different consequences of our theory. The theory S, the particular explanation for the results of the first test, is not eliminated by the recourse to a completely different implication of the theory. But it would probably have less weight in our thinking because of the increased credibility of our original theory.

Thus the basic logical process of science is the elimination of alternative theories (both those we know and those we do not) by investigating as many of the empirical consequences of each theory as is practical, always trying for the greatest possible variety in the implications tested.

Two Very General Alternative Theories: Statistical Inference

We are now in a position to discuss the logical role that statistical inference plays in science. There are two alternative theories that we always have to regard as possible explanations of any given set of observations, both of which give rise to *random distributions of the observations*. The first is that the observations were produced by *the way we designed our study,* especially by the *sample of observations we chose to make* out of those we could have made. In statistical theory, the observations we could have made are called either the population or the universe. The second alternative theory that we always have to take account of is that the observations were produced by *a large set of small influences operating in different directions.*[3]

The implication of this is that we always want to reject evidence if it can be explained either by the design of the research or by a large number of small, unorganized causes. Many observations made in daily life constitute such a small sample that any results might be explained by the selection of the sample from out of the total population of observations. For instance, Durkheim might have observed a small town in France to see whether Protestants killed themselves more often than Catholics. Whether we regard this as a sample of France's population (which it is, though an inefficient one) or the total population to which the theory applies, it is still true that any observations we make will have so few cases

---

[3] The original theory of random distribution was worked out for the second situation, of a large set of small causes without any internal organization or pattern, in the theory of errors of measurement. Gauss's notion was that errors of measurement (after the measuring instruments were perfected and checked) were the result of a large number of small forces, such as friction, perceptual errors, recording errors, and the like, which operated in different directions in the different measurements of a phenomenon. Recently, statistical theory has been mainly developed as a theory of samples from a population, so that some people are unable to understand how statistical inference applies when they have measured the whole population of observations to which their theory applies. This failure of the imagination very often happens among people whose orientation to statistics is for administrative, rather than scientific, purposes, in which they only want to know a parameter in an administratively defined population. The orientation to statistics taken here is roughly that called "Bayesian."

of suicide in them that they might give different results than a complete count of suicides in France. On the other hand, such a small number of suicides might have been produced by a large number of small causes of suicide. That is, a random distribution could explain our observations.

Since the theory of sampling and the theory of large numbers of small causes apply to so many phenomena, if they imply our observations and if our theory also implies them, then our theory is very little more believable than it was before.[4]

The theory of sampling and the theory of large numbers of small, unorganized causes are quite highly developed mathematically. By knowing how we collected the observations, or by knowing the number of observations, we can often say quite precisely what kinds of observations would be consistent with these two very general theories. If the observations we actually make are inconsistent with these derivations (in other words, if statistical theory implies not-B_1, and we observe B_1), then we eliminate *these* alternative theories.

The branch of statistics which is called the "design of experiments" deals with the problem of deriving from our theory consequences *which will not be implied* by either of the statistical theories (which are mathematically the same). It tries to specify which observations, if they were made, would be implied by our theory but not by statistical theory.[5]

The Crucial Experiment

The logic which we applied to statistical inference can be generalized to all cases in which we have *explicitly formulated alternative theories*. In many cases we can specify some of the most important alternatives to our own theory. If we can specify the

[4] Many people would say that it was no more believable than before, but often observations that are consistent with chance are inconsistent with those alternative theories that imply a strong tendency for the observations to be different from the random distribution. In the language of statistics, our observations establish a confidence interval which includes the null hypothesis. Theories which imply parameters outside the confidence interval are thereby "rejected," or at least rendered unlikely.

[5] Another part of the design of experiments in statistics deals with *turning other possible theories into statistical theories,* by a technique called *randomization.* Turning other theories into a statistical theory and then disproving the statistical theory is, of course, not the only way of disproving them, and it has nothing to do with the refutation of the sampling and large-group-of-small-causes explanations.

most important of alternative theories, then it is very inefficient to test our theory by picking empirical consequences at random, with the hope that some of them will be inconsistent with the main alternative theories. The rational thing to do is to look for those consequences of our theory whose *negation* is implied by the alternatives. We look for consequences, B_j, of our theory which will give us the logical situation shown below:

SITUATION V: THE CRUCIAL EXPERIMENT

A or C or $(D, E, \ldots)$
$(D, E, \ldots)$ unlikely
$A \Rightarrow B_j$
$C \Rightarrow$ not-B_j
B_j true

C false
A or $(D, E, \ldots)$ [$(D, E, \ldots)$ unlikely]
A very much more credible

By eliminating the most likely alternative theory, we increase the credibility of our theory much more than we do by eliminating alternatives at random by checking consequences of our theory without thinking.

Such a consequence of a theory (or, to speak more precisely, of both theories) is called a *crucial experiment* and is a description of a set of observations which will decide between two alternative theories, both of which according to present knowledge are quite likely. The purpose of the design of experiments in statistical theory is to construct crucial experiments between any given theory and statistical theory. In this case, usually, sampling theory (or some other theory reduced to sampling theory by randomization) plays the logical role of C above, and the design-of-experiments statistical worker searches for a B_j by working out the mathematical consequences of C as compared with A. Thus what is called the design of experiments in statistics is a particular example (and a particularly difficult example to understand) of the finding of crucial experiments.

Examples of Crucial Experiments

For more substantive examples, we can again turn to Durkheim's *Suicide*. The most popular alternative theory at the time Durkheim lived was that suicide was the result of mental illness (not further specified) or was caused by the same causes that caused mental illness. Durkheim reasoned that if this were the case, then the same populations that had high rates of mental illness ought to have high rates of suicide. Since, as it happened, the social causes of suicide that Durkheim was interested in did not, apparently, cause variations in rates of mental illness, *his* theory implied that the correlation between rates of mental illness and rates of suicide would be insignificant. Thus he could describe a set of observations (the relations between rates of mental illness and rates of suicide, for various regions) which would show one result (positive correlation) if mental illness caused suicide, and a different result (insignificant correlation) if social causes were operating. He then made these observations, and the correlation between mental illness rates and suicide rates was insignificant. This disproved the alternative theory (as it was stated) and made his theory much more credible.

Of course, only the theory that was explicitly posed as an alternative is disproved, and sometimes that theory can then be reformulated so as to be consistent with the new observations. In this case, for instance, it seems sensible to suppose that particular kinds of mental illness, such as depressive disorders, would be related to suicide. There is some evidence that depressive disorders, which account for a relatively small part of mental disease and hence do not affect the overall rates very much, are related to quite different social variables than is schizophrenia. Schizophrenia accounts for the bulk of the variation in overall mental disease rates. Thus it could very well be that a *different alternative theory* relating suicide and mental disease might be true, one relating suicide specifically to depressive mental disorders. Durkheim's data fundamentally show that suicide rates are not related to rates of schizophrenia.

Perhaps an even more elegant example from Durkheim is his analysis of the suicide rates of Jews. By this point in the monograph Durkheim has shown that urbanism, education, and employment in commerce are all positively related to suicide, which he has interpreted as evidence for his theory of individualism. Now, he argues, if there were some other explanation for these connections of urbanism, education, and commercial employment to suicide, they *should operate just as well in a highly solidary, but educated, urban, commercial group.* If, on the other hand, urbanism, education, and commercial employment are only indicators of individualism as opposed to solidarity, then when we find them in a highly solidary group they will not cause suicide. Thus if Durkheim can find a highly solidary, but educated, commercial, urban group, he can put a decisive test, a crucial experiment, to choose between his theory of individualism and very many of the alternative theories which would still be compatible with the data.

He argued that such a group were the Jews of France at his time. Because of their minority status, they formed a compact group with detailed, highly ritualized norms of daily conduct that were thoroughly enforced on each individual because the individual was almost always among his coreligionists. But the Jews were thoroughly urban, commercial, and much more highly educated than other Frenchmen. Consequently, Durkheim's theory predicted a very low suicide rate. Almost all other theories which could explain the relation of urbanism, education, and commercial employment to suicide would predict a very high rate. Consequently, when he showed that Jews at his time in France had very low suicide rates, he made his theory of individualism very much more credible.

Thus in the statistical design of experiments, in Durkheim's examination of mental disorders as causes of suicide, and in Durkheim's study of the suicide rates of Jews in France, we have the same logical situation. In each case we have explicitly developed the competing theory at least to such a level that we can derive some consequences from it. In the statistical design of experiments, this alternative theory is a theory of random distributions. In the case of mental infirmities and suicide the competing theory is that suicide is caused by, or has the same causes as, mental disorders in general. In the case of the Jews' suicide rates, the competition is that urbanism, education, and commercial employment will have the same effects on suicide, whatever their relation to individualism and social solidarity.

Then we choose one of the consequences of the theory we are testing that would contradict the alternative theory, and we make observations appropriate to checking *that* consequence of our theory in preference to checking all the consequences as we happen to think of them. If we are clever enough in inventing the alternative theories to make them inherently likely, and in deriving the consequences which will decide between them, we increase the efficiency of our observation for the advance of science very greatly.

Because the advance of science is much more economical when we can explicitly eliminate the most likely alternative theories, and because formulating the alternative theories and deriving their consequences is preeminently a theoretical task, the central gift of the great methodologist is his facility at formulating and deriving the consequences of alternative theories in such a way that the observations can actually be made to decide the question. Because two of the most important alternative theories are those which give rise to random distributions, methodology has come to be identified in the naive mind with statistical expertise. Statistical expertise is, of course, a particular kind of theoretical talent, a talent for deriving the implications of the theories which give rise to random distributions of one kind or another.

A strong esthetic reaction to crucial experiments is the central mark of the true scientist.

II / THE STRUCTURE OF CAUSAL THEORIES

Up to this point, we have not been concerned with the internal structure of our theory, called A above, but only with what happens to it as a whole when we conduct investigations to test it. In this section, we will analyze a particularly important class of theories, which are called *causal theories*. Not all scientific theories are causal theories in the sense in which we use the term here. By analyzing the internal logical structure of these theories, we can formulate more precisely how one derives empirical consequences from such theories. But before we can proceed with this analysis, we need to discuss the concept of a *variable* in scientific theories, because the *theoretical sentences*, or statements, of a causal theory are statements of a particular kind about the connection between scientific variables.

Definition of Variables

A "variable" in science is a *concept* which can have *various values,* and which is defined in such a way that *one can tell by*

means of observations which value it has in a particular occurrence.
As will develop later, a causal law is a statement that certain values
of two or more variables are connected in a certain way. The meaning of the terms of this definition can be better understood by
considering a wide variety of variables used in sociological theory.

The simplest kind of variable is one which has *two values,* which
can be represented as 1 and 0. Such a variable is commonly called
a dichotomy, since it cuts the observations into two classes. There
are first of all *natural* dichotomies, which we observe quite directly:
sex, citizen or noncitizen of a particular country, employed or not
employed, married or unmarried, all of which apply to people as
the units of observation, and such things as votes in the United
States (acts which can, usually, be classified as either Democratic
or Republican), legal cases which can be classified as in federal
or state jurisdiction, and so forth. The crucial point is that someone besides the investigator decides which of these classifications
someone, or something, belongs to. The classifications exist independently of the scientific purposes of the investigator.

Then there are conceptual variables with two categories, in which
the investigator himself creates the classification and places his observations in those two categories. For instance, in the comparative
study of politics votes for different parties in different countries are
often reduced to leftist votes and rightist votes; political scientists
classify monarchies as constitutional or not constitutional, or governments as totalitarian or nontotalitarian.

Then there are variables with two values which are explicitly
created as simplifications of variables which have more than two
values. Some of this simplification may be done by the society itself,
as in classifying people by age into minors and adults, or in simplifying the ranking system in the army into officers and men. Others
are created by the investigator himself, as when an investigator has
a scale of attitudes ranging from the extreme left to the extreme
right and divides the population into leftists and rightists by split-
ting his scale in the middle, or when he has a scale of the degree of
democracy of political systems and cuts it in the middle to distinguish dictatorships from democracies.

At the next level of complexity, we have variables which can
take on a definite, known, finite number of values, which are gener-

ally called classifications. Some of these again are natural variables, as would be a classification of the population of the world by country of citizenship, ranks in the army, brands of automobiles or some other defined product, or votes classified by party in a country with more than two parties. Some variables with several values are conceptual, such as classification of building as single-family dwellings, apartment houses, commercial buildings, factory buildings, buildings with more than one of these functions, and "other buildings"; or a classification of governments into communist, liberal, and traditional; or a classification of workers according to their occupations or according to the industries in which they work.

These variables can also be created by simplification of more complex variables, as when we divide incomes (a continuous variable) into high, medium, and low, or classify attitudes as rightist, leftist, and centrist. Finally, such variables can be created by combining two or more simpler variables into a complex variable. For instance, one could combine sex and marital status and obtain a variable with four values: married woman, married man, unmarried woman, unmarried man.

A third kind of variable is one which has exactly as many values as there are observations—that is, a complete ranking of the observations. An example would be rank in class at graduation.

Finally, there are continuous variables, or variables considered as continuous, such as the natural variables of income, age, floor area of a house, number of rooms in a house, years of employment in a firm; or such conceptual variables as intelligence quotient, degree of economic development of a country; or the constructed variables of the per cent in a given area voting for a candidate, or the size of a city.

For each of these types of variables we have a concept (e.g., sex, income) in terms of which we make observations, and we classify or order these observations in some way (e.g., into masculine and feminine, or into high, medium, and low income, or according to dollar income) so that each observation is connected with a single value of the variable.[6]

[6] Sidney Siegel, *Non-Parametric Statistics for the Behavioral Sciences* (New York: McGraw-Hill, 1956), gives a good discussion of the logical character of different kinds of variables.

Definition of Causal Laws

Now we are in a position to describe what we mean by a causal law. A causal law is a statement or proposition in a theory which says that there exist environments (the better described the environments, the more complete the law) in which a change in the value of one variable is associated with a change in the value of another variable and can produce this change without any change in other variables in the environment.[7] It will be useful to use an example from another science to see more exactly what is involved in this definition.

Let us take "The shining of the sun causes the temperature to rise." Here we have two variables, whether the sun shines or not and temperature. We will call sun shining x and temperature y and write $x \rightarrow y$. The first is a dichotomy, a simplification of a continuous variable of the degree of sunshine; the second is a continuous variable. Then the causal law stated above means the following set of statements:

1. A change in x (in some defined environments) *is associated* with a change in y—there is a correlation between the two variables. When the sun shines, the temperature is on the average higher than when it does not shine.

2. One can produce the change in temperature by making the sun shine, but one cannot make the sun shine by changing the temperature.

3. There does not have to be any change in other variables for the sun to have its effect on the temperature (though, of course, the sun will have other effects than its effect on the temperature unless we control them, and the temperature itself will cause other variables to change unless they are controlled).

Here one should note the following important points:

1. There can be environments in which the law does not apply.

---

[7] This definition is adapted from that of Russel Ackoff, *The Design of Social Research* (Chicago: University of Chicago Press, 1953), pp. 65–68. See also Herbert Simon, *Models of Man: Social and Rational* (New York: Wiley, 1957), chapter 3, pp. 50–61, and chapter 1, pp. 10–36.

It would not apply in a perfect vacuum, since temperature is not defined in such an environment.

2. The arrow with only one shaft, which we have used for causation, is quite different from the double-shafted arrow of logical implication, which we used above when discussing the *testing* of theories rather than their *formulation*.

3. The causal law can have variables of different classes, as dichotomies and continuous variables in this case.

4. There are other kinds of scientific theoretical propositions than causal laws, such as systems of simultaneous equations without exogenous variables, or laws of mutual dependence without causal priority such as the relationship between temperature, pressure, and volume in a gas, or indirect causation $(x \rightarrow z \rightarrow y)$, and so forth.

5. Variations in other variables can also cause variation in the caused variable, y, without falsifying the causal law. Any given dependent variable may be involved in a large number of causal laws.

6. Because of this, even though we know the causal law $x \rightarrow y$, we do not necessarily know that a *given* change in y that we observe is *in fact* caused by a variation in x, since it is quite possible that x does not vary in the environment we are investigating, or that the variations in y produced by variations in x are small relative to variations produced by other variables. For example, the sun can produce tides, but the major explanation for tides is the attraction of the moon. This means that even after a causal law is established, there is a further task of establishing which of the "natural" variations in y are *in fact* caused by x.

Observation in Support of Causal Theories

In order to derive observations sufficient to support or refute a causal theory, we must try to create observations of the following kinds:

1. We must observe *different values of the causal variable.* Unless there is variation in the causal variable, we cannot establish covariation. If one has a theory that individualism causes suicide, then one must observe at least two values of individualism, such as

Catholic and Protestant, educated and uneducated, commercial people and noncommercial, Jews and Gentiles. An observation of the suicide rates of Catholics alone, or of commercial people alone, is worthless for establishing covariation.

2. *Covariation:* We must observe variations in the dependent variable associated with these different values of the causal variable. Durkheim observed the suicide rates characteristic of groups with different degrees of individualism, thus classifying each group at the same time as high or low in individualism and as high or low in suicide rate.

3. *Causal Direction:* We must observe in some way that it is not possible to change the value of the causal variable by changing the supposed dependent variable, or that it *is* possible to change the value of the dependent variable by changing the causal variable.

4. *Nonspuriousness:* We must observe that there are not other variables in the environment which might cause changes in the dependent variable which change at the same time as the independent variable changes. There may be other effects of the causal variable which cannot be avoided, in which case one must try to show that they do not cause changes in the dependent variable. And there may also be effects of the dependent variable, in which case one also must try to establish the causal direction between the dependent variable and the possible confounding variable.

There are two main methods of observing *covariation,* the "experiment" and measurement of variables in their natural variations. The basic idea of the experiment is that the investigator himself changes the value of the causal variable for part of his observations, leaves it the same (or sets it at some other value) for another part, and measures the changes in the dependent variable.

In this way he has at least two values of the causal variable. These are often called the "treatment" and "control" observations, or the "experimental" and "control" observations. In the more advanced sciences usually the investigator sets several values of the causal variable to observe details of the variations of the dependent variable and has no "control" group. And he must measure variations in the dependent variable.[8] The great advantage of this method

---

[8] Experimentation is more efficient if he can also measure variations in the causal variable.

of observing for covariation of two variables is that it solves at the same time the problem of causal direction, though not the problem of spuriousness.

The second method of observing for covariation is observation of natural variations of the two variables. In this case it is absolutely necessary that both variables be measured, and that there be natural variations of sufficient magnitude in the causal variable to have measurable effects. Sometimes such observations of natural variations are done with the help of special measuring instruments, such as interviews, tests, or calipers, and sometimes they are made without special aids (*e.g.,* by watching social interaction, or by the inspection of animals in zoology). Observing variations without special observational aids is often called natural history and is the preferred method of many anthropologists, political scientists, and historians in the social sciences. In any case, in order to establish covariation, one must observe at least two values of the independent variable (preferably many cases of each of the two) and measure or observe the associated variation of the dependent variable.

There seem to be five main methods for establishing *causal direction:* experimental manipulation of the causal variable, manipulation of the dependent variable (together with knowledge of covariation), temporal priority of changes or of determination of the value in one of the variables, knowing from other investigation the causes of observed variations in the causal variable, and knowing other causes of variation in the dependent variable if these causes are uncorrelated with the variation in the independent variable. Each of these requires some explanation.

1. If we have manipulated the causal variable, then we know its cause in this particular case: our own action. If we know the cause of its variation (and if this cause cannot itself cause variations in the dependent variable), then we know that the covariation between the causal and the dependent variable must be due to the causal force of the causal variable.

2. Sometimes we cannot manipulate the causal variable—for instance, we may not be able to control the sunshine—but we can control the dependent variable—for instance, the temperature of a certain area. If we change the temperature of an area, and if the

sun does not come out or go in, then we know that the dependent variable does not cause the causal variable. If we know (through observing covariation) that there is some causal connection between the two variables, then the causal direction must go the other way around.

3. If we observe that the change in the causal variable (such as a rise in the price of cars) *precedes* changes in the dependent variable (such as an expansion in the production of cars), then we know that the second changes could not have produced the first change. Likewise if the value of some variable is determined, for some particular observations, at a time previous to observed differential changes of the dependent variable, then we know that the determination of the first variable caused (directly or indirectly) variations in the second variable. For instance, if we observe that children from higher-class families decide, during high school, to go to college with greater frequency than working-class children, we can establish causal direction if we have previously established that the class level of the family is mostly determined at the time the father enters the labor force.

4. If we know that the variation in the causal variable is due to other causes, as the variation of sunshine is due to the rotation of the earth on its axis, then we know that the variation in the temperature between day and night could not have caused the differences observed in the amount of sunlight between day and night. Hence we know that any observed covariation is due to sunshine causing variations in temperature.

5. If we know other causes of the dependent variable which are unrelated to the cause we are studying, then we can also establish causal direction. For all we need to do is to find observations in which the dependent variable varies (due to the other cause) without variation in the causal variable. For instance, differences in altitude cause systematic variations in temperature. If we choose an extremely dry climate, then the amount of sunshine will be equal on the heights and in the plains. If we observe covariation between altitude and temperature, and at given altitudes a covariation between sunshine and temperature, then we will have shown that some variations in temperature do not cause variations in the amount of sunshine, while variations of sunshine do cause variations in temperature.

It should be noted that some of these methods of establishing causal direction will show that the causal variable causes the variations in the dependent variable *even if* changes in the dependent variable can cause changes in the causal variable (especially the classical experiment, number 1 above, and sometimes number 3). Others will work only if there is no mutual causation (numbers 2, 4, and 5).

Finally, there are four main methods of establishing *nonspuriousness:* deliberate control of the value of possible spurious variables, control of possible spurious variables through randomization, control through knowing from the design of the investigation that the other variables will not vary between observations, and control through measurement of these variables and partialing out or correcting for their variation.

1. In the classical experiment as usually conceived in the physical sciences, other variables are deliberately controlled—for instance, the amount of impurities in a chemical reaction is deliberately set as near zero as possible, or temperature is controlled by air conditioning the laboratories. In order to do this, the variables which might cause variations in the dependent variable have to be pretty well known and they must be controllable through the deliberate intervention of the investigator. In general, such variables must be capable of being measured with high precision.

2. In control through randomization, one provides some sort of a *list* of the possible observed values of spurious variables and then chooses values from this list according to some random process for observation. For example, if we divide an experimental plot of land for a fertilization experiment into small plots, then we know that there is a value of natural fertility associated with each plot. Even though we cannot measure natural fertility (let us suppose), this provides us with a *list* of possible values of this spurious variable for various observations we can make. If we give each of these plots a number and choose which plots to apply artificial fertilizer to by using a table of random numbers, then we know that the values of natural fertility are controlled within certain statistical limits.[9]

[9] This is a rough way of talking about what is going on, and the degree of confidence we have in our conclusions will depend on the (unknown)

3. In control through knowing that all sets of observations have been exposed to the same values of third variables, even though we cannot control these variables, we ensure nonvariation of such variables and hence know that they could not have caused the variations in the dependent variable. For instance, in an agricultural experiment we may not be able to control the number of days of sunshine and rain to which fertilized and unfertilized plants are exposed, but we know enough about meteorology to know that if the plots are sufficiently close together they will be exposed to very small variations in weather.

4. Finally, we can measure third variables and compare covariation between our causal variable and the dependent variable only among observations where the third variable has identical values. Or if we know (or can compute from our data) the relation between the third variable and the dependent variable, we can correct the observed values of the dependent variable to take out the effect of the third variable and see whether there is still covariation between the causal variable and these corrected values. This is the *technique of partial correlation or standardization.*

In general, for any causal theory, then, one must derive empirical statements which specify observations which will establish covariation, causal direction, and nonspuriousness. The particular practical situation of the investigator, and the nature of the variables, will determine which of the various kinds of observations he will be able to make and which will be most efficient. There are also various ways of combining the above techniques of observation to get greater efficiency. For instance, if one can measure some of the important spurious variables but not others but can provide some sort of list of different values of these others which he cannot measure, then *stratified random sampling* will improve the efficiency of the randomizing method of eliminating spuriousness.

This completes our logical analysis of causal theories and of how one derives empirical propositions from them which can be com-

---

shape of the distribution of natural fertility among plots. To speak more precisely, we will know with a certain probability that natural fertility differences would not account for differences of a certain size in the yield of the artificially fertilized plots as compared to the yield of unfertilized plots.

pared with observations. But in causal theories, as well as in other theories, *concepts* appear. Since these are keys to relating theories to empirical consequences, we must briefly discuss the logic of concept formation and its relation to empirical statements.

III / SCIENTIFIC CONCEPTS

Above we defined a scientific variable as a concept which can take on various values such that we can tell by observations which value it has in a particular case. Such direct observational concepts are among the most important in any science, though philosophers of science are generally inclined to admit that there are other concepts ("unobservables") in many or most scientific theories. Such concepts are electron, cause, a person's predisposition, and the like. We will deal here only with observational concepts, with emphasis on variables and types (complexes of variables).

Change of Concepts as Theories Change

The first requirement for a concept is that it accurately reflect the forces actually operating in the world. That is, the definition of a concept is a hypothesis that a certain sort of thing causes other things of interest to us. Usually this means that we have some specific ideas about what we want to explain, and that a certain kind of antecedent condition will in fact produce such phenomena as effects. If our theory is then refuted, we change the theory, which means among other things that we change our concepts or formulate new ones which more exactly correspond to the forces apparently operating.

For example, we may start with the idea that socialization in the lower class, in general, encourages juvenile delinquency. But on closer observation we find great variations in the amount of delinquency of children from family environments which seem to be, in the relevant respects, as nearly identical as we can measure. But we observe that some of the most delinquent children live in certain neighborhoods and are far more concentrated than we would expect if only class factors were operating. We then form a concept of a delinquency-producing neighborhood and try to figure out how it might operate (so that we know what observations to make, what concept to form).

Suppose that on preliminary investigation of delinquency-producing neighborhoods, it seems that what is happening is that certain neighborhoods are places where delinquent teenage groups form and that individuals become delinquent mainly by learning from their teenage friends the values and practices of delinquency. So we move to a concept of a "delinquent subculture." When we have defined this sufficiently well and figured out how to measure it, we can return to the data to see whether working-class boys are any more likely to get into trouble than middle-class boys *when they have the same level of exposure to the delinquent subculture.*

But in order to decide how to conceptualize the delinquent subculture, we need to think again about how such a culture would work to produce delinquency. We might do this by specifying various values which we believe would motivate or justify delinquency, various skills which one might learn which, if he knew them, would make it more profitable to be a delinquent, and so forth. We would probably conduct investigations on the correlation of these values and these skills with delinquent behavior or with membership in known delinquent gangs. Once we had located a series of these values and skills, we would give a tentative definition of the delinquent subculture in terms of them.

But then we might notice that there were gangs with more or less the same values, with quite different rates of certain kinds of rational delinquency, according to the neighborhood they were located in (in other words, the delinquent subculture is not sufficient to explain all the variation in delinquency which varies with neighborhoods). Then we would be likely to redefine the concept of delinquency, to separate delinquencies caused by the delinquent subculture (perhaps vandalism, gang fighting, and so forth) and others which, though mostly occurring within it, require further explanation (rational crime). We might then form a concept of *opportunities* for rational crime made up of the existence of organized crime, markets for selling the numbers, and the like, in the neighborhood. This part of delinquency then would be explained by delinquent subcultures plus opportunities.[10]

As the science advances, it progressively redefines its concepts until they accurately represent the phenomena in the world. Both concepts defining the thing to be explained and the causal variables get redefined, until in the ideal case each concept represents phenomena which always have the same set of effects and the same set of causes, and all other characteristics of the observations are eliminated as irrelevant. Conceptual perfection cannot go on without the increase in knowledge about how the world works, for conceptual perfection is the location of phenomena with a unique set of causes and effects. It is quite useless to discuss concepts without reference to substantive theory about what goes on in the world, about what causes what. And such substantive theory is merely wind without observation ("research") to find out whether it is true or not.

Consequently every concept must be, either implicitly or explicitly, a *hypothesis* that specified phenomena, and no others, are, in some situations, causally operative. One does not formulate such concepts unless he has an idea that they cause something important or that they are caused by a distinct set of phenomena.

This means that concepts are in a constant state of flux as long as the causal theories are still in the process of development. And it means that the criteria for judging concepts are beliefs and evidence that the theories in which the concepts are involved are true. Usually when a theory proves inadequate, the concepts in it change (as, for instance, the concept of distance and time changed when relativity theory replaced Newtonian mechanics).

But because lower-level concepts are the part of a theory which directly corresponds to measurements or observations, they have some special characteristics. The practical and theoretical aspects of measurement and observation place certain requirements on the conceptual aspects of theories. We will discuss in turn the definition of *variables* and the definitions of *types*.

---

[10] This represents roughly the conceptual development of one branch of the theory of juvenile delinquency. The names of Sutherland, Solomon Kobrin, Albert Cohen, Cloward, and Ohlin are associated with the main stages in this development.

Conceptualization of Variables

As we recall from the discussion above, a variable is a concept which has various values, such that one can tell from observations what value it has in a specific case. Usually there are several different ways of telling which value of a variable appears in a specific observation (which usually ought to agree, if they can be carried out at the same time). In fact, the correspondence is never exact, and measurement theory deals with approximations and criteria of agreement.

In general, a science starts off with its variables defined by common sense, by the distinctions that people make in daily life. Because people, in order to live efficiently, have to take account of the causal forces at work in the world, they make distinctions which are institutionalized in the language they speak. This is the level of "natural" variables which we discussed above, in which the investigator uses the values of variables given him by the society.

For instance, in discussing delinquency above, we implicitly started with the concept defined by the society, in which "delinquency" is activity of which the police and courts take account, and "juvenile delinquency" is delinquency committed by people whom, because of their age, the law treats in a special way. But by the time we got the theory developed, we were forced to redefine the concepts because different kinds of action that concern the police turned out to have different causes (distinguishing between rational crime and subculturally caused crime).

One of the fundamental difficulties with applied research generally is that natural variables *that create administrative problems* generally are not the same variables *that have a unique set of causes*. Sometimes applied researchers formulate this 'by saying that a natural variable "has multiple causes." From a scientific point of view, this means that the applied researcher is trying to explain the wrong thing.

In general, variables may be measured either by their *causes* or by their *effects*. Measurement of variables by their causes is most important in experimental research, where we try to manipulate the independent variable, and measurement by effects is most important when we are measuring things as they occur naturally.

As an example of measurement by causes, a social psychologist might tell one group that "you will probably like each other" and another group that "you probably will not get along too well," in order to study the effects of social solidarity. Clearly he is measuring solidarity by its presumed causes (namely his statements to the subjects). On the other hand, intelligence presumably has the effect that a person is able to answer more questions of a certain kind on tests, and we use a series of these effects (a series of questions) to locate the underlying variable.

What this means, obviously, is that our measurement of any concept improves as our theories of its causes and effects improve. But there are certain techniques of improving measurement tools, without special theoretical analysis of the causal structure relating the underlying variable to those causes and effects by which we measure it.

These techniques depend on the idea that if two manifest observations are caused by the same underlying variable, there will be *covariation* between the observations, since there is causal covariation between the underlying variable and each of its effects. There will also be covariation between causes of an underlying variable and effects of that same variable. The techniques include factor analysis, Guttman scaling, latent structure analysis, item analysis, and so forth.[11]

We will not go into these techniques here but will only point out that in the long run these are all implicitly causal theories of one kind or another, utilized for the special purpose of measurement of underlying variables. We use these causes and effects for measurement because we are not interested in these effects, or these causes, of the variables under investigation. One exercise a student can use to practice his theorizing is to take a group of related scales and guess at the causal structure involved. In factor analysis, this is called "interpretation" of the factors. Many people who use other techniques do not realize that their measuring instruments have an internal causal structure and hence do not "interpret" their results.

[11] See Warren Torgerson, *Theory and Method of Scaling* (New York: Wiley, 1960).

The point here is that one uses the causes and effects of a variable to locate it, applying various techniques for analyzing the covariation between observations due to the observations' having common causes and common effects. This means that measurement is scientific theory in action for a specific purpose. The assumption of all these techniques is that if we can throw together enough minor causes and minor effects of an underlying variable (such as the minor effect of intelligence that it enables one to answer certain questions), those variables that really cause things and those that really are the result of a unique set of causes will turn up in our analysis. Then these are likely to be variables which cause the phenomena that we are really interested in explaining or which have a unique set of causes.

Further, the central way of increasing the covariation between observations that we use for measurement is to understand and conceptualize better the underlying causal structure. We can then obtain observations which are uniquely effects or causes of the variables actually operating and hence increase the covariation among observations. Thus the improvement of measurements is usually due to the advance of theory.

Measurement is not only a device for testing theory. It is a part of the theory.

Type-Concepts

A *type-concept* in scientific discourse is a concept which is constructed out of a *combination of the values of several variables.* Sometimes we find that in the world a whole series of variables has a set of values which are all the same in a large number of observations, and that if we find that one of the variables has a different value then all of them have different values. One group of type-concepts we are all familiar with is the chemical elements. If we isolate the elementary chemical substances and examine them, we observe that a large number of scientific variables such as valence, atomic weight, boiling and freezing points, specific gravity at a given temperature, number of atoms in a molecule, the strength of the bond they form in compounds, all go together. That is, all naturally occurring instances of elementary substances with an atomic weight near 1 have the same valence, the same freezing and boiling points, the same specific gravity, the same number of atoms in a molecule, and the same strength of the chemical bond. We would call all these instances "hydrogen." If we look then at the instances of elementary substances with an atomic weight around 4, we observe a different valence, different boiling and freezing points, a different specific gravity, and a different strength of the chemical bond in compounds. We call all these instances "helium."

This fact that a large variety of variables takes on a limited number of *combinations of values* means that we simplify our theory greatly by talking about hydrogen and helium and the other elements rather than talking about all the values of all the different variables. Whenever a large number of variables go together, so that specific values of one are always associated with specific values of the others, the creation of *typologies,* or sets of type-concepts, such as the chemical elements, is scientifically useful. Other examples from various sciences are diseases in medicine (the variables are the symptoms which form the syndrome of the disease); compounds in chemistry; rock types in geology; the state-descriptions of solid, liquid, and gas in physics; classifications of societies as hunting-and-gathering, nomadic-herding, agricultural, and industrial in anthropology; classifications of languages according to their root language in linguistics; cloud-types in meteorology; and so forth.

The simplification of scientific theory by such typologies is due to the fact that many times the operative variable, either as cause or effect, is the type rather than the variables which make up the type. For a wide variety of chemical and physical problems we can formulate our predictions in terms of whether the gas we are working with is hydrogen or helium, forgetting about most of the variables which define the qualities of the two gases. Likewise we presume that the different diseases with different syndromes have different causes, while all instances of a given disease have the same causes.

We may, of course, find out that we have been wrong in such a supposition. In that case, we usually try to construct a new, better typology. When the causes of polio were discovered precisely, for instance, it turned out to be at least three different diseases.

The first test of a type-concept, then, is that the variables that make it up be *in fact* connected to each other. We need to know that the variables have a combination of values in some instances and that these values are all the same in all such instances and have a different set of values in other instances. Thus in recent studies[12] evaluating Max Weber's type-concept of "bureaucracy," it has been discovered that part of the values of variables Weber used to construct his type-concept were in fact associated with each other, while another group of variables were not associated with these but were associated among themselves. Thus the concept had to be broken down into two different type-concepts ("rational" and "bureaucratic," or "professional" and "bureaucratic" administration).

The second criterion then is the criterion of all scientific concepts, that the typology be useful in the formulation of theories that are supported, that the type is indeed important as a cause or as an effect of other phenomena.

Types as a Convenience in Talking About Interaction Effects

There is another common use of typologies in scientific discourse which is not as fundamental as the simplification function—namely, to talk about *interaction effects* of two or more variables. By an "interaction effect" we mean that one variable has different effects, depending on the value some other variable has. For instance, people who are more interested in politics are more likely to attend political rallies for a candidate. But if people are very interested in politics but *favorable to the opposing candidate,* they are very unlikely to attend a political rally for the candidate. Thus variation in interest has different effects, depending on attitude toward the candidate.

It is often convenient in this situation, for simplicity in presentation, to create a new variable which takes account of both variables. That is, we define a new variable according to the *combinations*

---

[12] See the summary of studies by Stanley Udy and me in Peter Blau and Richard Scott, *Formal Organizations* (San Francisco: Chandler, 1962), especially pp. 207–08 on Stinchcombe and pp. 205–06 and 208–10 on Udy.

of values on other variables. Thus we might construct a variable in our example according to the following table:

INTEREST IN POLITICS	OPINIONS ON CANDIDATE *A*	
	Favorable	*Unfavorable*
High	Enthusiastic supporters	Enthusiastic opponents
Low	Apathetic followers	Apathetic opponents

Then if we were to relate this new variable to attendance at a political rally for candidate *A*, we would probably find that only the "enthusiastic supporters" were very likely to attend. That is, our typology constructed out of the two variables of interest and opinion would be more efficient than opinion alone or interest alone in predicting the attendance.

Such typologies for analyzing interaction effects are the most common typologies in sociology, and the fourfold table with types as entries in the cells is a standard tool of sociological theorizing. Notice that there is no statement in the table above that says that any combinations of values are more likely than any others. Nor is there anything comparable to the implicit statement in the periodic table of elements which says that elements with an atomic weight around 4 with a valence of $+1$ never occur. In typologies for analyzing interaction effects, all the combinations of values receive names and are presumed to be empirically possible.

There are, of course, other methods of handling interaction effects than the creation of typologies, since there are a large number of different ways of defining a new variable as a function of a combination of values on other variables. One of the most common ways of defining values of combinations with continuous variables is to form the product of the two. For instance, if we had a continuous measure of favorableness to candidate *A* and a continuous measure of political interest, then the product of these two variables would be high among the enthusiastic supporters and low in the other three cells, and thus would function in exactly the same way as our typology for predicting attendance at the rally.

Such typologies for handling interaction effects, then, are just one of a large class of ways of defining a new variable as a function of the combinations of values on other variables.

Examples of such nontypological combinations of variables to create a new variable would be the "cost of living" in a country (defined as a function of the prices of various goods), or "mean annual rainfall" (function of rainfall in various years). In each case the concept is useful because there are some effects of each of the variables which depend on the values of the others. The effect of a rise in the price of medical services on the welfare of workers, for instance, depends on whether other prices have gone up or down. A dry year will have different effects on what crops are planted the following spring if previous years have also been dry than if the area is a normally wet region. That is, there are interaction effects among the variables which make us want to use a function of their combinations as a theoretical variable rather than the variables themselves.

In summary, then, typologies have two radically different functions in scientific theory, one of which is fundamental, the other of which is just a convenience. In the first case a typology is a statement that a large number of variables have only a small number of combinations of values which actually occur, with all other combinations being rare or nonexistent. This results in a radical improvement in scientific theory. In the second case, a typology is merely a convenient way of writing a function of two or more variables in such a way that interaction effects can be simply stated.

IV / LEVELS OF GENERALITY IN SOCIAL THEORY

Up to this point we have discussed theories which are specific enough to have specific empirical consequences. We plan to spend much of our time at this level in this book, but it will be useful to have a general outline of all the various levels of generality which are included in the term "theory" as it is commonly used in sociology. Many of the debates and frictions among sociological researchers are really debates about the level of generality it is fruitful to work at. And many of the exchanges of criticisms, though apparently about whether or not some particular theory is true, are actually conflicts over levels of generality.

Confusions over levels of generality quite often lead people to believe they have refuted something when they have not. To take a currently popular example, many people argue that since Marx predicted that the increasing misery of the workers would lead to their radicalization, and since this prediction turned out to be false, "Marxian theory" has been disproved. What has been disproved, of course, is only that part of Marxian theory which implied that prediction. Examining Marx's argument on this point, we find it rather difficult to tell exactly what he does base this prediction on, but it seems to be his Ricardian analysis of the labor market. Thus there is certainly something wrong with the bald prediction, and very probably something wrong with Marx's version of Ricardo's theory of the price of labor. But it is quite possible that nothing is wrong with, for instance, his theory of politics as an expression of the class struggle, or with his theory that *if* there were increasing misery, *then* there would be a proletarian revolution. What has happened in this case (and it happens just as much to Freud as to Marx) is that people regard all elements of Marxian (or Freudian) theory as equally involved in every one of Marx's (or Freud's) hypotheses. Thus they refute, for instance, Marx's theory of politics by examining a consequence of his economic theory, or Freud's theory of the unconscious by refuting a specific theory of compulsive behavior. Many such problems can be avoided if we classify the elements of a man's thought according to the level of generality and use this distinction to guide our analysis of exactly what has happened, logically speaking, when a specific hypothesis of a theory has been refuted.

An Outline of Levels of Generality

It seems to me to be useful to classify elements of theories into the following seven levels of generality:

1. General ideas about causality, about what can be accepted as a fact, about what forms of logical inference are valid, and other similar philosophical presuppositions of scientific theories. This

chapter, for instance, is an example of writing at such a level. The general argument of Marx that the material world exists and all observable phenomena have material causes would be another example at this level.

2. General causal imageries, about the kinds of causes and causal structures that work for explaining phenomena of many varieties. Examples are: the idea of classical physics that causes cannot work from a distance without intermediaries; the sociological notion that some things are, or are not, to be explained by their consequences ("functional" theories); the idea that the physical environment is important in shaping animal and human behavior; or Marx's imagery that social relations in productive activities create interests and motives that people take to other areas of life.

3. Broad distinctions among classes of phenomena thought to have a distinctive type of explanation or to be the phenomena among which to search for causes of other phenomena. For instance, Freud distinguished between consciously controlled behavior and behavior that was not consciously monitored (slips of the tongue, dreams, hysterical symptoms, and reactions to projective techniques such as free associations) and held that the latter had a different set of causes from the former. Or Marx distinguished a set of authority relations and rights of appropriation ("property relations" or "relations of production") which he thought had a large number of effects and in turn were caused in a systematic way by the historical stage of development of the economy.

4. Ideas that the causes of one broad class of phenomena are likely to be found among variables in another broad class of phenomena. For instance, Freudian theory urges that the explanation of most behavior not controlled consciously is in the structure of unconscious motives, especially sexual, derived from repressions of these motives in infancy. Or Marx argued that most political phenomena are to be explained by variations in property relations.

5. Theories that one in particular of the variables within a broad class of phenomena explains a particular variable (or set of variables) in another class of phenomena. For instance, Marx argued that Bonapartism ("populist dictatorship," we would call it today)

was caused by a predominance of a "petty bourgeois" mode of production (one characterized by small businessmen and small farmers). He thought a petty bourgeoisie (especially one made up of small peasants) was both equalitarian and had great difficulty organizing as a class, needing therefore a democratically oriented dictator. Or Freud argued that hysterical paralysis was caused by a repression of a strong wish to do something involving the paralyzed member.

6. The empirical consequences of theories, describing the observations that could be made if the theory were true. Thus Marx argued that if petty bourgeois production causes Bonapartism, then Louis Bonaparte in France would be heavily supported by petty bourgeois groups. A modern Marxist would argue in turn that the development of Bonapartism in Egypt or Mexico would have also been supported by small peasants and small businessmen. Or in Freud the empirical hypothesis would be that analysis of dreams, slips of the tongue, or free associations would reveal repressed wishes involving the paralyzed member in a particular case of hysterical paralysis.

7. Assertions that the observations in a particular case support, or refute, the empirical specification of level six. Thus Marx's assertions that in fact the petty bourgeois groups supported Louis Bonaparte, or Freud's assertion that in his case studies repressed wishes were indeed found, are of this order.

Levels of Critiques

A refutation or critique of a theory may touch any one of these levels. For the sake of illustration, let us go systematically through critiques at different levels, both for the Marxian theory of Bonapartism and for the Freudian theory of hysterical paralysis.

At the most general philosophical level, Lenin thought that Mach's philosophy of science attacked the materialist basis of Marxism, and that such petty bourgeois idealism led indirectly to considering the state as a mystical body, above mere class interest.

Skipping down to the fourth level, a critique might argue that the same mode of production tends to cause different political phenomena at different times in world history, depending on the world ideological environment. For instance, radical movements are different after the 1917 Bolshevik Revolution than they were before. Thus the critique asserts that the causes of political forms are to be found in the reigning ideas of an age, rather than in the means of production. Marx would call such an argument also "idealistic," but it is clearly a different level of idealistic deviation from Marxism than Mach's.

An argument that populist dictatorships in the modern world (e.g., in Egypt) are very often supported by the proletariat attacks one of Marx's theories at the fifth level. It does not necessarily challenge the fourth-level assumption that groups with a distinctive position in the productive system will have a distinctive politics. It merely says that Bonapartism in particular is one of the political expressions of the proletariat.

An argument that Marx incorrectly chose his indicators of a petty bourgeois productive structure, and that France in 1851 was really a feudal structure, would attack Marx at the sixth level. It says that the empirical assertion that France should have strong Bonapartist movements does not follow from the theoretical proposition that petty bourgeois modes of production ought to produce Bonapartist movements, for France was not in fact petty bourgeois. Likewise an argument that similar productive arrangements occur in the modern world and should produce Bonapartist movements is a modification at the sixth level. Countries with a large rural population and a land tenure system similar to that of France in the 1850's would include, in the 1960's: Haiti, Mexico, Formosa, Egypt, Ghana, Java in Indonesia, and perhaps India. An argument that these countries do not produce Bonapartist movements, yet should be included among countries with a petty bourgeois productive structure, would be an attack at the sixth level. This argument does not seem to me to show much promise.

An argument that Marx misinterpreted the facts about mid-nineteenth-century French political life and that it was really big business and big landowners who supported Louis Bonaparte would be an attack at the seventh level. The argument would agree that the facts ought to be the way Marx says they ought to be. But it says that in the real world the facts are some different way.

An argument that Freud had mistaken, say, a repressed fear for a repressed sexual wish in one of his case studies would be an argument at the seventh level. It would be asserting that the facts are not as Freud says.

A derivation of new facts that Freud had not considered would be an attack (if the results came out negatively) at the sixth level. For instance, if Freud's theory were right, then it should be true that responses of hysterical paralysis patients to thematic apperception tests should differ from the responses of nonhysterical patients, by showing evidence of repressed sexually significant wishes using the paralyzed member. A critique that derived this consequence and then attacked the theory because this consequence is not true attacks at a higher level than a mere disputing of the facts.

The critique would immediately be moved up to the fifth level, if Freud were to accept this as a valid deduction from his theory. If the argument remains at the level of whether or not the thematic apperception results do derive from the theory, it need not move up.

An argument then might or might not develop at the fourth level. There are still other variables in the broad class of subconscious motives which might serve as alternatives to the repressed wish as explanations of hysterical symptoms. Proving that particular subconscious motives do not appear among hysterical patients on thematic apperception tests more frequently than among normals does not prove that some other motives may not appear more frequently. But one could assert that there are no such differences, nor any other evidence that subconscious motivations differ between hysterics and normals. Such an assertion of no subconscious differences would attack Freud on the fourth level.

An argument that both conscious and unconscious phenomena are learned in exactly the same way, according to the laws of learning psychology and reinforcement schedules, would be an attack at the third level. It would argue that exactly the same causes explain behavior which Freud classed in two distinct broad classes. It would argue that whether a piece of behavior was consciously monitored or not played no role in its explanation.

An argument that one cannot believe functional explanations of behavior, explanations by motives or other subjective orientations toward the ends of action, would be an attack at the second level. Behaviorism in psychology was such an attack.

An argument which says that since Freudian theory involves concepts which are unobservable (such as the ego and the id) it is all just a mystification would be an attack on fundamental philosophical postulates about what kinds of conceptual entities can enter into science.

It is extremely rare that a refutation at a lower level involves a refutation all the way back to the first principles of the philosophy of science. How much a theory is damaged by the refutation of a particular part always has to be analyzed logically.[13]

V / CONCLUSIONS

In this chapter our purpose has been to formulate the logical tools needed to evaluate scientific theories, as a guide to the work of constructing these theories in such a form that they can be tested. In the first section we assumed that we could derive empirical statements from a theory we wanted to test. Then we analyzed what happened to our degree of belief in a theory when different kinds of consequences of the theory were compared with the facts. If a consequence of a theory turns out to be false, the

---

[13] A good recent example of difficulties in this respect is George Homans and David Schneider, *Marriage, Authority, and Final Causes: A Study of Unilateral Cross Cousin Marriage* (Glencoe, Ill.: Free Press, 1955). They try to refute a particular "functional" theory that cross-cousin marriage is to be explained by its consequence that it ensures the regular and systematic exchange of women among families in certain kinds of kinship structures. Then they argue that they have shown that nothing is explained by its consequences. That is, after examining (and apparently refuting) a theory at level five (Rodney Needham argues that they in turn failed at level seven in assessing the facts of the case), they jumped up to level two to argue that this refutation showed the lack of usefulness of a general causal imagery. The general usefulness of a causal imagery is not, of course, involved in a failure of some particular theory which uses that causal imagery. We do not wish here either to judge whether their conclusions on functionalism are right (we will treat them later) or to evaluate their anthropological evidence. Our only point is that, if one accepts their evidence, they have only refuted a theory of the functions of cross-cousin marriage and have not shown that nothing is ever caused by its functions.

theory is falsified. If it turns out to be true, the theory becomes more credible. If several similar consequences turn out to be true, the theory becomes substantially more credible, for then more alternative theories are eliminated. The more different the consequences of a theory which are checked are, the more alternative theories are eliminated, and consequently checking many different consequences increases the credibility of a theory greatly.

But if an empirical consequence of a theory we are checking is also a consequence of either of the theories which generate random distributions (sampling or a large group of small causes), then the credibility of our theory is increased very little. Hence statistical significance of a set of observations (proof that they are unlikely to be explained by random distributions) is usually a minimum requirement for regarding the observations as substantial support for a theory.

If we can formulate the main alternatives to a theory, then we increase our scientific efficiency greatly by using crucial experiments. A crucial experiment is a set of observations which will give one result if one of the main alternative theories is true, and a different result if another is true.

Then we turned to the internal structure of one important class of scientific theories—namely, causal theories. In order to analyze such theories, we had first to define a scientific variable. A scientific variable is a concept which has several values. The concept and its values are defined in such a way that there is at least one way to tell what value an observation has in a particular instance (that is, at least one way to "measure" it). A causal law, then, is a statement that a change in the value of one variable is sufficient to produce a change in the value of another, without the operation of intermediate causes.

Observations in support of causal theories must support three elements: they must establish *covariation, causal direction,* and *nonspuriousness.* The two main ways of establishing covariation are experiment and measurement of simultaneous natural variation of two variables. The main methods of establishing causal direction are: manipulation of the independent variable, manipulation of the dependent variable together with knowledge of covariation, temporal priority of the causal variable, knowledge of the causes of the causal variable, and knowledge of some other causes of the dependent variable which are not correlated with the cause we are studying. The main methods of establishing nonspuriousness are: deliberate control of possible spurious variables, control through randomization, control through knowledge that values of the possible spurious variable stay the same in various observations, and control through measurement of the spurious variable and either adjustment of the results for such spurious effects or partial analysis.

Then we turned to the next lower level in scientific theories, that of concepts. First we pointed out that the purpose of a concept is to identify phenomena which have identical causes or identical effects in some scientific field. Consequently concepts change as fast as the theories change, for as we locate the cause or the effects of phenomena more exactly, we must divide up phenomena differently. The test of a concept is how many supported scientific statements it occurs in.

The measurement of concepts is generally by either the causes of the phenomena or by their effects. The improvement of measurements and the refinement of concepts thus constitute a particular case of improvement of causal knowledge. However, the particular environment in which this investigation goes on has given rise to special devices for sorting out the causes and effects of a variable that are most directly related to the underlying variable, such as scaling techniques and factor analysis. All these devices depend on the fact that the direct effects or the direct causes of a variable we want to measure are likely to have high covariation with that variable, and hence high covariation with each other.

There are two main kinds of type-concepts, which use a combination of values on several variables to create a new variable. One of these, exemplified by the chemical elements, asserts that in the real world only a few of the many logically possible combinations of a number of variables actually occur; it gives names to each of these combinations. The other is a simple way of writing a new variable as a function of two or more others; it makes no assertions about the world. This last kind of type-concept is especially useful in talking about interaction effects of two or more variables, in which a change of a variable has a different effect depending on the values of other variables.

In the final section we turned to the general problem of how to analyze more exactly what has happened to a whole theoretical structure when some particular derivation has been disproved. One important device for analyzing what happens is the classification of the elements of a theory according to their level of generality, ranging from general philosophical presuppositions down to assertions about what happened in a particular observation. A theoretical argument can be attacked at any one of these levels, but much confusion in scientific discourse has its origin in refuting a hypothesis at one level and believing that one has refuted a theoretical proposition at another level. The whole problem of the logical structure of complex theoretical systems has received very little fruitful analysis.

Although this chapter has touched on some problems currently discussed in the philosophy of science, we have tried to leave aside philosophical and epistemological problems whenever we could. Our purpose has not been to outline the ultimate justification for scientific belief, but to outline how scientific belief systems operate in practical fact, so that we can use this knowledge in constructing social theories.

CHAPTER THREE

Complex Causal Structures: Demographic, Functional, and Historicist Explanations of Social Phenomena

In this chapter we will try to show that theories of sufficient complexity to be interesting and powerful can be built out of the components outlined in the preceding chapter. We will decompose demographic, functional, and historicist explanations into causal connections between variables. When we have done this, we can study each causal link by the means appropriate to the single-link theories of the preceding chapter, by deriving consequences to be checked against the facts.

In addition, more complex causal structures give rise to quite different overall patterns in the data on social phenomena. For instance, as we will see, functional types of causal structures give rise to a pattern in which the *consequences* of structures tend to be constant in a given situation, but the *structures themselves* have great variety and variability. This variability of one of the elements of the explanation has led many people to conceive that functional explanations are of a radically different kind from other explanations, to think them somehow "soft" or philosophically unsatisfying.

57

Their belief is rooted in a misunderstanding of the structure of multiple causal links in functional theories.[1]

We will suggest diagnostic clues in the pattern of data on social phenomena which indicate the appropriateness of such complex structures. These patterns of data are strict logical derivations from the complex causal structures involved and have no necessary element of "intuition" or "judgment" or "approaches" about them. Complex theories have empirical consequences just as do simple theories, and deriving these consequences is simply a problem of understanding the logical structure of the theory exactly. Complex theories are important for sociological research because most interesting social phenomena show the patterns of data generated by the more complex theories of this chapter, rather than simple one-link causal structures of the sort treated before.

First we will deal with a two-component theoretical structure, demographic explanations. In demographic explanations one set of causal processes determines the *numbers of people* of different kinds, while a second determines a *proportionality factor* by which these numbers of people are multiplied to get the effective causal force. After outlining the basic causal structure, we will deal with two main variants of demographic explanations. A closed demographic explanation is one in which the number of people of certain kinds is the result of past demographic processes. An instance is population growth, where the size of a population is the result of past population size and a proportionality factor of the past birth rate. An incomplete demographic explanation is one in which the causes determining the numbers of people of the relevant kinds are quite separate from the causes of rates or proportionality factors.

Second, we will deal with functional explanations, in which a structure or an activity is caused (indirectly) by its consequences.

[1] This has had the unfortunate consequence that rigorous research has been pretty much confined to the simple one-link causal theories of the preceding chapter, while the interesting theoretical work has gone on with "soft" research procedures. The main exception is the magnificent study *Union Democracy*. One way of describing this chapter is that in it we will try to teach everyone to write such books. Seymour M. Lipset, Martin A. Trow, and James S. Coleman, *Union Democracy: The Internal Politics of the International Typographical Union* (Glencoe, Ill.: Free Press, 1956).

Obviously such a theory involves a causal loop of some kind. In addition, it is clear that a consequence of a structure cannot enter into its causation as a variable if that consequence is maintained anyway—that is, if the consequence would come about whether the structure were there or not. Thus some "tension" tending to disturb the consequence is an inherent part of functional explanations. Functional explanations thus consist of causal links among three variables: (1) a *structure* or *structure activity* which has as a consequence the maintenance of (2) a *homeostatic variable,* which in turn would not be maintained without the structure because of (3) *tensions* which tend to disturb it.

A quick example may make this clearer. Claude Bernard[2] gave a functional explanation of certain structures in the liver in terms of maintaining blood sugar levels constant. The blood coming into the liver from the digestive system varied widely in sugar content, with variations in eating and digestion. Animals which do not maintain fairly constant blood sugar levels (*e.g.,* diabetics) are much more likely to die, and hence there is selection for animals with effective livers. Here the *structure activity* is the storage of sugar, the *homeostatic variable* is blood sugar level, and the *tension* is the wide variability of digestive activity. The consequence of liver functioning is causally linked to producing animals with functional liver structures (or some equivalent), creating the functional causal loop, by natural biological selection. If digestive activity were constant, there would be no selection in favor of animals with functional livers, and we would not expect to find them. Thus the tension is a necessary part of the explanation of the presence of functional structures.

From this three-component causal structure, we will go on to causal structures of an infinite character. Many social phenomena regenerate themselves from year to year. The United States is the richest country in the world this year mainly because it was the richest last year, for example. Such infinite self-replicating causal loops tend to preserve on into the future the historical causes which got them started. We have called such infinite self-replicating causal structures "historicist" explanations. They are the kinds of causal

[2] Claude Bernard, *An Introduction to the Study of Experimental Medicine* (New York: Macmillan, 1927).

structures which make "tradition" a powerful source of explanations of social phenomena. Another way of describing such explanations, then, would be that they identify where the causal energy comes from which preserves "traditions."

In the appendix to this chapter, we will describe a set of mathematical procedures for dealing with the kinds of graphs used here to represent causal structures. These procedures have been called the algebra of *linear directed graphs*. Manipulation of such graphs is the source of much of the logical content of the verbal parts of the chapter, especially the parts on functional explanations. However, the verbal parts can easily be understood without the mathematical apparatus that generated much of them. Readers who hope to do creative work in the logic of functional theory would be well advised to study this branch of mathematics. Some additional new results in functional theory will be derived in the appendix, by way of illustration of the power of the procedure.

I / DEMOGRAPHIC EXPLANATIONS OF SOCIAL PHENOMENA

By a demographic causal theory, we mean one in which a causal force is assumed to be *proportional to the number of people* of a certain kind. The number of people of that kind is, in the general case, determined by other causal processes. Thus the explanation of many social phenomena breaks down into two distinct problems of causal explanation: (a) explaining how many people of a given kind there are, and (b) explaining the proportionality between numbers of different kinds of people and the causal force producing the phenomenon. The illustrations in Table 3.1 indicate a number of features of demographic explanations. First, the second column indicates why we call them demographic. They involve *describing the population* (*demo* is a root for "people," *graphic* for "describe") in terms of the numbers of people in those categories of the population which have distinct proportionality factors. Because we know that women have very few children at some ages (below about 15 and above about 45), and many more at other ages, common sense tells us that our theories will be much more refined if we describe the population first in terms of its age and sex structure. Because we know that in all economies different indus-

TABLE 3.1

Illustrations of demographic explanations

To explain	Kinds of people whose number must be specified	Proportionality factors
Number of births	Women of reproductive ages	Age-specific birth rates
Gross national product	Labor force in various industries	Industry productivities
Number of students at a given level	Age groups in population corresponding to level	School attendance ratios and level distributions by age
Votes for left parties	Eligible voters in various social classes and ethnic groups	Proportions of social groups voting left

tries add different amounts of value per man per year to the product, it is useful to describe the industrial structure before analyzing productivity. Because very few 40-year-olds, but relatively many 18-year-olds, will enter college, it is useful to describe the detailed age structure of the population in predicting freshmen enrollment. Because many societies either do not have many factory workers or do not permit workers to vote, and because workers are more likely to vote for left parties, it is useful in comparing political systems to describe the structure of classes and the structure of eligibility to vote. Thus demographic explanation is most valuable when the proportionality factors for different groups of the population are markedly different and when populations differ in their internal structure.

The second feature is that we do not think that the proportionality factors depend in an immediate way on the numbers of people in various categories. If people changed their fertility so that women in more numerous age groups had fewer children and if when the number of women went down each had more children, so as to maintain a given number of births, a demographic explanation would not be very useful. What we would want to know in that case would be why the number of births remained constant, and what forces determined the size of that number. For instance, one would not try to predict the total amount the society would pay to physicians by projecting the number of physicians and multiplying it by a constant income factor. For we imagine that, by reason of supply and demand mechanisms, the more physicians there are, the less each will earn. Thus a relative causal autonomy of the numbers and the proportionality factor is required to make a demographic explanation useful.

Note, however, that the proportionality factor need not be a constant, unchanging quantity. For instance, with economic development, all the proportionality factors in Table 3.1 change. Birth rates tend to go down, productivities go up, school attendance ratios increase, and votes by workers for extreme left parties often decrease. The point is that these changes are relatively autonomous from changes in the numbers of people in different categories.

A third common feature characterizes three of the four proportionality factors and is strategically very important: they are inherently time-dependent. Age-specific birth rates are usually given in numbers of children per woman-year in that age group. This is because we know that a thousand women of a given age will have about five times more births in five years than in one year, that births are time-dependent phenomena. Likewise, productivities are almost always stated on a man-year basis, because in the normal course of events a man will produce five times as much in five years as in one. And the reason that the proportion of students of a given age entering college is an important figure is that people usually enter college exactly once during a year, or not at all during that year.

The reason that time-dependent phenomena are usefully treated demographically is that the number of people in a given category during a given year is a direct measure of the number of man-category-years. Thus anything time-dependent tends to have an overall causal force proportional to numbers of people, which is an indirect measure of the amount of time.

The Simplest Integrated Demographic Theory: Population Growth with Negligible Reproductive Cycles

Let us now consider a simple case of a theory which integrates into the *same* theoretical structure both the numbers of units in a population and a proportionality factor. Let us conceive of the proportionality factor as a birth rate, so that the number of people in the population at t_1 is equal to the number at t_0 (a previous time), plus the number "born" in the time between t_0 and t_1 (we will take care of deaths later). Let us also assume that practically as soon as new units are added to the population, they start to reproduce.[3]

Then if we call the time difference between t_0 and t_1 "Δt," and the difference in population between t_0 and t_1 "ΔP," and the instantaneous birth rate α, we have

$$\Delta P = P_0 \alpha \, \Delta t \tag{1}$$

The change in population is equal to the population at t_0, multiplied by the birth rate during the period, which is $\alpha \, \Delta t$. Those familiar with the calculus will be able to see immediately that integrating this expression will give us an exponential growth of population (or exponential decline, if the "birth rate" is negative).

We can easily modify this theory to take account of deaths, if the death rate is constant, by merely subtracting the death rate from the birth rate, and substituting the difference for α above. If the birth rate is higher than the death rate, the population will expand at an increasing rate as time goes on. If the death rate is higher, the population will die out as a negative exponential, declining at a decreasing rate. See Figure 3.1.

When the number of people in social groups depends on the number of people in those groups in the past in a simple way, then very simple combined theories incorporating both processes can be constructed. Slight variations in the processes postulated give rise to other patterns of development, which are easy to formulate formally and are often very useful approximations to reality.[4]

[3] This is grossly untrue for human populations, and consequently the theory developed here does not apply to them without modification. If the age-specific birth rate is constant, the overall birth rate will be constant, or constantly cyclical, and the theory can be modified to take account of age by modifying only the birth rate. For some of the implications of inconstant birth and death rates, combined with long reproductive cycles, see Norman Ryder, "Notes on the Concept of a Population," *American Journal of Sociology,* Vol. 69 (March, 1964), pp. 447–63.

[4] A good nonmathematical introduction to many of these theories is Kenneth Boulding, "The Malthusian Model as a General System," *Social and Economic Studies,* Vol. 4, No. 3 (September, 1955); also a Bobbs-Merrill reprint.

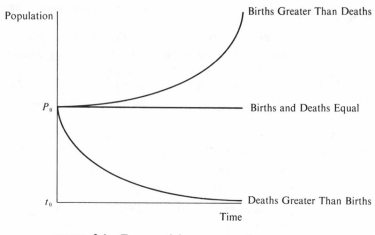

FIGURE 3.1 Exponential approximations to population growth curves for populations with negligible reproductive cycles and constant birth and death rates.

A More Complex Integrated Demographic Theory

Let us now go on to a slightly more complicated case of an integrated or closed demographic theory. Let us suppose that all the people in one part of the population come from either that part of the population in the past or another part. And let us suppose that all the people from that other part come either from the first part in the past or from that other part itself. We can diagram this situation as in Figure 3.2.[5]

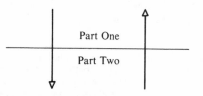

FIGURE 3.2 A closed population with transitions between parts.

[5] This diagram and the ideas developed in this section are all based on James S. Coleman, *Introduction to Mathematical Sociology* (New York: Free Press, 1964), chapters 4–9. The diagram, modified here, appears on p. 106.

The arrows represent a certain number of people moving from Part I of the population to Part II, and some moving from Part II to Part I. At some future time, the number of people in Part I will be the number who were in at the beginning, minus the number who have left to Part II (the downward arrow), plus the number who have come in from Part II (the upward arrow).

Now we may suppose, as is usual in demographic theories, that the number moving *from* Part I in a given time period is determined by the *number of people* in Part I at the beginning of the time period and a *proportionality factor* (usually called a "transition rate") which moves a certain proportion of the people in Part I over into Part II. Likewise we may suppose that the number moving into Part I from Part II will depend on the number of people in Part II at that time, multiplied by a proportionality factor (or "transition rate"). If we call the transition rate from I to II, q_{12}, and that from II to I, q_{21}, and if we call the numbers in the parts n_1 and n_2, respectively, the number moving would be:

from Part I to Part II: $q_{12}n_1$
from Part II to Part I: $q_{21}n_2$

Where will the change of n_1 and n_2 stop? It will clearly stop when the numbers moving out of a part equal the numbers moving into it. Or it will stop when

$$q_{12}n_1 = q_{21}n_2 \qquad (2)$$

That is, it will stop when

$$\frac{n_1}{n_2} = \frac{q_{21}}{q_{12}} \qquad (3)$$

This is one of the most important results in the whole area of demographic explanations. When a demographic causal process

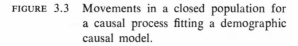

FIGURE 3.3   Movements in a closed population for a causal process fitting a demographic causal model.

operates as in the diagram and we let it operate long enough to come to a stop,[6] *the relative numbers of people are a measure of the relative sizes of the proportionality factors.*

With this knowledge, we can answer for example the following questions about polling often put by intelligent and thoughtful people.

1. Why can pollsters use a poll from a month before an election to predict the division of the vote, when a great many people change their minds during the final week?

2. Why can pollsters usually divide the "Don't Know" answers among the candidates in the same proportions as those who answered, and still predict the election percentages with reasonable accuracy?

3. Why can sociologists use differences between groups in the proportion saying "Agree" to a question to measure differences in the causal force toward agreement in those groups, even though people change a great deal in their agreement to the question over short periods of time?

The answer to each of these is that the underlying causal forces, the proportionality factors, or transition rates, are well measured by the relative numbers of people answering "Republican" or "Democrat," or "Agree" and "Disagree." The changes during the last week, the division of the "Don't Know" answers, the group differences in agreement to a question, all are approximately governed by those same causal forces. Hence the proportions are stable in the face of much individual change.

Here we have treated a special kind of demographic theory of very wide applicability and generality.[7] The key conditions for its applicability without modification are these:

1. The population is classified into exhaustive categories, all of which are recruited from each other.

---

[6] We can approximately check this by repeated interviews using the same questions. If the same number change from "no" to "yes" as change from "yes" to "no," we can infer that the process has come to a stop.

[7] Further modifications of theories of this general nature, with many examples, are treated in Coleman, *op. cit.* Some acquaintance with the calculus is useful in reading his treatment.

2. The proportions of people of one category moving into another category per unit of time are approximately constant.

When these two conditions are met, we find a very simple example of an emergent property of a social group. The proportions of people in the parts of the population tend to constancy (or equilibrium) in the face of a good deal of individual change. This means that the pollster who takes a "snapshot" of the population at a given time is not really measuring the ephemeral and changing characteristics of individuals. Instead, he is measuring a balance of causal forces characterizing the group. This group property is usually much more stable and reliable than the characteristics of the individuals.[8]

This point is important and intuitively difficult for many people, so it bears repeating. If a pollster had to say that the people he found to be Democrats a month before the election would still be

[8] Perhaps it would be useful to outline why we can very often explain aggregate phenomena very well, when our understanding of individual behavior is very imperfect. We can note that this is precisely the situation that Gauss was in when discussing errors of measurement, as mentioned in Chapter Two. Gauss did not know very well the idiosyncratic causes which bore on the individual measurements of physical quantities. But he showed that the behavior of a large aggregate of poorly understood measurements could be understood very well.

Suppose that we have a causal force, f, which bears on every member of an aggregate (in Gauss's case, f was the influence of the size of the thing measured on the measurements). Then also for each individual there is a large number of idiosyncratic causes (for Gauss, these were random measurement errors due to many small causes). The effect in the population would then look like this:

INDIVIDUAL	CAUSAL FORCE BEARING ON INDIVIDUAL
1	$f + i_1$
2	$f + i_2$
3	$f + i_3$
.	.
.	.
.	.
n	$f + i_n$

Some of the idiosyncratic forces (the i's) will tend in the opposite direction from f, some in the same direction. If we have a good theory of the systematic forces, the average of these idiosyncratic forces will be zero. Let us suppose that the "average" size of these idiosyncratic forces is σ (actually in statistical theory, σ refers to the square root of the mean square of the forces). Gauss showed that under these conditions, with

Democrats at the time of the election, he would shortly be out of business. It is only because he can usually say that his poll results measure the underlying causal forces, approximately in equilibrium, that there is any stability in poll results. The stability of a population proportion only very rarely depends on the stability of the individual characteristics on which it is based. A great deal of the stability of social phenomena depends on such equilibria of

---

reasonable restrictions on the distribution of idiosyncratic forces, the *mean* force bearing on the individual is $f + \dfrac{\sigma}{\sqrt{n}}$. So the aggregate force bearing on the entire group would be $nf + \sqrt{n}\ \sigma$.

Now let us suppose that the idiosyncratic forces that we do not understand are four times as large as the systematic forces that we do understand—that is, $\sigma = 4f$. Consider the aggregate force exerted on populations of different sizes. The entry at the left is the number of people in the population we are studying, n. In column (1) is the systematic force applied to that population, nf. In column (2) is the total effect of the idiosyncratic forces, $\sqrt{n}\ 4f$, since $\sigma = 4f$. In column (3) is the ratio of the idiosyncratic forces we do not understand to the systematic forces which we do understand.

Population of size	(1) Systematic force	(2) Idiosyncratic force	(3) Ratio (2)/(1)
1	f	$4f$	4.0
100	$100f$	$40f$	0.4
10,000	$10,000f$	$400f$	0.04
1,000,000	$1,000,000f$	$4000f$	0.004

As the size of the population increases from 1 to 100, the influence of the unknown individual idiosyncratic behavior decreases from four times as large as the known part to four-tenths as large as the known part. As we go to an aggregate of a million, even if we understand only the systematic one-fifth of individual behavior as assumed in the table, the part we do not understand of the aggregate behavior decreases to less than 1 per cent (0.004).

Thus a psychologist explaining migration decisions of individuals might regard himself as massively ignorant, knowing only one-fifth of what goes on. A labor economist explaining the migration behavior of an aggregate of a million people can, with exactly the same theory, regard himself as a genius for having explained over 99 per cent of the aggregate behavior.

The conflict between the view that one has explained only a fifth of the behavior and the view that one has explained 99 per cent of the behavior is apparently a permanent feature of the social sciences. I take the 99 per cent, or aggregate, view.

forces of change. A grasp of how this can come about is essential for potential social theorists.

Incomplete or Open Demographic Explanations: Rates, Quantities, and Proportions

By an incomplete or open demographic explanation, we mean one in which the numbers of people are not determined by the action over time of the same causal process involved in the proportionality factors. The circle of explanation is not closed. We need two separate theories of the determinants of numbers of people of different kinds and the proportionality factors to be applied to them. The examples given in Table 3.1 are incomplete demographic explanations. There are three main kinds of such incomplete explanations: those explaining rates (*e.g.,* births per year), those explaining quantities (*e.g.,* gross national product per year), and those explaining proportions (*e.g.,* proportion voting left).

By a *rate,* we mean the frequency of a given event in a given time period. By a *quantity,* we mean some aspect of social behavior which can be added, multiplied, and divided, such as dollar value or tonnage. By a *proportion,* we mean the fraction of some group of people having a given characteristic. Usually we are interested in proportions that are relatively stable features of a population.

Rates: Many events happen with different frequencies per year to different kinds of people. The frequency of giving birth is nearly zero for women less than 15 years old and for women more than 45 years old. Hence any analysis of the birth rate per year which ignores the sex ratio or the age distribution of women is likely to be foolish. Unmarried women have a lower birth rate per year than married women in most social groups, so separation of the population of women in the fertile ages by whether or not they are married is often fruitful.

There are three main intellectual purposes in analyzing rates according to a classification of the population. First, we may want to *eliminate* the effects of different numbers of people in various categories, in order to study the causes of variations of the proportionality factors in populations of different structure. Second, we may want to *predict gross rates* when group-specific rates are approximately constant. Third, we may want to use variations among groups in rates as *clues in the search for causes* of the proportionality factors.

We very often achieve *elimination* of different structures of population groups by studying the whole set of proportionality factors for each of the subgroups. For instance, Table 3.2 gives

TABLE 3.2

Fertility of women 40 and over by farm background and income: Detroit, 1952–58*

| Income of head of family | TWO-GENERATION URBANITES | | FARM MIGRANTS | | Proportion of farm migrants within each category |
	Average no. of children	No. of cases	Average no. of children	No. of cases	
Under $3000	2.36	(134)	3.21	(99)	42%
$3000–$4999	2.04	(276)	2.85	(158)	36%
$5000–$6999	2.15	(292)	2.61	(100)	26%
$7000+	2.19	(329)	2.24	(72)	18%

* Source: David Goldberg, "The Fertility of Two-Generation Urbanites," *Population Studies*, Vol. 12 (1958–59), p. 217. Two-generation urbanites were identified as families in which the husband's father had had a nonfarm occupation when the husband was growing up. All others were identified as farm migrants to the cities. None of the differences in fertility by income are statistically significant for the two-generation urbanites.

some data on birth rates (per woman-reproductive-life, rather than the usual per year basis) for families of urban and rural extraction living in the Detroit area. Here we want to eliminate the well-known influences which cause higher proportions of rural-born people to be in the lower classes in cities, and the well-known higher birth rates of rural people, so as to study the birth rates of the social classes with ruralism eliminated.

We see in the first column of figures that there are no important differences in fertility by social class among urban-born people. All the significant difference in fertility by social class is accounted for by the different composition of the social classes in terms of urban-rural origins. Rural migrants have higher birth rates and are disproportionately concentrated in the lower classes. Further, those rural migrants who have achieved high incomes have adopted an urban fertility pattern, practically identical to that of the *lower-class* urban-born people and very similar to that of all urban people.

Thus this analysis by demographic techniques locates two separate kinds of causal forces. One, which we wanted to eliminate, is that there are more rural-born people in the lower classes and rural-born people have higher birth rates. This is a causal force proportional to the numbers of rural migrants in the different social classes, and it explains most of the differences among the social classes in birth rates. The second kind of causal force identified is one which operates on the proportionality factors, the birth rates. Rural migrants have different birth rates according to the social classes they have attained. This suggests that successful adaptation to urban social life by migrant rural families both (a) encourages occupational success and (b) involves the adoption of urban patterns of fertility control. But among urban-born people, no differences of any importance in the birth rates appear.

Rather than explaining why lower-class people have higher birth rates (perhaps by some theory of their inferior intelligence, their greater impulsiveness, or some other such variable), we have to explain the higher birth rates of people of rural extraction. That is, the problem of explaining social class differences in fertility in cities turns out to be the *same theoretical problem* as explaining the higher birth rates of rural areas.

This same finding can be used for the other two purposes outlined above. It will lead us to make different predictions about what is likely to happen to gross social class differences in fertility as the proportion of the urban population that is of rural extraction decreases. The differences will probably disappear. It also casts doubt on the old-fashioned inferences of dysgenic consequences of social class differences in fertility, because it is not likely that rural migrants are of genetically inferior stock to urban people. It is far more likely that their being in the lower classes is caused by their recent migration, rather than by their inferior mental equipment.

Another way of eliminating the effects of population structure is "standardization." [9] By taking the group-specific rates within the population, and applying them to create a fictional birth rate which represents what *would happen* if the populations had the same structure, we eliminate the differences in structure. That is, we could construct an "origin standardized" birth rate for each social class in Table 3.2 by imagining that each social class had the same proportion of rural-born people as one of the social classes, or as the general Detroit population of that age. The main limitation of this method is that it cannot take account of "interaction" effects. That is, in Table 3.2 we would lose the information that social class has no effect in the urban-born population but a substantial effect in the farm-migrant population.[10] Origin-standardized birth rates calculated from Table 3.2 would show a lessened, but still substantial, variation by social class in the birth rate, because variations in the rural-born birth rate would show up in the standardized rates.

Besides this purpose of isolating group-specific rates so that we can investigate the causes of those rates, we may instead (or also) have the purpose of understanding or *predicting gross rates* when the group-specific rates are approximately constant. For example, the age-specific mortality rates from heart disease are approximately constant across societies. Medical science has not (yet) had much effect on these rates. But societies with high birth rates have many more young people in them; societies with low birth rates have more old people.[11] Hence the gross rate of heart disease increases as the birth rate declines. A fact like this is of no help in explaining the age-specific rate of heart disease. But it may

[9] Morris Rosenberg, "Test Factor Standardization as a Method of Interpretation," *Social Forces*, Vol. 41 (October, 1962), pp. 53–61.

[10] David Goldberg, "The Fertility of Two-Generation Urbanites," *Population Studies*, Vol. 12 (1958–59).

[11] The intuitive idea that societies with lower death rates have more old people is wrong (except that it happens that they also have low birth rates). Lower death rates are mainly achieved by saving children and young people, and hence have the same sort of effect as high birth rates. The life expectancy of a man of 60 is almost the same in poor societies as in rich societies. It is the life expectancy of the new-born children which is most affected by improved medical care and sanitation. Thus, the first effect of a decline in mortality, with birth rates constant, is to produce a younger population. Only when birth rates decline does the average age of the population increase.

be very useful indeed in planning hospital needs, in deciding the number of internists to train, and the like. In addition, a negative correlation between birth rates and heart disease rates is, at first blush, a queer fact that we may want to understand, in order not to be led into fanciful theories of the degeneracy of modern societies that are losing both their reproductive and physical vigor. Demographic explanations often explain quite simply such peculiar behavior of gross rates.

A third purpose is to *use variations among groups in rates as clues in the search for causes of rates.* This is one main purpose of epidemiological research, which studies disease rates. For example, it has been discovered that certain cervical cancers in women are virtually absent among nuns, very infrequent among Jews, intermediate in the white non-Jewish population, and very frequent among Negroes. This suggests that some aspect of sexual practices may account for the cancers. Several hypotheses come to mind. Perhaps it has to do with cleanliness and circumcision. But one suggestive hypothesis is that the pattern above (and several other patterns not reported here) are very similar to the pattern of the rates of venereal diseases. Groups with low sexual contacts (*e.g.,* nuns) and endogamous groups with high family stability (*e.g.,* Jews) have low rates of both venereal disease and cervical cancers. Groups with unstable families and a high proportion of men and women with multiple sexual partners during their lifetimes (*e.g.,* U.S. Negroes) have higher rates of both venereal diseases and of cervical cancers. To an epidemiologist this might suggest looking for various mechanisms of transmission of such cancers, similar in form to those involved in venereal infections.[12]

Quantities: Suppose one were interested in explaining why, in very many underdeveloped countries, a single "primate" city is very much larger than other cities and is the main focus of industrial and commercial development. We know that industrial and commercial development is very much dependent on the size of the market, in dollars or pesos or whatever. How might demographic analysis help?

---

[12] Clyde Martin, "Marital and Coital Factors in Cervical Cancer," unpublished Ph.D. thesis, (Johns Hopkins University, 1966). Considerably more evidence related to this hypothesis is presented there.

It is known[13] that in poorer countries the *ratio* of urban to rural incomes is much higher than in richer countries. That is, urban per capita yearly income in a country like Honduras or Mexico may be 3 to 8 times as great as rural yearly income per capita. In a country like the United States, it is only about $1\frac{1}{2}$ times as great. In addition, we know that the proportion of income spent on goods produced outside the home increases very rapidly with income. That is, very poor people, especially very poor rural people, spend most of their income on things produced at home. Richer rural people spend much more of their income for things produced outside the home.

In Table 3.3, we present some rough calculations of the relative

TABLE 3.3

Approximate relative weight in the market of urban and rural people in poor and rich countries

	URBAN PERSON			RURAL PERSON		
	(1)	(2)	(3)	(1)	(2)	(3)
	Income index	Market proportion	Weight in market (1) × (2)	Income index	Market proportion	Weight in market (1) × (2)
Poor country (*e.g.*, Honduras)	1.0	1.0	1.0	.25	.50	.125
Rich country (*e.g.*, U.S.)	1.0	1.0	1.0	.67	.90	.60

weight in the market of urban and rural people in a poor country, and compare it with the situation in a rich country. If a rural person in Honduras makes about a quarter as much as an urban person and spends half of that on food grown at home, then his weight in the market is only one-eighth that of his urban colleague. In the United States, the rural person makes about two-thirds as much as

[13] Simon Kuznetz, "Industrial Distribution of National Product and Labor Force," part 2 of "Quantitative Aspects of the Economic Growth of Nations," in *Economic Development and Cultural Change,* Vol. 11 (January, 1963), pp. 32–50, especially 36–39.

his urban colleague and spends about nine-tenths of that income in the market. His market weight then is about six-tenths that of his urban colleague.

The differences between these weights will be even greater if we are considering industries producing or trading in luxury goods, such as cars, household appliances, jewelry, shoes, and education. These things are luxuries in the sense that richer people spend a great deal more on them than do poorer people. Since it is exactly these luxury industries that are being newly established (more basic nonluxury industries had large markets when the country was poorer, and hence were established first), their markets will be even more concentrated in the cities. Thus especially for new luxury industries the market in a poor country will be almost entirely urban, while the market in rich countries will be significantly rural. Multiplying out these market weights by the size of population will give the proportion of the market which is urban rather than rural.

When the causal force is a quantity such as income, and when the total quantity is a causal force as in the case of market size, and when great inequalities characterize the distribution of that quantity among people (as with income in poorer countries), a demographic analysis is often useful. In this case, by breaking up the total income by rural vs. urban, we see that the market is more highly concentrated in urban people, especially for those goods being newly introduced into the economy (the luxuries), in poorer countries than in richer countries. And this heavier weighting of urban people in the market may outweigh the simple fact that there are more rural people in poorer countries. Even though the country is more rural, the market of that country may well be more urban. Hence new industries and new commerce tend to be established in these cities. This further concentrates the market and maintains the income differentials. Such a heavily weighted feedback process can result in explosive growth of central primate cities, while regional cities, more dependent on rural markets, lag further behind than they would in advanced countries.

Thus back of the growth of the great primate cities of the underdeveloped world, we can see a process operating which can be understood by a demographic explanation (this is not, of course,

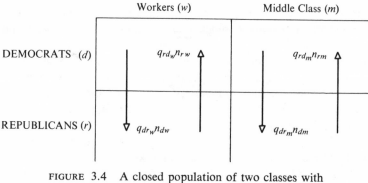

	Workers (w)	Middle Class (m)
DEMOCRATS (d)	$q_{rd_w} n_{rw}$ ⬆	$q_{rd_m} n_{rm}$ ⬆
REPUBLICANS (r)	⬇ $q_{dr_w} n_{dw}$	⬇ $q_{dr_m} n_{dm}$

FIGURE 3.4   A closed population of two classes with a different balance of forces in the classes.

the only process explaining such explosive growth). But in this case the proportionality factor is a quantity (of income spent in the market), rather than a frequency of an event.

Proportions: The most conceptually satisfactory way to deal with different proportions in different subcategories of a population is to repeat the transition rate analysis above in each of the subgroups.[14] For example, suppose we are interested in the *proportion Democratic* among workers and middle-class people. We have on the one hand some theory (perhaps of economic development or of extension of citizenship rights) which predicts for us the number of workers and middle-class people in the electorate. Now we want to analyze the proportions in each subcategory who are Democrats. For simplicity, let us assume that there are only Republicans and Democrats and that during the period we are analyzing no one changes social class (or that the rates at which they change classes are sufficiently slow that we can ignore them). Then we can construct a diagram similar to Figure 3.2 for each class.

That is, among Democratic workers in a given time period, a proportion q_{dr_w} change to Republican (the subscript dr means Democrat-to-Republican, while the subscript w specifies that this transition rate applies to workers). Among Republican workers, a proportion q_{rd_w} change to Democrats. If we let this process operate long enough, it will stop when the same number of workers change from Democrat to Republican as change in the

[14] This again follows Coleman, *op. cit.*

opposite direction. If we call the number of workers who are Democrats n_{dw} and the number of workers Republicans n_{rw}, then there will be no more change in the proportion Democratic when

$$q_{dr_w} n_{dw} = q_{rd_w} n_{rw} \qquad (4)$$

or when

$$\frac{n_{dw}}{n_{rw}} = \frac{q_{rd_w}}{q_{dr_w}} \qquad (5)$$

[Compare equations (2) and (3) above.] By the same reasoning, the proportion Democratic among middle-class people will become stable when

$$\frac{n_{dm}}{n_{rm}} = \frac{q_{rd_m}}{q_{dr_m}} \qquad (6)$$

We find that in fact the proportion Democratic among workers is higher than the proportion Democratic in the middle class, and that these proportions are fairly stable over the short run (even though many people in both classes are changing preferences). This indicates that the causal force q_{rd_w} is larger than q_{rd_m}, or that q_{dr_w} is smaller than q_{dr_m}, or both. That is, either the causal force toward being a Democrat is larger for workers, or the causal force away from being a Democrat is smaller for workers, or both.

Stability in the pattern of proportions can thus be expected whenever the causal forces operating in a group are relatively stable. It does not necessarily mean that individuals are deep-dyed Democrats or Republicans, and that such deep-dyed Democrats are more common among workers. It can mean that (in that case, the q's will be small). But the stability of proportions, and of differences in proportions among social groups, is compatible with a great deal of freedom, indecision, discussion, and mind-changing among individuals.

Formulating the problem of proportions in terms of a balance of forces of individual changes, rather than in terms of the numbers of people of a given kind, is the first step to wisdom. The second step is, clearly, finding the causal forces which produce the equilibrium observed at a given time.[15]

Essentially, then, analyzing a population proportion turns into a problem of classifying that population into categories that have

---

[15] For a more complete treatment, see Coleman, *ibid.*, especially chapters 9–12.

different balances of causal forces operating to change individuals. As the number of people exposed to the balance of causal forces characteristic of a subgroup increases, that subgroup's balance becomes more important for the total population. But a change, for instance, in the number of middle-class people in a society is quite a different thing from a change in the balance of Republican and Democratic causal forces *among* middle-class people. By a demographic analysis of population proportions, we avoid mixing these two things up.

It is useful in carrying out such an analysis of proportions to draw diagrams like that in Figure 3.4. First, it reminds one that his results may indicate a balance of forces rather than qualities of individuals. And it suggests the following series of questions:

1. How confident am I that the present situation reflects a *long enough operation* of these transition rates so that the numbers of people reflect the relative causal forces operating now (the q's)?

2. Which of the variables I have here are *relatively permanent* characteristics of individuals (low q's; *e.g.,* race), and which are *relatively ephemeral* (high q's; *e.g.,* political preference). What does this imply about *causal direction* of the association between them? If both are relatively ephemeral, what causal processes probably connect them? Can one be regarded as causally prior (*i.e.,* that its transition rates are the same in all categories of the other variable)? What evidence would show this?

3. What is the *nature of the causal force* represented by the ratio of the q's? Do people probably leave one category for reasons different from their reasons for leaving another?

4. Are any of the transition rates (the q's) likely to be zero? If so, and if there are any people left in the cells with zero arrows pointing inward, then the process is *not* in equilibrium. This immediately demands temporal analysis. How did the people get into the cell? When did the last people move? What causal force is left out of the theory?

Demographic Explanation Summarized

The basic structure of demographic explanations, then, is that two different sorts of causal processes determine the *number of people* to whom a causal force is applied and the *size of that causal force,* the proportionality factor. In particular, most sociologically important causal forces vary a great deal among *different kinds of people.* Changes in the distribution of kinds of people have a different theoretical meaning from changes of the causal forces applied to those people.

It makes a great deal of difference theoretically whether the birth rate declines because there are fewer women in reproductive ages or because each fertile woman has fewer children per year. Because these are different causally, they give rise to different predictions about the future. Likewise we will predict something quite different about social class differences in fertility if we know that they really measure rural-urban fertility differences, because the proportion of rural-born people in cities is declining much more rapidly than the proportion of working-class people. Hence we will expect social class differences in fertility to disappear in advanced societies.

This breaking apart of explanation into two components is also characteristic of the conceptual structure of complete or closed demographic explanations. Even though the number of people depends on the previous birth rate, it also depends on the size of the population at a previous time. Even if new Republicans were recruited only from among Democrats, the number of new Republicans would depend on the number of Democrats at a previous time as well as on the forces making people change. This conceptual independence becomes quite a practical independence when the numbers of people of a certain kind (say, workers) are determined by quite different causal forces (say, industrialization) in incomplete demographic explanations from those which determine a proportionality factor which applies to them (say, proportion Democratic).

A wide variety of causal theories in sociology are of this complex structure, rather than of the simple causal relations analyzed in the preceding chapter. But these are the simplest and most primitive of complex causal structures in social explanation. Next we turn to a set of theoretical structures with three components and three kinds of causal relations among them. These are the causal structures characteristic of functional explanations of social phenomena.

II / FUNCTIONAL CAUSAL IMAGERY

By a functional explanation we mean one in which the *consequences* of some behavior or social arrangement are essential elements of the *causes* of that behavior. The commonest kind of functional explanation in everyday life is that of motivation, of "wanting." We explain the behavior of the famous chicken by his wanting the consequence of being on the other side of the road.

When we say that someone wants a car, that generals want to win a war, that people generally want not to be sick, and use this to explain their behavior, we are saying that the consequences of their behavior are its principal cause. When we use such an explanation, we expect that if one kind of behavior does not have those consequences, a person will try another kind of behavior. Under different situations, the same want may explain very different kinds of behavior. In one war theater, a general who wants to win may use heavy naval artillery, in another bombers, in another infiltration and psychological warfare, in another large land armies. Whenever we find *uniformity of the consequences* of action but *great variety of the behavior causing those consequences,* a functional explanation in which the consequence serves as a cause is suggested.

In analyzing the concept of want, Heider[16] proposes the criterion of equifinality. That is, if various means are perceived to lead to the same end, and the subject tries one of these after another until he reaches the end, and then the subject stops changing among behaviors, common-sense psychology interprets the subject's behavior with the word "wants."

Let us consider some social phenomena that are thought to exhibit this characteristic of equifinality.

1. There seems to be, in all societies, some man who is ultimately responsible for the welfare of a given child (often such responsibility is called "sociological fatherhood"). But sometimes the man is the biological father, sometimes a stepfather (the new

[16] Fritz Heider, *The Psychology of Interpersonal Relations* (New York: Wiley, 1958).

husband of the mother), sometimes the mother's brother, sometimes the patriarch of a large household who may be a grandfather,
granduncle, or other older relative. The variety of means with the
same consequence suggests that a functional explanation in terms
of providing a sociological father is appropriate for analyzing
family patterns.[17]

2. All organizations try to pursue their goals in the face of
uncertainty and variability of the environment and try to reduce
the uncertainty. But sometimes they do it by research on the uncertain factors, sometimes by flexibility in adapting to changing
factors, sometimes by buying or conquering the organization or
country producing the uncertainty, and sometimes by leveling
the uncertain factor by, for instance, keeping adequate inventories to even out fluctuating supply. Such an equifinal pattern suggests a functional explanation of organizational behavior in terms
of uncertainty reduction.[18]

3. All societies in which there is something substantial to inherit
(land, the kingship, money) provide some set of rules of inheritance
which determine more or less uniquely who is to inherit each good.
But some societies provide succession through the father's line,
some through the mother's, some through election by a defined
group, some by wills enforced by court proceedings, some through
passing rights to the next younger brother, some by redivision
within the whole community. This combination suggests that unique
determination of the inheritor of different rights is almost always
achieved, though the means may vary. That is, it suggests a functional explanation of inheritance patterns.[19]

4. In most social groups there are some roles or positions into
which a youth is never admitted without previous training for
competence, rules of behavior, standards of performance, attitudes,
and values. But in some social groups this socialization is mostly
done by the family, in some by schools and universities, in some by

---

[17] See Bronislaw Malinowski, "Parenthood, the Basis of the Social Structure,"
in V. F. Calverton and Samuel D. Schmalhauser (eds.), *The New Generation* (New York: McCauley, 1930), pp. 137–38.

[18] See James Thompson, *Organizations in Action* (New York: McGraw-Hill,
1967), *passim*.

[19] See A. R. Radcliffe-Brown, *Structure and Function in Primitive Society:
Essays and Addresses* (New York: Free Press, 1963), pp. 32–48 on
"Patrilineal and Matrilineal Succession."

a "basic training" period in which one deals with simulated environments (*e.g.,* targets rather than the enemy), in some by apprenticeship, in some by a group of future peers (*e.g.,* fraternities). The unity of consequences of a variety of devices suggests a functional explanation of patterns of training in terms of training requirements of positions.[20]

Indications for the Use of Functional Imagery

Functional causal imagery is thus indicated whenever one sees (or thinks he sees) a pattern of equifinality in social phenomena. The next question to ask is what clues there are to a pattern of equifinality. It is simplest to see these in the simple case analyzed by Heider: how do we judge that a person "really wants" something? That is, how do we every day diagnose an equifinality motivational cause in other people? Then we can locate analogous situations in other explanations that do not involve wanting.[21]

1. If increased difficulty in achieving the end leads to increased activity, an equifinal structure is indicated. When someone really wants something, he is willing to put forth more effort when getting it is harder. When somebody really wants something, there is a positive correlation between how hard it is to get and how hard he works to get it. This is how we tell, for instance, that people really want to breathe, even though they do not put forth much effort to breathe most of the time. We recognize increased effort by the variety of means tried, by the amount of time invested, by psychological preoccupation with getting it, by the search for new knowledge about getting it, by the willingness to sacrifice other things to get it, and so forth.

An illustration for a social phenomenon is given by Malinowski. He saw that Trobriand islanders engaged in many more magical practices before going on highly dangerous fishing expeditions on

---

[20] Talcott Parsons, *Family, Socialization, and Interaction Process* (Glencoe, Ill.: Free Press, 1955), pp. 42–131, especially pp. 50–53, 98–101, and 124–25.

[21] Note that we are analyzing wanting as a special case of equifinality or causal centrality of consequences. It is *not true* that equifinal causal structures indicate wanting, as we will show in considerable detail later.

the high seas than when they fished with poison in the lagoon. This observation led him to conjecture that people tend to maintain a conviction that they control the outcome of their activities, that they reduce anxiety. When controlling outcomes becomes harder (when the outcome is uncertain), they tend to maintain this conviction of control by magical appeals to supernatural forces. Hence societies will concentrate magical rituals to control the environment in those areas where their actual control is least.[22]

Another illustration: Firm succession rules reduce conflict over inheritance of property. People will fight harder over large amounts of property than over small amounts. It is therefore harder to prevent conflicts when there are great properties involved. Therefore, the observation that succession rules are usually firmer, clearer, better enforced, and better obeyed in the landed upper classes than in the poor rural lower classes suggests a functional explanation of succession rules. Society, so to speak, tries harder to resolve succession conflicts when they are more severe.

2. If the end is achieved in spite of causes tending to keep it from being achieved, an equifinal structure is indicated. Even if we do not know that a man has put forth great effort, the fact that he overcame great difficulties and hindrances and still achieved the end is evidence that he really wanted the end. Thus if we know a man has earned a college degree even though his father died early and he had to support his family, we would judge he really wanted an education.

Suppose we observe that a production line in a wooden toy factory works pretty steadily, even though we know that the raw materials are shipped in the spring and summer from sawmills and the demand is highest before Christmas. We infer that there must be compensating devices which level out supply and demand variations. We would be well advised to look for structures whose functions were to level these input and output variations.

A very general cause of political apathy in various countries is the illiteracy, isolation, and poor organization of rural areas. If we observe that in Mexico the electoral participation of farmers is often higher than that of urban people, and that this high participa-

---

[22] Bronislaw Malinowski, *Magic, Science and Religion* (Boston: Beacon Press, 1948).

tion is reflected in other ways such as government programs to help farmers, we begin to look for social arrangements whose function is to incorporate farmers into the political system. If we note at the same time the peculiar Mexican rural institution of the *ejido* (communities that are given land taken from large landowners), we will probably examine this institution to see if it has this function.[23]

3. If a variety of explanations or purposes, or inadequate and inconsistent purposes, are offered by people behaving to explain their behavior, an equifinal structure is indicated.[24] When a young man gives different explanations of his purpose in dating a woman (*e.g.,* one to his fraternity and one to the woman) and various inadequate explanations of his canceling some dates, the woman sensibly infers some latent, unmentioned want motivating the dating. Likewise when corporate managers explain their wants in terms of economic development before Congress but talk quite a different language to stockholders, we likewise suspect latent wants.

When an anthropologist studying another culture finds a pattern of marriage, say marriage of a cousin on the father's side, he may ask the people why this pattern is practiced. If some say it is because it is approved in their religion, others say that the two partners will know each other better, others say it keeps property in the family, and others give still other explanations, he suspects that the pattern achieves some latent end. His suspicion will be reinforced if he finds that the religious texts do not approve that marriage pattern, that other cultures with the same religion do not practice it, that the society makes no other provision for people who know each other well to marry, that property does not usually pass out of families when people marry someone else, and so forth. The latent function might be to preserve the solidarity and status of the lineage, for instance.[25]

---

[23] Linda Mirin and Arthur L. Stinchcombe, "The Political Mobilization of Mexican Peasants," unpublished paper.

[24] Robert K. Merton, *Social Theory and Social Structure*, revised and enlarged edition, (New York: Free Press, 1963), pp. 19–84, on "Manifest and Latent Functions."

[25] Richard B. Scott, "Social Status and Father's Brother's Daughter Marriage in the Middle East," (1965), unpublished manuscript, Johns Hopkins University.

If "grassroots administration" is highly touted in only some of the programs of a government agency (*e.g.,* in dealing with agricultural programs but not with power programs), and if only certain kinds of local people are included in the "grassroots" (*e.g.,* wealthy farmers but not tenant farmers), the analyst suspects that a latent function is served by the incorporation of farmers. The function might be obtaining the political support of strategic farm groups for the agency.[26]

4. If it is known that some causal process is operating which selects patterns of behavior according to their consequences, an equifinal structure is indicated. We know that if people do not want profits, there are many tax advantages in organizing nonprofit corporations. Hence if some group organizes itself as a business corporation, we infer that it wants profits and that it will probably change its activities if necessary to get them. That is, we know that the population of business corporations is selected according to the consequences which are causally crucial in motivating their behavior. The existence of a business corporation as a business corporation allows us to infer a good deal about its wants. To take a different example, we know that evolution wipes out species whose members do no want to eat. Hence the fact that a species exists lets us infer that its members want to eat. That is, when we know there are processes selecting out certain functional behavior, it is strategic to look for those functions in any bit of behavior we find in that selective context.

Types of Social Selection Processes

It will be useful to outline some of the mechanisms which generally select patterns of social behavior according to their consequences, so as to be able to recognize generally when the fourth principle applies to social activity. This outline will also be useful for getting ideas about the nature of reverse causal links from consequences back to structures, a sore point in functional theory.[27]

---

[26] Philip Selznick, *TVA and the Grassroots: A Study in the Sociology of Formal Organization* (Berkeley: University of California Press, 1949).

[27] George Homans, "Social Behavior as Exchange," *American Journal of Sociology,* Vol. 63 (May, 1958), pp. 597–606.

1. A behavior or a structure may be selected by biological natural selection, if its consequences increase the number of children with that behavior or structure living to reproduce. It has been suggested that the reflex of smiling in small babies and the impulse to respond favorably to a baby's smile in adults give a biological evolutionary advantage. Children may live to reproduce more often if they smile at their parents, and if their parents respond to smiles with loving care. Unsmiling babies and babies of parents who do not respond to smiling may more often be dashed against the cave wall.

2. Behavior may be selected by the differential survival of social groups with that behavior, because of its favorable consequences. For instance, firms which level input and output variations in order to run a production line at a steady rate may survive market competition better than those which do not, because of the lower costs of steady production. Hence there could be social selection for those structures within firms which level variations in production.

3. Behavior may be selected by its consequences being what people want, so that they plan their behavior to get the consequences. This planning in turn may be at the aggregate level, as in constitution-writing, or at an individual and small-group level, as when a whole class of individuals arrives at solutions for its succession problems.

4. Without planning, people may find consequences of behavior satisfying. Thus church services might be maintained without much planning to achieve theological ends, because people find the social interaction, or the respectability, satisfying.

5. With or without planning, a pattern may have pleasant consequences for other people, who reward the behavior. Thus without planning or analysis, a wife often learns what her family likes to eat by the way they react to what she serves. Quite complex patterns of behavior ruled by subtle chemical principles may be worked out on a pure "my husband doesn't like that" basis.

6. When reward from others is combined with benefited people's control over the conditions of existence of the behavior, a powerful evolutionary principle operates. The market selects, with great efficiency, the behavior of firms according to the consequences of that behavior for customers. And the labor market rewards the favor-

able consequences of education for productivity with sufficient power to be the main motivational base of the school system. If a firm's behavior does not have consequences sufficient to motivate people to pay for them, it goes broke.

Thus whenever a pattern of behavior occurs repeatedly in one of these situations which tends to select behavior by its consequences, it is very likely to have a functional explanation, an explanation in terms of its consequences. And it is likely to show the features of equifinality characteristic of such functional causal structures, as outlined above. For instance, craft systems appear archaic to a modern bureaucratic, business school eye. Yet they persist in extremely competitive market systems such as the construction, machine tool, entertainment, and publishing industries. (They also persist in some less competitive industries, such as railroads.) It has been suggested that craft institutions provide careers for workers where the firms, because of their instability, cannot. Careers in turn are essential to motivate workers to develop a high level of competence.[28]

The Logic of Functional Explanation

Inspecting the explanations above, we can locate the following essential elements in functional explanations:

1. The consequence or end which tends to be maintained, which in turn functions indirectly as a cause of the behavior or structure to be explained. Let us call this H, for "homeostatic" variable. A homeostatic variable is one which tends to be stable in empirical reality, even though there are forces which tend to change it.

2. The structure or behavior which has a causal impact on H, which we are usually trying to explain. Let us call this structure S. The causal connection between S and H is that S tends to maintain H. We can diagram this as in Figure 3.5.

[28] Arthur L. Stinchcombe, "Bureaucratic and Craft Administration of Production: A Comparative Study," *Administrative Science Quarterly*, Vol. 4 (September, 1959), pp. 168–87. The evidence presented there shows that the high level of variability of the construction industry, the tension which disturbs career stability, is negatively associated with a bureaucratic style of administration, which is a functional alternative to craft systems for providing knowledge at the work level.

S $\bullet$ —— $+$ —— $\triangleright$ —— $\bullet$ H

FIGURE 3.5   The connection of structure to homeostatic variable.

3. Other causal forces, tensions or difficulties, which tend to upset H, to keep it from happening regularly unless the structure causes it. If H would be maintained anyway, there is unlikely to be a structure especially concerned with maintaining it. Clean-air committees do not grow up in farm areas. Let us call these upsetting tensions T. The causal structure to this point is, then, given in Figure 3.6.

4. A causal process, evolution, competition, satisfaction, reward from others, or planning and wanting, which causes those S's maintaining H to be selected or reinforced. These forces become stronger when the consequence is not maintained, thus increasing the activity of the structure or selecting for it more strongly. Since this force is stronger when H is not naturally maintained (when T is higher) and decreases when H is maintained, it is a causal force with negative direction from H to S.

What propositions can we derive from Figure 3.7?

1. As T (or tension) increases, H (or the homeostatic variable) is not naturally maintained. The nonmaintenance of H increases the causal force operating to increase the level of activity of the structure, S. That is, the greater the tension, the higher the level of structure activity, or the more elaborated the structure. Compare this with the principle of increased difficulty in achieving the end leading to increased activity, mentioned earlier as an indicator of wanting. Thus as objective uncertainty (T) increases, anxiety

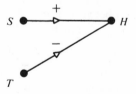

FIGURE 3.6   Contrasting effects of structure and
tension on homeostatic variables.

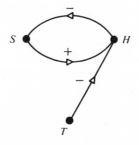

FIGURE 3.7 The elementary causal structure of a complete functional explanation.

(H^-) increases, so magic (S) increases. Or as the amount of property in dispute (T) increases, social peace (H) declines, and the certainty of succession rules (S) tends to increase. The proposition above held to indicate the appropriateness of functional explanations is a logical derivation from a causal theory with the form represented by Figure 3.7.

2. If T is high, or varies, but H remains constant, it is likely that some compensating causal loop of the nature of that between S and H exists. Compare this consequence of a looped causal structure with the principle of the end being achieved in spite of causes tending to keep it from being achieved, an indicator of wanting. That is, it is a derivation from the causal structure represented by Figure 3.7 that H will tend to remain constant even when T is large or varies. Thus if production of a plant (H) is stable, even though supply of raw materials (T) varies, then structures for leveling inputs (S) are likely to be operating.

3. If a structure is maintained by an unrecognized selective process from H, it will be stable as long as the tensions continue. People may often give explanations unrelated to H or T. Compare this consequence with the principle of the variety of explanations or purposes (or inadequate and inconsistent purposes) offered as an explanation of a pattern of behavior by people who are behaving that was offered above as an indicator of wanting.

4. If a selective causal connection between H and S exists, such that S's are selected or reinforced if they maintain H, then S's found in that situation will be more likely to be functional for maintaining H. That is, it is a logical derivation from a causal theory of the

89

form of Figure 3.7 that S's will be disproportionately selected from among those which maintain H. In addition, if there are no tensions upsetting H, then the selective or reinforcing process will not work to select functional structures. The common-sense theory that Gardens of Eden will not select and reward efficient work is logically correct, although it does not apply to tropical climates as commonly supposed. The reason population density is lower in the tropics is that it is harder to make a living there. Compare this consequence of a looped causal structure with the argument above on the selective conditions under which one will expect functional structures. Thus if we know that reduced costs (H) are strongly selected for in competitive industries (a strong reverse causal arrow from H to S), and that craft institutions (S) exist in some of those industries, this combination suggests that there is some cause which tends to push costs up (for example, career disorganization of skilled workers in fluctuating industries) (T), which is compensated for by a causal connection between craft institutions and reduced costs.

5. If several structures have the consequence of maintaining H, they will *all* tend to be caused by a functional causal system. Both sweating (S_1) and dilation of surface blood vessels (S_2) are selected for when body temperature is a homeostatic variable (H), especially when external temperatures (T) are highly variable (*e.g.,* among land animals as opposed to water animals—sweating would not be selected for among water animals because the causal connection between S_1 and H does not exist in water). That is, the equifinality feature, the causal priority of consequences, is a logical derivative of a causal theory of the form that is outlined in Figure 3.7.

All the peculiar results which distinguish functional explanations can thus be derived from a causal theory with the structure outlined in Figure 3.7. There are a wide variety of social, psychological, and biological processes which can serve as a reverse causal link between homeostatic variables and functional structures. Hence there is nothing any more philosophically confusing, nor anything any less empirical or scientific, about functional explanations than about other causal explanations. Functional explanations are merely a special case of causal theory, whose peculiar structure creates some interesting special results. But these are empirical results, which can be tested against the facts.

A Comment on the Conservative Nature of Functional Explanation

There have been some unfortunate confusions about the nature of homeostasis and of the equilibrium between tensions and functional structures. Many of these derive from a feeling that functional arguments assert that homeostatic variables constitute a list of good things about societies, and that focusing on the positive consequences of existing institutions tends in a conservative direction. This conservative cast of functional theory is not logically necessary, but it is an inherent rhetorical opportunity in the theory. In political discourse, the defenders of a structure or a practice will point out its positive consequences. They will point to selective processes, the market and voting being special favorites, which tend to preserve functional structures, as evidence that whatever is, is right. And they will view with alarm the tensions which would upset certain homeostatic variables—greed, external danger, the requirements of efficiency in dealing with the environment, latent civil war, the destructive passions of man's nature, and the like.

This selective affinity between functional explanations and conservative social thought often involves sloppy functionalism. Tensions are exaggerated, the goodness of homeostatic variables is overemphasized, the selective power of the market is exaggerated, the causal efficiency of existing structures in maintaining the homeostatic variable is overestimated. Such scientific sloppiness is a legitimate object of attack, just as the scientific sloppiness of much radical political rhetoric is an object of attack.

But there is something more fundamental going on here than mere scientific mistakes, and in order to deal with it we must analyze more exactly the conceptual status of homeostatic variables.

First, a homeostatic variable in a functional explanation is merely *factually* maintained, in spite of tensions tending to cause its disruption. Factual maintenance implies only that there is some *causally effective* selective force, not that there is a causal force which selects out good things. Natural selection selects out foxes and wolves for their causal efficiency in getting enough food to live to reproductive age. Shepherds need not agree that this is a good thing. One's attitude toward natural selection, and toward the selectively efficient red tooth and claw, depends on whether he loves sheep or wolves. Conservatives love wolves.

Second, usually the selective process takes place over a longer time span than the consequences of a structure. This difference in time span is most obvious if we compare the quickness with which the liver reacts to reduce the blood sugar level after a meal with the time span of millenia in which the dominance of animals with livers was established. The difference in time span means that the social or biological species dominant at a given time may well be on their way out. Clearly increased navigational skills, larger fishing boats, weather predictions, and lifeboats are alternatives to magic for reducing the anxiety of going out on the high seas. Almost everyone who has tried both prefers to set to sea in a modern ocean liner without the blessing of the gods, than in a canoe with the best of supernatural protection. Dinosaurs were clearly functional structures at one time, but that did not prevent their eventual extinction by more functional structures. A functional social structure such as canoe magic may, as easily as not, be a dinosaur.

Finally, functions may become irrelevant because the tensions to which they respond disappear. Usually they disappear because some other structure is handling or preventing the tensions. Many social practices to handle the consequences of infectious diseases for family life, or for individual functioning, disappear as modern medicine advances. There is less need to make sure that the young children of a widow have a sociological father, because there are many fewer young widows. Imprisonment for mental patients, and all the social structures that secure it, may become archaic as chemical control over the behavior of mental patients improves. But also, many tensions disappear through natural processes. We no longer have many of the devices worked out in the nineteenth century for handling ethnic tensions between Catholic immigrants and Protestants, because the level of religious tension is much lower. Many mutual help structures which were very important in rural life are functionally superfluous in urban life. In short, a functional structure may be functional for a function that no longer needs to be served, which no longer operates as a selective force for new structures.

Functions for homeostatic variables that we do not, as citizens, want to see preserved, functions better served by some other structure, or functions to relieve tensions that have disappeared, all may serve as scientific *explanations* of the existence of a structure. They are hardly rhetorical advantages of existing structures. In fact, one style of radical debunking of the status quo is pointing out that structures are functional for some ignoble end. This may perhaps become clearer when we treat the logical structure of Marxian analysis in the following section, for most of Marx's radical rhetoric consists in the assertion that social structures are preserved because they are functional for the enemies of the proletariat.

Marxian Functionalism: Functional Arguments in a System of Unequal Power

The fundamental starting point of Marxian analysis of social structures is that many things have good consequences for some people and bad consequences for others. If we look over the course of history, we find that such social structures change. The Marxian theory of history attempts to explain why structures giving advantages to one group are destroyed and replaced by structures giving advantages to other groups. The idea of power is essential to the Marxian analysis. None of the functional explanations above took account of the distribution of power.

The Marxian postulates about power can be briefly summarized as follows: (1) The relative power of social classes is determined by the mode of production, by the authority system required by a given technology, and by who owns the productive property. (2) The mode of production changes over time with advancing technology, extension of the market, larger units of production, and the like. (3) Hence the distribution of power among classes changes systematically over historical time.

The reason changing power distributions cause changes in insti-

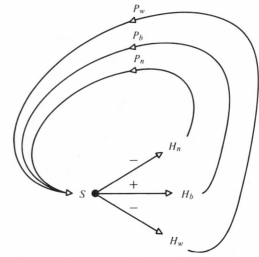

FIGURE 3.8   The causal loop structure of Marxian functionalism.

tutions ("superstructure") is that *the greater the power of a class, the more effective that class is as a cause of social structures.* Hence consequences for powerful classes have more effect in maintaining a social structure than do consequences for less powerful classes. Figure 3.8 illustrates the incorporation of power into a functional argument.

Let us suppose that the S analyzed here is parliamentary republicanism as a form of government. Marx called this system "bourgeois democracy" and argued that it served the interests of the bourgeoisie.[29]

The H_n in the diagram represents the consequences of parliamentary democracy for the nobles. P_n stands for the power of the nobles. That is, H_n is the set of variables which tend to be criteria of selection used by nobles in deciding where to exert their causal, selective power over institutions. P_n is the degree of selective force which nobles represent. Hence the causal effect in maintaining S,

[29] Cf., for example, Karl Marx, *The Eighteenth Brumaire of Louis Bonaparte,* translated by Eden and Ceder Paul (London: G. Allen Unwin Ltd., 1926), or Marx, *Communist Manifesto* (Chicago: Regnery, 1949).

for that part of S's consequences which affect the nobles, is a product of how good the consequences of S are for the nobles times the power of the nobles as a selective force. According to Marx's argument, the consequences of parliamentary democracy were negative for nobles, since it allowed urban interests to be represented and to invade the authority system of noble estates, to tax noble incomes, to protect peasants, and so forth. Hence insofar as noble power made them an effective cause of what happened in society, there was a selection process *against* bourgeois democracy. The closer the consequences of a structure (parliament) approached those of bourgeois democracy, the more pressure nobles would put on to change the structure. (In the diagram I have used a notation so that if the consequences for a group are unfavorable, the arrow between the structure and H for that group is given a negative sign.)

In like fashion, in accordance with Marx's analysis, the consequences for the bourgeoisie were positive, because they could resolve their conflicting economic interests by parliamentary compromise but could present a united front against workers and nobles. But Marx argued that the consequences of parliamentary democracy were negative for the workers, because its structure (especially in his time, when workers did not have votes) did not represent their interests as well as unions or the dictatorship of the proletariat. (I do not agree, but this is irrelevant to the logical structure of the argument.)

Now let us see what happens when we vary the distribution of power among the classes. For the sake of convenience, let us represent both the consequences for the different classes and their power by numbers. Under the feudal mode of production we would have something like the situation in Table 3.4. The consequences in the first column are multiplied by the power of the class in the second column to get the causal force supporting or undermining the structure. In this situation, the net result is to discourage parliamentary structures.

But the evolution of technology, the extension of markets, and the organization of factory production all tend to redistribute power in favor of the bourgeoisie. The fate of parliamentary democracy is therefore quite different in the capitalist stage of development.

TABLE 3.4

Parliamentary democracy (S) *in feudal mode of production*

Class	Consequences of S for the class	Power of the class	Causal force supporting (+) or undermining (−) S
Nobles	−1	5	−5
Bourgeoisie	+1	2	+2
Proletariat	−1	0	0
NET CAUSAL FORCE			−3

In this situation, the bourgeoisie imposes its preferred form of government over the opposition of the nobles.

As the dynamics of bourgeois development continue, the proletariat is concentrated into larger factories where it organizes unions. As these unions are fought by the bourgeois government, they unite into political movements of a socialist character. Meanwhile the bourgeoisie is getting smaller, and its innovating role in

TABLE 3.5

Parliamentary democracy (S) *in bourgeois mode of production*

Class	Consequences of S for the class	Power of the class	Causal force supporting (+) or undermining (−) S
Nobles	−1	2	−2
Bourgeoisie	+1	5	+5
Proletariat	−1	0	0
NET CAUSAL FORCE			+3

production becomes less important as the internal structure of factories becomes more "socialized." Its power is further sapped by the growth in severity of crises; the inherent instability of capitalist markets gets extended to the whole economy. Workers' increasing numbers and increasing organization change the distribution of power again, this time in favor of the proletariat. We will get, according to Marx, a situation like that in Table 3.6. Thus

TABLE 3.6

Parliamentary democracy (S) *under late monopolistic capitalism and socialism*

Class	Consequences of S *for the class*	Power of *the class*	Causal force supporting (+) or undermining (−) S
Nobles	−1	0	0
Bourgeoisie	+1	2	+2
Proletariat	−1	5	−5
NET CAUSAL FORCE			−3

Marx expected that the growing power of the proletariat would undermine bourgeois democracy and lead to a workers' revolution in which it would be replaced by a socialist government of a non-parliamentary type (in particular, without representation of bourgeois interests).

Marx and Marxists have applied this form of argument to forms of government, ideas about society ("ideology"), religion, family structures, property systems, international relations and warfare, revolutionary conflicts, and other parts of the superstructure of society. The approach is summarized in the famous phrase, "The ruling ideas of any age are the ideas of its ruling class." [30]

The elegance and economy of the theoretical scheme have gripped the minds of social thinkers on purely esthetic grounds ever since Marx wrote. Historical movements of governments, ideas, and institutions are determined by the organization of production and its effects on the power distribution. Yet the detailed study of the consequences of institutions for different classes is a logically inherent part of the explanation of them and renders the analytical engine marvelously flexible.

Our purpose here is not to judge whether Marx's judgments of the consequences of structures for different classes were accurate. Nor is it to evaluate his theory of the dependence of the power distribution on the arrangements of production. My own opinion is that he made serious mistakes in both these aspects of his analysis, but that he was mostly right.

[30] Marx, *Communist Manifesto*, p. 31.

Instead our purpose is to point out the general theoretical strategy of classifying men *according to how important they are as causes of social arrangements.* Consequences for powerful men, for shapers of society, are obviously more important in functional explanations of a structure than consequences for causally insignificant men. Consequences of social structures in universities for professors are likely more important than consequences for students. The rapid decrease of university teaching loads shows this. Consequences for physicians are likely to be causally more important than those for patients. The poor patient with an interesting disease can get extraordinary medical care at university hospitals, because his care has consequences for physicians, while equal suffering by poor patients with ordinary diseases gets brief treatment in a cost-conscious county hospital.

A word should be said about the role of tensions in Marxian functionalism. The main source of tension is clearly the support of other classes for structures which harm a given class. The potential causes for disturbance of noble hegemony are the competitors for hegemony, the bourgeoisie and the proletariat. This great explicitness about the sources of tensions, and the fugitive (if logically necessary) role tensions have played in most other functionalist writing, has led many people to mistakenly distinguish Marx from functionalism on this ground. But Malinowski cannot get by without uncertainty, nor Radcliffe-Brown without succession disputes, any more easily than Marx can get by without class conflict.

Graphically one can identify the tension for nobles in Figure 3.8 by starting at *S*, tracing around the bourgeois loop back to *S*, and then running up the noble loop. Tracing loops does not, of course, aid in understanding what is going on in the world, but it shows Figure 3.8 to be a representation of the theory and a strict analogue to Figure 3.7. The greater the power of the bourgeoisie, and the more in conflict their interests with respect to the consequences of the structure, the higher the tension. This is as it should be.

Summary

Functional theories explain phenomena by their consequences. They are very generally useful in explaining social phenomena because there are many chains of reverse causation which select patterns of behavior by their consequences: biological evolution; social evolution; individual and collective planning to achieve the consequences; satisfaction to the actor from the consequences with consequent operative conditioning; satisfaction to others who reward the actor; and satisfaction to others combined with social selection in a market system. Each of these common processes select out and reinforce behavior or social structures according to their consequences. This means that it is always a good bet, in trying to explain a social phenomenon, to look at its consequences.

There are a number of quick strategies for making a preliminary check of a functional theory, to see whether it is at all likely. We may repeat them here. First, if many different behaviors or structures are found in different groups, or within the same group, which all have the same consequence, this suggests that the consequence is causally crucial, the variations accidental. If we change the situation, the behavior will change, but it will change to another behavior with the same consequence. Second, if the level of activity of a structure varies with the tension which tends to keep a consequence of that structure from happening, this would also be a derivation from a functional theory. Third, if we find a consequence remaining steady even though one of its causes is varying, this again would be a logical derivation from a functional theory. We should start looking for the feedback loop from the consequence to a structure tending to maintain it. Fourth, if people give erratic and unconvincing reasons for a structure, but the structure keeps functioning when those reasons do not apply, it is likely to be caused by some of its unrecognized consequences. Fifth, any structure that occurs in a system we know to be highly selective by certain consequences is likely to have those consequences and to have been selected for that reason. Thus if we find a social pattern in a highly competitive industry, we would be well advised not to be arrogant about the favorable consequences of a change until we understand the functions of the existing structures.

But, as Marx realized, some consequences are more consequential than others. Structures often persist in spite of their having negative consequences ("dysfunctions") for some people. By negative consequences we do not mean necessarily bad consequences, but merely those which, in the absence of other positive consequences, would tend to select *against* the structure. When we find such negative consequences, we want somehow to add up the positive and negative to get a net causal force maintaining the structure. Marx's key observation is that in adding up such consequences it is necessary to weight them by the power of the groups that get the positive consequences and the power of the groups with negative consequences. This is such a fundamental modification of the mood of functional analysis that the similarity of the logic has been overlooked by many people.[31]

Functional explanations are thus complex forms of causal theories. They involve causal connections between three variables with a special causal priority of the consequences of activity in the total explanation. There has been a good deal of philosophical confusion about such explanations, mainly due to the theorists' lack of imagination in realizing the variety of reverse causal processes which can select behavior or structures according to their consequences.[32]

With the experience gained so far in more and more complex logical structures of theory, we are prepared to tackle an even more difficult kind of explanation. In a "historicist" structure of explanation, we must deal with an infinite (or near infinite) number of causal connections. This is not as difficult as it sounds if we restrict the infinite part to causal processes of a simple, self-replicating kind. One particular type of self-replicating process, as we will see, is created by a functional causal structure.

What we will address next is the causal structure of explanations of social phenomena by "tradition," by what has been done by a group in the past. Because it is so logically complex, and because

[31] Merton, *op. cit.*, does not overlook it.

[32] Also there are philosophical prejudices about the time order of variables on which naive people get hung up. As an exercise, the student may want to state the reverse causal processes above so that the consequence which is a cause of behavior happens before a given piece of behavior. This is not a difficult exercise. Also, many people unthinkingly suppose that the *only* causal system with an equifinality structure is a wanting structure. Trying to imagine whole societies wanting some consequence understandably mixes them up. But clearly equifinality is an abstract characteristic of many kinds of causal systems, and forcing a detailed analogy to wanting merely shows a determination to be confused.

much explanation by means of tradition is dependent on an exact understanding of the functional causal structure, explanations by tradition have generally been misconceived. In order to avoid eliciting these past confusions in the reader, we will speak of "historicist" explanations.

III / HISTORICIST CAUSAL IMAGERY

We very often observe social phenomena that stay the same from year to year. Often the best prediction we can make is that "this year will be just like last year." The United States will have a two-party electoral system this year because it had a two-party system last year. France will have a multiparty system this year because it had a multiparty system last year.

There are two main ways to explain why this year is like last year. One is that this year's phenomena are produced by a system of constant causes, the same causes that produced last year's phenomena. For instance, if we ask why cotton this year will be produced in the same areas that produced cotton last year, we find a series of causes of cotton production that stay fairly constant: the angle of the sun, the supply of water, the cotton plant's physiology, the approximately constant amount of clothes people wear, the cost advantage of cotton over wool and synthetics, the cheapness of Negro labor in the South and of Mexican labor in the Southwest, and the like. Some of these causes might, of course, change in the fairly short run. But mostly they do not. Thus the stability of the geographical distribution of cotton (and consequently of the social effects of cotton plantation systems) is a consequence of the constancy of the causes and conditions of cotton cultivation. We will not be interested here in constancy produced by a constant system of causes.

The second main type of explanation for this year's being like last year is that some social patterns cause their own reproduction. For instance, after one takes out all the variation in voting among counties that can be explained by their social composition and industrial base, rural Michigan and North Dakota and the hills of Tennessee are much more Republican than other parts of the country. After taking out the effects of social variables, Minnesota and Montana are much more Democratic than other parts of the country. There is evidence that the poverty-stricken hill country of the Border States has been disproportionately Republican ever since the Civil War.[33]

Likewise the electoral laws that maintain a two-party system here and a multiparty system in France seem to generate the sources of their own support. It is well known that the results of the movements and wars of the Reformation still determine which European countries are predominantly Catholic, which predominantly Protestant. Men vote like their fathers, go to the church of their fathers, feel loyalty to the land of their fathers, live in wealthy or poor countries according to the wealth of the country their fathers lived in, choose Yale over Harvard because their fathers went to Yale, and are ruled by the English common law rather than continental civil law according as their fathers were ruled by one or the other.

The frequency with which social patterns reproduce themselves from year to year, even when they are not caused by a set of constant causes, suggests an apparently simple variety of social explanation. Some set of causes *once* determined a social pattern (*e.g.,* the Reformation determined Protestantism in North Europe, Catholicism in South Europe). Then ever since, what existed in one year produced the same thing the next year (*e.g.,* each year each country had the same dominant religion it had the year before). We will call such theories "historicist explanations."

The original causes in such an explanation may be of any kind. The line between Catholics and Protestants may have been determined by military variables such as mountain ranges, by functional processes such as the usefulness of Protestantism to the commercial middle classes, by reasons of state when a king wanted to "throw off the Roman yoke" and appoint his own bishops, by the fact that Martin Luther's German was high art while his Polish was bad, and so forth. Such explanations of the start of traditions may or may not be sociological. But the reasons that traditions get maintained are sociological. Thus the problem of explanation breaks

[33] V. O. Key, *Southern Politics* (New York: Knopf, 1949), especially pp. 280–85 on "Mountain Republicans."

down into two causal components. The first is the particular circumstances which caused a tradition to be started. The second is the general process by which social patterns reproduce themselves. We will be primarily occupied with these general self-reproductive processes here.

The Causal Structure of Historicist Explanations

By a historicist explanation I mean, then, one in which an *effect* created by causes at some previous period *becomes a cause of that same effect* in succeeding periods. A commonplace example is marriage. Most men are married to a certain woman this year because they were married to her last year. The processes of courtship cause a historical event, a wedding, at one period. This event is a transition to the state of "married to a particular woman." Then this effect becomes a cause of the same effect in succeeding periods. We can diagram this causal structure as in Figure 3.9.

In Figure 3.9, *x* is an original historical cause of *y*; *D* stands for a "delayor" so that *y* at a given time operates as a cause in the following time period; and the 1 on the returning arrow indicates that *y* as a cause in the succeeding period reproduces itself as an effect.

The infinite loop created by the *D* and 1 arrows gives the historicist causal structure its distinctive features. Our main purpose in this part of the chapter is to suggest the main kinds of social processes that can create such infinite, self-replicating causal loops and thereby suggest when historical research and historicist explanations will be most appropriate. Or to put it in the language more common in sociological and anthropological theorizing, we

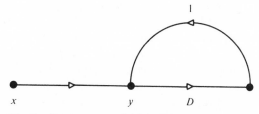

FIGURE 3.9   The basic structure of historicist explanations.

will explore the causal structure of situations in which "survivals," deposits of past history in the social structure of the present, are most likely to be found. Or to put it in a final way, we will show how to derive empirical propositions about the conditions under which traditions will tend to be preserved, and about the conditions under which they will decay.

"Survivals" and Functional Explanations

We must deal first with the relation between historicist and functional explanations, because most of the interesting causal structures explaining the persistence of tradition are special cases of functional explanations. When functional analysis was first introduced explicitly into anthropology, it was an *alternative* to historicist explanation.[34] We will show in this section that a functional process will give rise to infinite self-replicating causal loops. Far from being an alternative, a functional causal structure generally *implies* a historicist structure.

Consider some social structure or practice which fills a need (maintains a variable for which there is an effective reverse selective causal process) in a society and is maintained for that reason. It may be maintained because people have learned that they get good effects from the practice, because someone thought it up and keeps it going himself, because other groups without some equivalent to fulfill the need died out, or for any other reason. Consider, for example, magical practices which allay anxieties. *Once the anxieties are allayed,* they no longer are a selective principle encouraging anxiety-allaying practices. Contented men setting out to sea under the protection of the gods have no reason to look for new gods until it is too late.

Particularly where there are no objective criteria of functional effectiveness (as in allaying anxiety), any social practice which has few negative consequences will tend to be continued if it serves the function. Hence any magical practice which allays anxiety will tend to regenerate itself, for its competitors will have little anxiety to feed on. That is why we find, in magical and religious practices, great variability in practices among societies and intense tradition-

[34] Cf. Radcliffe-Brown, *op. cit.*

alism within them. Religion has important social functions, but almost any religion can perform them adequately.

This pattern of immense variety and intense traditionalism in the religious and magical sphere and in family organization is what led the classical anthropologists to look for historical causes. They were abetted in this penchant by the historical cast of the content of most religious ideologies. For instance, American religion supposedly has its roots in some events that happened in Palestine some thousands of years ago.

The key contribution of the functionalists, Malinowski and Radcliffe-Brown especially, was to point out that such practices were maintained by their consequences, and that the *interesting* part of the historicist explanation was the process creating the self-regenerating loop, not the original cause. Neither, of course, denied that the original causes must have been there. They argued only that we probably could not find them for technical reasons of lack of documents, and that even if we could the result was trivial because the practices might as easily have been something else and still served the same function.

To restate this argument another way, *which* of a set of functional alternatives is found in a particular society is generally determined by historical events. But once a functional alternative becomes established, it tends to eliminate the causes of the other alternatives and thus to regenerate itself.

Such an argument applies to most marriages. There are usually a large number of men who might serve perfectly well as a husband for a given woman. Once one of them starts to serve the functions of a husband, the intensity of search for another is greatly reduced. Her heart does not speed up as much when she comes into contact with an eligible man. Exactly because men are, to a large extent, functional alternatives for a woman, we find that the husband of any 50-year-old woman can be quite well predicted from knowledge of what eligible young men lived nearby when she was about 20. We find that the proportion of mixed Jewish-Gentile marriages among middle-aged couples is much more determined by the (low) intermarriage rates of the 1930's than by the (higher) intermarriage rates of the 1960's.

Likewise the function of providing political leaders who are responsive to the wishes of the people can be performed by either two-party or multiparty electoral systems. But if in the United States we have responsive political leaders under our two-party system, where will motivation for a social movement of electoral reform come from? And if the French or Italians have responsive leaders, why should they waste their energies instituting a two-party system? Whatever historical causes instituted one system in one place and the other in another are still effective, because in most respects they are functional alternatives.

The causal structure tending to preserve functional alternatives suggests, though it does not uniquely determine, the nature of the original historical process which got it started. If a survival has been preserved because it fulfills a function, then it was probably originally established by search behavior for a pattern of activity which fulfilled it. As we have discussed previously, this search pattern might have been a conscious attempt to solve the problems posed by the need. Or it might have been more or less random experiment reinforced and guided by an occasional success. Or it might have been social selection, with surviving examples of social structures fulfilling the need, and with dead social structures having failed.

That is, the usual form of the historicist causal structure which will apply to any of a set of functional alternatives will be that given in Figure 3.10.

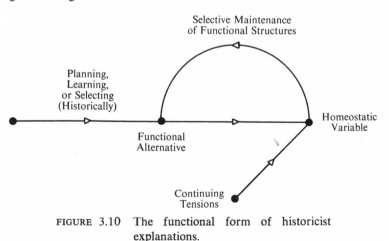

FIGURE 3.10 The functional form of historicist explanations.

Empirical Derivations from Functional Historicism

The first sort of empirical derivation from the functional form of historicism is that which excited the classic functionalists. Most things which are historically preserved in a group will show an equifinal causal structure, with all its implications outlined above. Variable and erratic features of societies are much less likely to be functional. Hence self-replicating or traditional phenomena are more likely to show: a variety of structures or practices with equivalent consequences; covariation between tensions and level of structure activity; nonvariation in the consequences of a structure in spite of variation in some of the other causes of this consequence; and a variety of unconvincing explanations by the people involved about why the practice is carried out. Variable and erratic phenomena are less likely to show these equifinal features.

A second set of derivations can be made about the conditions under which traditions will atrophy or change. If tensions are reduced—for instance, by improved navigation—functional structures which compensated for these tensions will atrophy. A more causally efficient functional structure will tend to eliminate previous structures serving the same function, once it gets started. The introduction of new kinds of selective processes (e.g., scientific tests of beliefs) will tend to switch the causal balance from one functional alternative to another. If, for any reason, a homeostatic variables ceases to be a source of selective force (e.g., if capacity to defend oneself is eliminated as a selective criterion by the Pax Britannica, or if cost minimization is eliminated as a selective principle in the economy by socialism or government protection), then alternatives maintained by their functions for that variable will atrophy (as craft institutions in the construction industry have atrophied in the Soviet Union). They may be replaced by structures more functional for other homeostatic variables (e.g., human welfare instead of defense, or job security instead of cost reduction).

Institutions and Historicist Explanations

By an "institution" I mean a structure in which powerful people are committed to some value or interest. The key to institutionalizing a value is to concentrate power in the hands of those who believe in that value. It can be arranged that they should believe in it by surrounding powerful roles with rewards and punishments that make it in their interest to believe in the value. Whatever values or interests are defended by the various power centers of a society or group are said to be institutionalized in that group. We will examine in Chapter Four the internal structure of the concept "institution." For the present, our interest is in the relation of institutions to the way effects regenerate themselves from year to year.

The relation between institutions and the preservation of historical patterns can be seen in the religious patterns of Europe. The countries which are now Protestant are countries whose kings were Protestant after the wars following the Reformation. Where the Protestants were militarily defeated, or where the king was never converted, Catholicism continued to be institutionalized. That is, the power centers of the society defended the practices and organizations that spread Catholicism and discouraged those that spread Protestantism. Conversely, where the Protestants won, Protestantism was institutionalized. The intimate interrelation between the results of historical wars (obviously power phenomena) and present religious patterns (obviously value phenomena) suggests that power has a great deal to do with the historical preservation of patterns of values. We would like to understand theoretically how this comes about.

The Mechanisms of Institutional Self-replication

It will be useful to break down the problem of how institutions regenerate themselves into three: (1) How does it happen that succeeding generations of power-holders have the same values? (2) What advantages do values defended by power-holders have in gaining popular support, which regenerates the value by socialization of new generations of the public? (3) What advantages do values defended by power-holders have in being embodied in the activities of future generations, whether they gain popular support or not?

If power-holders of the next generation tend to have the same values as past power-holders, any effectiveness that power has in the following generation will work in the same direction as current institutions. If power this year is used to commit the population to a value, the population itself in socializing its successors will preserve the value. And if activities of the society embody the value, any functions of those activities for other values and interests, or any inertia in activities as such, will tend to preserve patterns related to a value into the next generation. All three processes create infinite self-replicating loops.

1. Power-holders shape their successors in power by (a) control over selection, (b) control over socialization of elites, (c) control over the conditions of incumbency in a powerful role, and (d) their symbolic value as ego-ideals for ambitious young men.

1(a). Power-holders tend to select out men with the same values and interests as themselves for both disinterested and interested reasons.[35] The disinterested reasons are both direct and indirect. Directly, they want to preserve things they think valuable into the next generation, and they deliberately select people to do so. Indirectly, they feel comfortable with, associate with, and understand the morality and trustworthiness of men like themselves.

Their interested reasons are likewise both direct and indirect. Directly, their own interests, power, and values are safer if the potential Young Turks are on their side, preselected to defend their seniors. Indirectly, men try to get favorable positions for their sons, relatives, and friends, who are likely to have the same values and interests because of family or small-group solidarity. Thus morality and interest coincide to produce a strong tendency for men in power to be succeeded by men of the same interests and persuasion.

1(b). Power-holders control the socialization of their successors both by design and by accident. By design they often set up schools, or tutors, or religious retreats, or informal instruction by seniors,

---

[35] See Philip Selznick, *Leadership in Administration: A Sociological Interpretation* (Evanston, Ill.: Row, Peterson, 1957). The conception of institutions, used here is based on that developed by Selznick. There are some other ways of conceiving institutions, but Selznick developed this one specifically to account for the historical preservation of values in organizations. The other notions of institution, having as their core the idea of role expectations, do not lend themselves to the explanation of historical continuity of institutions and hence are inferior to Selznick's conception.

or apprenticeships to power-holders, or whatnot. By accident, the very selective principles for elites become rewards and sanctions governing the whole course of socialization. Ambitious men come to believe whatever is necessary to get ahead, attend those schools where one learns the values needed to get ahead, and produce evidence in speech and behavior that they love the right things. If a man of his own volition pursues something which requires holding some value to get, he usually comes to be quite convinced of the sacredness of that value.

1(c). When power-holders finally have selected and socialized men who believe, they can provide against corruption of this purity by arranging the role-set of the new incumbent so he is obliged to follow the values. The successors to the Federalist presidents still had to deal with the Supreme Court and Congress, for the Federalists had established conditions of incumbency in the presidency. In other countries kings had to deal with bishops and vassals, bishops with kings and aristocrats, and aristocrats with kings and bishops. Under these conditions, the successor's powers are crippled if he does not live up to the values institutionalized in the role (*i.e.,* correlated with power over activities of the role). This is why, of course, the question of the conditions of incumbency in power is almost always the focus of constitutions and the subject matter of elections. Power-holders of this generation control the values of power-holders in future generations by constitution-writing.

1(d). In *War and Peace,* Tolstoy gives the following account of a young nobleman's reaction during a review of troops by the Tsar:

> When the Tsar was only twenty paces away, and Nikolay saw clearly in every detail the handsome, young, and happy face of the Emperor, he experienced a feeling of tenderness and ecstasy such as he had never known before. Everything in the Tsar—every feature, every movement—seemed to him full of charm.
>
> Halting before the Pavlograd regiment, the Tsar said something in French to the Austrian Emperor and smiled.
>
> Seeing that smile, Rostov unconsciously began to smile himself and felt an even stronger rush of love for his Emperor. He longed to express his love for the Tsar in some way. He knew

it was impossible, and he wanted to cry. The Tsar called up the colonel of the regiment and said a few words to him.

"By God! what would happen to me if the Emperor were to address me!" thought Rostov; "I should die of happiness."

The Tsar addressed the officers, too.

"All of you, gentlemen" (every word sounded to Rostov like heavenly music), "I thank you with all my heart."

How happy Rostov would have been if he could have died on the spot for his Emperor.

"You have won the flags of St. George and will be worthy of them."

"Only to die, to die for him!" thought Rostov.

.   .   .

The Tsar stood for several seconds facing the hussars, as though he were hesitating.

"How could the Emperor hesitate?" Rostov wondered; but then, even that hesitation seemed to him majestic and enchanting, like all the Tsar did.

.   .   .

After the review they all felt more certain of victory than they could have been after two decisive victories.[36]

Such a feeling of awe, wonder, and worship toward powerful people—tsars, millionaires,[37] geniuses, stars, or bosses—tends to make them into models or ego-ideals which children, adolescents, and schizophrenics model themselves after. It is Napoleon and God who classically appear in the delusions of paranoids. Power makes a man extraordinary, and people imitate extraordinary men, thus regenerating institutions over the generations.

By selection, socialization, controlling conditions of incumbency, and hero worship, succeeding generations of power-holders tend to regenerate the same institutions. Insofar as institutions have effects, and insofar as they are social phenomena themselves, these processes give rise to infinite self-replicating causal loops. His-

[36] Leo Tolstoy, *War and Peace* (New York: Modern Library, n.d.), pp. 223–24.

[37] Jane Austen describes the emotions created in young ladies by rich young men in most of her novels. The emotions seem to be quite disinterested, and friends of a woman betrothed to such a man find him attractive.

toricist explanations are particularly crucial in explaining the institutional structure of society. Probably that is why so many historians either study institutions or study the wars and revolutions that change institutions.

For deriving empirical consequences from such observations, it is convenient to state these relationships in terms of the variable causal force of the infinite loop. Institutions will tend to be preserved *to the degree that* power-holders select their successors, *to the degree that* they control socialization for elite positions, *to the degree that* they control the conditions of incumbency of their successors, *to the degree that* they become heroes after whom potential leaders model themselves. That is, empirical propositions which can be derived from this analysis take the form of an interaction effect between what values become institutionalized historically and how efficiently institutions preserve themselves. Some of the variables which determine this efficiency of self-replication are those of control over selection, control over socialization, control over conditions of incumbency, and capacity to inspire awe.

Institutions will be historically fragile when institutional elites do not control their successors in these ways. For instance, institutions are generally precarious in the face of conquest, for the conquerors are rarely selected, socialized, or admitted to their office by their predecessors. And they have their own heroes.

2. Institutions and value patterns are partly sustained because the population at large believes in them. Popular faith is not nearly as important as democratic ideology would lead us to hope, nor as conservative apologetics for institutions would imply. Most men are trying to get by, regarding the institutional conditions of life as given and worrying about value questions on Sunday mornings, if at all. But under some conditions, when power fails through military threat, revolution, or corruption and sloth in institutional centers, popular belief can be an important force for regenerating institutions. Popular belief is to a considerable degree a residue of institutionalized belief. We need to understand how this residue is created.

Power-backed beliefs or values have a number of advantages over other beliefs and values for influencing popular belief. (a) They have preferred access to all media of communication and socialization which require resources, for power is another word for control over resources. (b) They have the advantage that power-holders generally have no other job than making policy and preserving values. This means that institutionalized values get full-time attention and thought while uninstitutionalized values depend on amateurs. (c) The factors above which regenerate values in the elite have a latent effect on the general population, especially when all of them want to grow up to be president. Hence selection, control over elite socialization, constitutional provisions about incumbency, and hero worship indirectly socialize the general population, especially its most ambitious part.

2(a). The proposition that resource-using communication and socialization tend to popularize institutional values implies that the less spontaneous and private socialization is, the more popular institutionalized values will be. Religious congregations as compared with household gods, educational systems as compared with family training, mass media as compared with rumor, all are more resource-using means of socialization. Hence we would expect that institutionalized values would be more popularly supported, the more developed such structures were. In societies with familial or tribal religions, poorly developed educational systems, and little mass media, we would therefore expect institutional structures to be much more fragile, much more affected by wars, revolutions, and redistributions of power.

This is, of course, what we find. When Protestant Germany conquered Catholic France and Poland in the Second World War, the effects were nothing like the effects during the Reformation. The dizzying rapidity of changes in constitutions in Latin America during the nineteenth century, when mass religion, mass education, and mass communication were rare, is proverbial. But the difference between nineteenth-century Latin America and feudal Europe was not so much in the rate of change as in the practice of writing the changes down. We are now seeing the same sort of institutional instability in new African countries.

Thus the self-replicating character of institutions in the face of military shocks depends very much on the degree to which socialization and communication in the society are resource-intensive or spontaneous. Spontaneous socialization produces "spontaneity" in institutional life.

2(b). The amount of social energy devoted to a value is mainly determined by whether it is defended by full-time workers or by amateurs. One of the main advantages of full-time workers is their greater degree of reflection and rationality. One of the main determinants of what a man thinks about is what he gets paid for thinking about. Directly or indirectly, power-holders in institutions get paid for thinking about how to achieve and preserve the values and interests embodied in an institution. The more elaborate an argument in favor of a value, the more extensive the data collection on which a solution to a problem is based, the more explicitly alternatives are explored and evaluated, and the longer the time span planned for, the more likely is it that the analysis was done by somebody who gets paid for it. The greater rationality with which values embodied in institutions are defended and disseminated is one of their main advantages in competition with alternative values.

Rational defense is effective not because the public is devoted to rational argument. The advantages of rationality are twofold. First, that section of the public which leads opinion is more likely to be swayed by rational argument than are followers. In particular, leaders of *other* institutions are paid to think full time about their values and the relation of them to other institutions. Rationality of leadership is especially important for working out inter-institutional relations and hence getting one's own values associated with and defended by other institutionalized values.

Second, and even more important, the longer the time span under consideration, the more important popular support is likely to be. Those values which depend on spontaneous social action by amateurs are likely to be defended only when some concrete problem or interest is touched. Lenin observed this when he pointed out that the masses spontaneously could reach only the level of "trade union consciousness." Hence little of the resources devoted to such values will be spent on such long-run activities as the development and dissemination of doctrine. Not only do institutionalized values have more resources devoted to them but a larger proportion of those resources are likely to be devoted to influencing popular opinion and controlling popular socialization.

2(c) Selection, socialization, incumbency in power, and hero worship in elite socialization affect public opinion indirectly. They have their effect by influencing the perceived rewards and punishments which control mass action in the population and by providing models of appropriate behavior for ambitious men in the public. Anyone who has some aspirations to get into the elite, or into the class of retainers and kept men of the elite, must satisfy the selective criteria by which such men get ahead. Many are called, but few are chosen. Thus many will be exposed to anticipatory socialization for elite positions they will never hold.

In addition, elite schools and etiquette provide models for mass schools and etiquette, and powerful men tend to be heroes to the masses as well as to potential members of the elite.

We will, then, expect that institutions will tend to regenerate themselves by means of disseminating support for the value in the general public to the degree that resource-using modes of communication are important in socialization of the general public, to the degree that values defended by power-holders are more rationally defended by men who spend full time at it, and to the degree that hope of elite status or awe for power-holders motivates the general public to model its socialization on that for the elite.

We would expect such institutional self-replicating forces to be greatest in modern societies, because resource-using modes of socialization are more common, because in modern societies recruitment to the elite generally involves systematic training in rational thought in colleges and universities (and perhaps less leisure and more work among the elite), and because more of the population can aspire to elite status when fewer channels are blocked off on ascriptive grounds. Considerable evidence does indicate that institutions are more stable in modern societies and that support for these institutions is probably more widely distributed in the general population.[38] Traditionalism of institutions combined with rapid changes in the means and mechanisms of institutions is characteristic of modern societies.

3. In addition to controlling the values of future members of

[38] See Seymour M. Lipset, *Political Man: The Social Bases of Politics* (Garden City, N.Y.: Doubleday, 1960), especially pp. 27–63 on "Economic Development and Democracy," for the relationship between economic development and governmental stability in modern times. Government stability in rich countries probably indicates higher general support for the institutional structure, for it is also true that economic development is associated with democratic electoral systems. If there is both greater stability and also greater constitutional dependence on popular support in modern societies, then there is probably greater popular satisfaction with the institutional structure in modern societies.

the elite and influencing popular belief, institutional power-holders have some capacity to control the *activities* of future generations, whatever those future generations may happen to believe. There are two possible causal links between control over activities in the present and the structure of activities and values in the future. (a) Activities established by current power-holders, embodying their values, may serve other functions than serving those values. Such additional functions will preserve the activities, even if commitment to the values is low. (b) People become committed to what they are doing, perhaps in order to reduce cognitive dissonance, so that one way to socialize people to a value is to get them to act in terms of that value without belief and allow belief to follow.

3(a). Consider the conquest of Latin America by the Catholic kings of Spain and Portugal. This conquest established the Catholic Church as an institution in Latin America and allowed Catholic priests to institute Catholic ritual practices, build Catholic churches, missions, and schools, and otherwise set up Catholic activities. It also allowed them to destroy or incorporate alternative religious practices with which the Indians had met their religious needs, relieved their anxieties, and established a moral order. After the substitution took place, religious needs, educational needs, relief from anxiety, and the establishment of a moral order all were functions of Catholic religious practice. That is, activities not previously in the culture of the Americas were established by the use of power. But once established, these activities served various social and psychological functions and served them regardless of the level of theological sophistication of the population. These functions then could, and did, maintain Catholic religious practices in the Latin-American countries even after the prop of the king's army was taken away during the nineteenth century.

To put the argument in other words, institutional leaders can take advantage of the tendency of functional alternatives to create infinite self-replicating loops, either deliberately or by accident. If some activity they establish, embodying the values they defend, serves one or more crucial social or psychological functions, it will tend to be preserved from generation to generation just as will a functional alternative established by spontaneous social processes. Most institutional leaders are well aware that they can preserve a pattern by making it useful.

3(b). Benjamin Franklin somewhere comments that one can establish friendships by borrowing something from a man, taking good care of it, and returning it on time and in good shape. If a man is induced to act friendly, he tends to become friendly. This is an illustration of an apparent general human tendency to believe in whatever one has been induced to do.[39] Thus by using institutional power to institute a set of activities, one may socialize the general population to believe in the values connected to those activities. Believing in them, the population will tend to do them again next year even when the support of power is taken away.

Summary of Empirical Derivations from Institutional-Historicist Theories

Thus we will expect institutions to replicate themselves to the degree that:

1. Powerful people secure successors of the same persuasion
   (a) by selection of their successors,
   (b) by controlling socialization of their successors,
   (c) by controlling the conditions of incumbency of their successors,
   (d) by being heroes and ego-ideals to potential successors.
2. Powerful people influence popular belief

[39] There are various formulations of this tendency. C. Wright Mills formulated it in terms of each man working out a "vocabulary of motives" to justify his own activities. C. Wright Mills, "Language, Logic and Culture," *American Sociological Review,* Vol. 4 (October, 1939), pp. 670–80. The general formulation of "balance theory" developed by Fritz Heider derives this observation from a general balance proposition. A man is attached to his own actions, and explanations of his actions are attached to those actions by society. Since men in general tend to become attached to things which are attached to something they are attached to (more simply, since attachment tends to be a transitive relation), they will tend to become attached to socially given explanations of their actions. These explanations will often be the values which justify the actions. Another formulation of the proposition can be made in terms of cognitive dissonance, that carrying out of an action without believing the explanation produces dissonance, and people in general reduce dissonance. One of the most interesting studies of this is Leon Festinger *et al., When Prophecy Fails* (Minneapolis: University of Minnesota Press, 1956). People who carried out actions thinking that the world would come to an end tended to believe that it would even more strongly after the prophecy failed.

   (a) by controlling the content of resource-using media of socialization,

   (b) by rationally devoting resources to long-run stability, because they defend the value full time,

   (c) by shaping the conditions of socialization of the general population indirectly through the public's hopes for elite status and their hero worship.

3. Powerful people determine the structure of social activity,

   (a) thereby serving other social functions besides the value in question,

   (b) eliciting commitment to the activities, and hence to the values embodied in them.

Of course, different elites have different capacities to influence future generations in these ways, because they have different amounts of power, because their skills in socialization or activity-creating differ, and because other social conditions favor or do not favor the operation of one or more of these processes. We will expect infinite self-regenerating causal loops, and hence the appropriateness of "historicist" explanations, to vary with the degree to which the processes specified take place. Institutional change (*i.e.*, a change in which values are correlated with amount of power)[40] will tend to take place at a lower rate, the more prevalent the above processes are.

Historical Causes in Institutional-Historicist Explanations

The original historical circumstances tending to produce self-replicating institutions are mainly those which determine an original correlation between power and values for a sufficient period

---

[40] By "institutional change" we mean a change in the correlation between a value and a power. As the situation changes, a solid institution will adapt to it, and the outer forms will change. As long as this does not decrease the correlation between a given value and power, we will not call it institutional change. For instance, a research university may so adjust to the new federal and foundation sources of research money that half or more of its funds come from these new sources. This would be institutional change only if the accompanying shifts in power within the university were such as to increase the correlation between research commitments and influence on university policy.

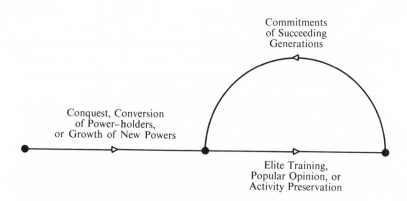

Commitments
of Succeeding
Generations

Conquest, Conversion
of Power–holders,
or Growth of New Powers

Elite Training,
Popular Opinion, or
Activity Preservation

FIGURE 3.11   The institutional-historicist causal
structure.

of time for the self-replicating processes to start to work. These circumstances seem to be of three main types. First, a distinct group with common values or interests may conquer power, from inside or outside a society or group, by military or constitutional means. Second, a group of power-holders may be converted to a new set of values, either suddenly by missionary effort or gradually as considerations of state create ideological problems and solutions.[41] Third, new kinds of power may be created by groups with a distinct set of values and interests. Before trade unions were organized, no one had the power to call a strike. Trade union leaders did not usurp a power that someone had; they created a new one. This new source of power was associated with egalitarian values and workers' interests (in varying mixes) because of the nature of the people who organized it.

Thus, in the case of institutions, the basic form of historicist explanation takes the special form shown in Figure 3.11.

Institutional and Functional Historicism

The institutional explanation for the preservation of historically created structures is a special and complex form of functional explanation. For when we say that people who hold certain values are powerful, we mean merely that their decisions are much more

[41] A good case study of such a process is Selznick, *TVA and the Grassroots.*

important causes of social behavior than are the decisions of weak people. The descriptions of the advantages of powerful people given above are descriptions of why, in particular, they are more effective as causes of the behavior of succeeding generations. And when we analyze why they want social activities to be in accord with their values and interests, it is almost always because the *consequences* of those activities are important to their values and interests.

The graph above could be redrawn in the same form as Figure 3.10 at the end of the section on functional survivals. But the functional loop would be differentiated according to the power of the various groups in a fashion similar to Figure 3.8 representing Marxian theory. It may be useful experience for the reader to construct the elaborated functional form of the above graph, or (what is the same thing) to add a historical branch to the graph of Marxian theory. The complete structure is rather messy, and the essential point can be seen in the simplified graph in Figure 3.11.

Sunk Costs and Historicist Explanations

If we ask why, this year, the United States is a much richer country than, say, Nicaragua, it is clearly because last year's resources in the United States have lasted into this year. The skills of the population, physical capital, functional organizational and institutional structures, a residential distribution appropriate to an industrial economy—all these are resources this year because they were resources last year. The historical preservation of differences in wealth suggests that resources generally tend to produce a historicist causal structure. We will analyze some aspects of such a suggestion in this section.

When an action in the past has given rise to a permanently useful resource, we speak of this resource as a "sunk cost." "Sunk cost" means that the costs of the original creation of the resource are no longer recoverable and consequently ought not enter into current calculations of rational policy. Quite often such permanent resources are specialized, and they are useful only for the pattern of activity they were designed for. Such specialized sunk costs include especially skills developed in an activity, permanent or semipermanent modifications of the physical environment (*e.g.*, dams, roadbeds, channels and harbors, cleared land), specialized social systems with the bugs worked out of them, reputations and good will, and so forth. If these sunk costs make a traditional pattern of action cheaper, and if new patterns are not enough more profitable to justify throwing away the resource, the sunk costs tend to preserve a pattern of action from one year to the next.

The Conditions of the Permanence of Resources

Resources can be permanent in two different ways. First, they can be physically or psychologically unchanging. This is a relatively rare situation, but graded beds for roads come close.

Second, and far more important, they may be self-generating. Perhaps the clearest case here is language. Competence in a common language is a resource which allows cultural activity and commerce to be carried on much more cheaply and efficiently. Each year new entrants into the society are motivated to learn the language in order to participate in the common culture and commerce. They also learn spontaneously in the family. Thus the succeeding generation also has the same resource. The recreation of the same linguistic resource in succeeding generations means that patterns of cultural production and commerce established in one generation tend to be preserved in the next. All resources which are improved with use, especially skills, tend to regenerate themselves.

In addition, there are resources which, in order to be used at all, must be maintained. Roads, railroads, harbors, canals, channels, irrigation and other water supply systems, some kinds of dams, power equipment and transmission lines, and to some extent housing will fail to work very soon if they are not maintained. That is, a decision not to regenerate the resource is nearly the same as the decision not to use it at all. In any period in which the cost of regenerating such a resource is smaller than the cost of investing in a new pattern of activity, the resource will tend to be maintained. Thus "permanence" of a resource comes about by means of constant effort.

Finally, there are resources which facilitate their own production, besides making other activity more effective. A good example at a high level of abstraction is the resource of liberty. If liberty is established, groups can more easily form to agitate for, or sue in the courts for, the continuation of their liberties or an extension of them. Liberty means that the capacity to resist oppression is widely distributed. This capacity is a resource for the pursuit of many ends, including more liberty. But also, oppression once established tends toward permanent suppression of liberties. Thus if "the price of liberty is eternal vigilance," such vigilance is much easier in liberal societies, for it is easier to create and defend liberties if many already exist, and it is more difficult to create them in an oppressive society.

Specialized resources for a given pattern of activity tend to be "permanent" when they are (1) physically or psychologically unchanging, or (2) self-regenerating, either because (a) they improve with use (*e.g.*, skills), or (b) they must be maintained in order to be used in any period (*e.g.*, canals), or (c) they are a resource useful in their own production (*e.g.*, knowledge, liberty, many basic industrial materials). Under these conditions, resources do not depreciate. Thus we cannot, in any given time period, decide whether to put new investments into old and new activities on the same basis. Old activities have an advantage from sunk costs, even if a new activity would be more profitable than the old if we were starting from scratch.[42]

---

[42] More formally, compare the rate of return on new investments in the old activity (operating expenses and maintenance), r_o, with the rate of return, r_n, on the total investment in a new activity (facilities and operating expenses and maintenance). In any given period, we will use the old resource if $r_o > r_n$—that is, *unless* the rate of return on the new investment is so high as to compensate for the added investment. As we move from this time period to the next, we have to ask whether the old investment depreciates—that is, whether r_o falls. If it falls, then the competitive position of the new activity will improve and the new activity will take over at the margin. r_o will fall unless (a) the resource has negative depreciation, so that the rate of return increases with use (*e.g.*, skill), or (b) the resource has zero depreciation (an unchanging modification of the environment), or (c) the regeneration of the resource is cheaper than it would be to build anew because (1) the regeneration itself has high productivity, as when minor maintenance makes the whole resource usable, or (2) because the resource itself makes marginal regeneration cheaper. I

Thus we will expect sunk costs to preserve historically determined patterns of activity whenever they create a productive resource which either does not decay, or which regenerates itself rather than depreciating, or which is cheaper to maintain in each time period than to change over to a new pattern of activity.

Aside from these characteristics of the old resource, certain features of new activities in general may make them more expensive. The most important are *risk* and *the work of thinking*. The poorer the capacity of people to predict the consequences of an innovation, the more likely they are to (rationally) prefer what they already have, whose consequences they can predict from their experience. Therefore the development of science, technology, market analysis, and predictable legal consequences of contracts tends to decrease preference for old patterns of activity and to make historicist explanations less useful. Historicist predictions of the kinds of vehicles used in American society, where science is well developed, are much worse that historicist predictions about civil legal procedure. The consequences of an innovation in civil procedure are not known because of the incompetence of modern economics to predict economic effects of legal changes.

The Historical Sources of Sunk Costs

The basic historical process that begins this kind of self-replicating process is resource creation. Most resources are created by deliberate investment, though some are created as a by-product of some other process. Thus the basic historicist causal structure takes the particular form given in Figure 3.12.

Let us refer back to the impressive, if somewhat obvious, example of the continuity of international income differences. A set of firms which have invested in the United States will often not move to Nicaragua even if the natural advantages of Nicaragua

---

suppose that conditions could be formulated more precisely by means of the appropriate differential equations. The mathematical regions could be identified in which an older, less productive resource would expand to absorb increases in demand, would remain stable while the new activity took over at the margin, would decline gradually to be eventually replaced and/or would be replaced immediately. But this is a topic for economists.

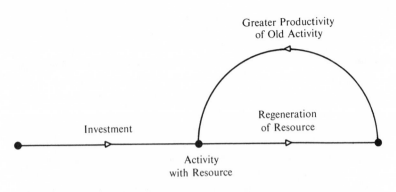

FIGURE 3.12 The sunk-costs historicist causal structure.

are greater. For this new activity in Nicaragua would have to have enough natural advantages to overcome gross differences in sunk costs. The sunk costs include self-regenerating skills of the population and physical resources. Physical resources are continuously maintained because their maintenance is more productive than investing the same money in new resources in Nicaragua, and because the resource base of the United States makes the production of replacements much cheaper there than in Nicaragua. In addition, investment in the United States is much less risky because the amount known (particularly the amount known by the relevant investors) about the future of the United States and what will work there is much greater than the amount known about Nicaragua.

Figure 3.12 may be elaborated into a functional graph of the form (Figure 3.10) for functional survivals. The tension is clearly the "need" for the product of the investment. If this need disappears, sunk costs cannot keep people using the old investment with the old pattern of activity. But such a graph should have explicitly a loop for the old investment and a loop for the new alternative, subordinate loops for the self-regeneration of resources, and further attached loops for the costs of each. For the main difference between activities with old resources and those with new is that the old activities have fewer negative consequences, fewer other good things that have to be forgone in order to satisfy the need. Further, if one is inclined to be pedantic, consequences for powerful people (investors) and weaker people (the public) can

124

be separated. In sum, every complication so far introduced can be incorporated into the graph of such an explanation. One could draw on for several pages.

Micro-historicism and Cohort Analysis

Many of the people most concerned with historicist causal structures have focused on macroscopic problems of social structure: the explanation of constitutions, party systems, societal religious structures, or national differences in productivity and income. But as we noted at the beginning of this part, micro-structures such as marriages often have historical continuity of characteristics. All the types of infinite self-replicating causal loops described above can apply to structures smaller than societies.

In an organization, a historical pattern of behavior which satisfies a functional need of the organization cuts the selective forces working for a new solution. In organizations as in societies, invaders or revolutionaries can take over centers of power, power-holders can be converted to new values or develop new interests, and new sources of power can be developed by distinctive subsections of the organization. These institutions within the organization have historical continuity for the same reasons as institutions in societies. Investments are made in the organization which create self-regenerating resources and thus induce the organization to continue in the same line of activity from year to year because of sunk costs.

This continuity of the characteristics of microscopic social structures has very interesting theoretical consequences. For *the causal forces operating on the first branch of the historicist causal structure vary with time.* Let us consider again the example of intermarriage among religious groups. We can summarize the causal forces operating on the courtship branch of marriage by a coefficient representing the proportion of intermarriages in a group, the a_i in Figure 3.13. After these causal forces operate, we enter the infinite loop of marriage. The results of such a conception are graphed in Figure 3.13.

If we ignore deaths and divorces in order to see the logic, the marriages that exist during time period 4 will be the sum of the n_1

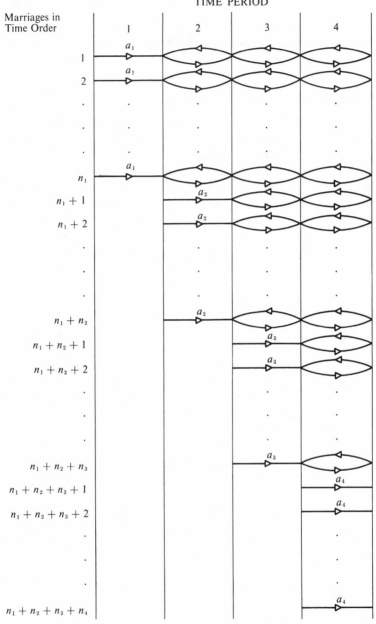

FIGURE 3.13 Historicist causal structures for microsociological units, producing differentiated cohorts.

marriages contracted in time period 1, plus the n_2 marriages in time period 2, plus the n_3 marriages in time period 3, plus the new marriages of time period 4. But the marriages of time period 1 were contracted under the causal forces represented by an inter-marriage rate a_1 and have since that time reproduced their characteristics. Those contracted in time period 2 were subject to causal forces proportional to a_2 and have since reproduced their characteristics in succeeding time periods. The marriages of time period 3 carry the causal force of a_3 into succeeding time periods. Only those contracted during time period 4 represent the causal forces operating on courtship during the present period.

If the rates a_1, a_2, a_3, and a_4 are substantially different, then a classification of marriages having different dates of courtship will locate *marriages having different causal sources.* An overall proportion of mixed marriages will not correspond to any causally unique force, but rather to a hash of forces operating at different times. In order to make causal sense out of current proportions of mixed marriages, we obviously must classify marriages by their age (the age of the marriage, of course, not the ages of the people). Such "generations" of identifiable units, classified by the time at which some self-regenerating characteristic was determined, are called "cohorts." [43]

Thus when a historicist causal structure applies to the *units of a population of social structures,* that population at a given time consists of age strata or cohorts which are a deposit of historical forces. Furthermore, those characteristics related to age strata in such a population of social structures are likely to be those to which a historicist causal structure applies. The connection of age and historical causes provides three main types of research

---

[43] Cohorts are useful not only when a characteristic is permanent but also when a characteristic develops in a predetermined time pattern. For instance, reproduction is partially determined by age since birth, so cohorts are basic categories for analyzing reproductive behavior. Most American corporations seem to grow at a relatively constant rate, so their sizes are largely determined by their size at founding (mainly technologically determined) and by number of years since founding. On cohort analysis in demography, see Norman Ryder, *op. cit.* On the size distribution of firms, see Herbert A. Simon and Charles Bonini, "The Size Distribution of Business Firms," *American Economic Review,* Vol. 48 (September, 1958), pp. 607–17. More precisely, Simon gives evidence that there is a relatively constant *distribution* of rates of growth of a set of firms.

opportunities. First, obviously, the historicist causal loop for those variables which tend to be related to cohort membership can be investigated. Second, the structure and dynamics of that population as a population can be more precisely analyzed by use of classification by age strata or cohorts.

Third, the operation of causal forces in the past can often be illuminated by the analysis of age strata of social structures, creating a "paleontology" of social structures. Suppose we find [44] that the social structure of newer industries involves a much higher proportion of professionals in their management, while older industries have few professionals. That is, textiles or railroads or retail trade have many fewer professionals than automobiles or chemicals or aircraft or computer production. This suggests immediately that systematic abstract knowledge learned in colleges has been a much more important causal force in industry-creation in recent times than it was before the turn of the century. This is paleontological evidence for J. A. Schumpeter's famous conjecture on the "routinization of innovation" [45] in modern times. The age strata of industries then reflect the historical process of rationalization of economic life which Max Weber took to be central to the process of modernization.[46] The extreme stage of rationalization is reached when, as in modern times, new industries are created on the basis of abstract bodies of knowledge developed and taught in colleges and universities.

Paleontological evidence of historical changes in courtship practices may be obtained from age strata of marriages. Age strata of colleges reflect the historical development of college financing from private to public. Age strata of trade unions reflect historical changes in the capacity to organize craftsmen and industrial

[44] As we do. See my chapter on "Social Structure and Organizations," in James March (ed.), *Handbook of Organizations* (Chicago: Rand McNally, 1965), pp. 142–93. O. Dudley Duncan called my attention to the logical similarities of this study to cohort analysis in demography.

[45] Cf. Joseph Alois Schumpeter, *Capitalism, Socialism and Democracy* (New York: Harper, 1950).

[46] This is a recurrent theme in Weber's work. One of the earliest statements is in his definition of captitalism in *The Protestant Ethic and the Spirit of Capitalism,* translated by Talcott Parsons (New York: Scribner's, 1958), and in his discussion of the impact of Protestant theology on magical practices in that study.

workers. Probably age strata of schools still reflect the historical evolution of teaching philosophies; age strata of civil-rights organizations, the historical evolution of the Negro movement; age strata of housing, historical architectural styles; age strata of people's friendship relations, the evolution during their life-cycle of the criteria of friendship; and so forth.

IV / THE PROBLEM OF THE CHOICE OF VARIABLES IN CAUSAL EXPLANATIONS

We have come as far as it is strategic to go here in explicating the causal structure of sociological explanations. The remaining chapters of the book are devoted to the contents of such structures, the causal forces that we plug into them. For the elegance and power of an explanation can be only as good as the causal connections among variables allow it to be. An exact conceptual representation of the operative causal forces is of great importance. A demographic explanation with the population classified by a causally irrelevant criterion is only a source of confusion. An exact definition of which aspect of a structure has the relevant consequences, and exactly which consequences have selective force for structures, is essential for formulating a valuable functional theory. And an exact understanding of the relations between power and values and a clear formulation of that relation for the problem at hand are crucial for building a sensible institutional-historicist explanation.

A mathematician or logician might be satisfied to leave all the dots in our graphs with the names x, y, z, S, H, T, Part I of the population, and so forth. A scientist is, at most, half way to a theory when he understands the appropriate logical form. The big trick is to fill in the x's and the H's with concepts formed in such a way that they have unique sets of causes and unique effects, so that the logical structure, when applied to the real world, is both cleaned of irrelevancy and adequate in explanatory power.

Concept formation in sociology, where causal forces are the product of somewhat invisible features of the social structure, is difficult, because most people's intuition psychologizes the phenomena. Most people find it easier to identify good or bad executives than good or bad administrative structures. Most people find it easier to think of ambitious and lazy people than to think of opportunity structures and their effects on ambition. Most people think of radical and moderate workers more easily than the ratio of illegal to legal channels of political access in a society.

Because of this failure of the intuition,[47] we are peculiarly dependent on logical reasoning to form concepts for explaining social phenomena. In the following chapter we turn to the conceptual apparatus for dealing with concepts of power—that is, concepts having to do with differences among individuals or groups in the causal effectiveness of their decisions in determining how social action is carried on.

TECHNICAL APPENDIX TO CHAPTER THREE / THE LINEAR DIRECTED GRAPH APPROACH TO COMPLEX CAUSAL STRUCTURES

The purpose of this appendix is to discuss the manipulation of the causal diagrams that have been frequently used in this chapter. Such structures are treated by an algebra of *linear operators*. This algebra is treated in texts on systems theory or electrical circuit theory in engineering. Mathematically, it rests on the theory of systems of linear equations, and to be strictly applicable requires that each causal force have a linear effect on the variable involved. However, the linearity restriction is not very severe, since variables may often be transformed so that their relations are linear,[48] and many nonlinear effects are approximately linear in the range of interest.

The linear graph treatment of complex causal theories has the

---

[47] Some people raise their lack of sociological intuition to the philosophical principle that only individual behavior and motives are real. I have never been able to understand, let alone sympathize with, their position. It seems to me analogous to maintaining that rocks aren't real, because they are structures of atoms, and that Newtonian theories of rocks flying through the air are not satisfactory until reduced to quantum mechanics. At any rate, our concepts here will be about rocks, not about atoms.

[48] For a general introductory treatment, with many examples, see W. H. Huggins and Doris Entwisle, *Introductory Systems and Design* (in press). As an example of a nonlinear effect which can be transformed, an effect which is the product of two variables can be transformed into a linear effect by taking logarithms.

advantage of representing the overall structure of a theory in an intuitively easy fashion, much easier to understand than a statement of the same theory in terms of a system of linear equations. The algebra of such graphs is often easier to manipulate to get a solution than the equivalent algebra of systems of equations.

The Basic Idea of a Linear Graph

The basic units of a linear graph are *nodes* which represent *variables,* and *arrows* which represent the *operator* which acts on a variable to translate it into another variable. For instance, the graph

$$x \bullet \overset{A}{\longrightarrow} \bullet\ y \qquad\qquad \text{I}$$

is written algebraically

$$xA = y \tag{1}$$

It means that A is an "operator" (in our case, a linear coefficient) which gives us the value of y for a given value of x. This operator is the mathematical equivalent to the causal connection between the variables x and y. As a linear equation,[49] it would have the form

$$y = ax \tag{2}$$

[49] Equations of the form:

$$y = ax + b \tag{3}$$

may be translated into graphical form by adding a constant source node whose signal equals 1. Then the linear operator B, operating on this node, produces a constant effect on y equal to b.

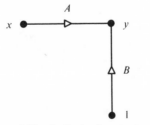

$$\qquad\qquad\qquad\qquad\qquad\qquad \text{II}$$

Then the graph is treated identically to the graphs analyzed below. Also, we can consider that all variables are *measured* net of their constant causes, thus simplifying the graphical manipulation. For simplicity, we have ignored constant causes in the graphs that follow.

The total effect or value of a variable is the sum of the effects of the arrows entering its node. Thus the graph

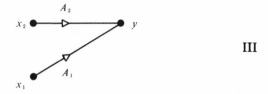

III

means that the value of y is the sum of x_1A_1 plus x_2A_2,

$$y = x_1A_1 + x_2A_2 \qquad (4)$$

or, in terms of a linear equation,

$$y = a_1x_1 + a_2x_2 \qquad (5)$$

A variable is affected *only* by adding arrows coming into it, and no account is taken of arrows going out of it. (This corresponds to the notion of direction implied in the word "cause" and is one reason such graphs are so intuitively appealing.)

Chain or Cascade Graphs

When a variable x_1 causes a variable x_2, and x_2 in its turn causes y, each operating in a linear fashion, we draw it as follows:

IV

Algebraically, this may be written

$$\begin{aligned} x_1A_1 &= x_2 \\ x_2A_2 &= y \end{aligned} \qquad (6)$$

But by certain properties of linear operators, we may translate this graph in several different ways, preserving that part of the information that we are interested in.

First, the above graph may be written "absorbing" the *node* x_2 (*i.e.,* we are not interested in x_2 at the moment). Algebraically, this would be

$$(x_1A_1)A_2 = y \qquad (7)$$

Equation (7) means that we operate first on x_1 with the operator A_1, and then on the result with A_2, in order to get the value of y.

But it happens that linear operators are commutative. That is, we get the same result by applying these operators in any order. Hence (dropping the parentheses, which only served to indicate order) we may write the relation between x_1 and y (absorbing x_2) as

$$x_1A_1A_2 = x_1A_2A_1 = y \tag{8}$$

In the graph notation, this is equivalent to (this is Graph IV with x_2 absorbed)

$$
\begin{array}{c}
A_1A_2 \\
x_1 \;\bullet\!\!\longrightarrow\!\!\bullet
\end{array}
$$

or

$$
\begin{array}{c}
A_2A_1 \\
x_1 \;\bullet\!\!\longrightarrow\!\!\bullet\; y
\end{array}
$$

V

Except for omitting all mention of x_2, this graph is strictly equivalent to Graph IV.

Absorption of nodes corresponds to the algebraic operation of eliminating a variable from a system of equations, as we do in ordinary solutions of such equations. The fact that upon absorption of nodes the operators of intermediate links in the chain commute is the basis of manipulation of such graphs.

Reduction of More Complex Graphs

This technique of absorbing nodes is very useful for *reducing* complex graphs to get at the connection between two variables. For instance, suppose we have a theory that says that four independent variables are related to each other and to a dependent variable (y) as follows:

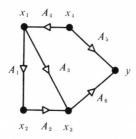

VI

Then suppose we ask the question of what would happen if *we* introduced from outside this system a change in x_1 of a given size. In particular, we want to know what to predict about the change in y. First we add to the graph an outside "source" of x_1, which we can call x_1', and a "tap" to draw off the effect of this on y, calling it y'. We need merely to absorb the appropriate nodes, remembering that the effects of two arrows entering a given node add, to the following reduction.

Graph VI with added taps.

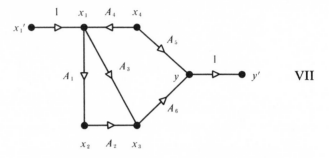

VII

Absorbing x_3 from Graph VII.

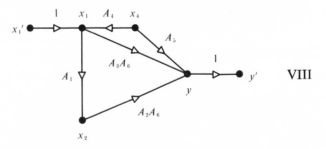

VIII

Absorbing x_2 from Graph VIII.

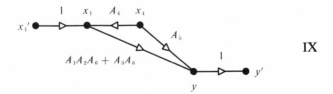

IX

Absorbing x_1.

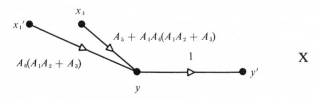

X

Absorbing y, and ignoring the effect of x_4, which does not change.

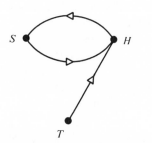

XI

Hence the effect of an exogenous introduction of a change in the variable x_1 (represented above by x_1') would be $x_1' A_6(A_1A_2 + A_3)$ on a measurement of y after the change was introduced. The composite operator $A_6(A_1A_2 + A_3)$ is called the "graph transmittance" from x_1 to y. It is equivalent to the total causal force of exogenous variation of x_1 on y, given the other causal relations of the graph. It is equivalent to the solution of the system of equations represented by the graph, for y' in terms of x'.

Loops in Linear Graphs

Let us consider a graph introduced earlier to represent a functional theory:

XII

Here S represents "structure activity" which compensates for changes in the homeostatic variable H. An exogenous tension, T, produces variations in H. Structures are selected out because they have the consequence of modifying the value of H to compensate for variations induced by T. In one of the examples above, H is anxiety, T is uncertainty in fishing which produces anxiety, and S is magical activity selected out because it reduces anxiety.

In order to translate Graph XII into a linear graph, we assume that all relations are linear and that the operators are as in Graph XIII.

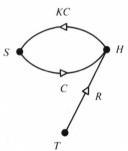

XIII

The assumption here is that the structure activity, S, has an effect proportional to C on the homeostatic variable H. Then the selective effect of being able to maintain H is proportional to its effectiveness in maintaining it (C again) and an operator K which says how effective the maintenance of H is as a selective cause. Thus if H is a powerful variable, such as anxiety about death, we would expect powerful selective effects (large K). If, on the other hand, H is the variable of cleanliness in the house, disturbed by the tensions of the mess children make, we would expect it to have a small selective effect (small K). This is merely saying that social variables which are very important to happiness or survival will tend to select structures that maintain them very strongly. Variables of smaller importance will have much weaker effects in encouraging functional structures. T in the graph is assumed to have an effect proportional to R on the homeostatic variable.

The Relations Between Tensions and Homeostasis in Functional Structures

Now let us study the effects of an induced change in T on the homeostatic variable, H. Adding a source and tap gives us Graph XIV.

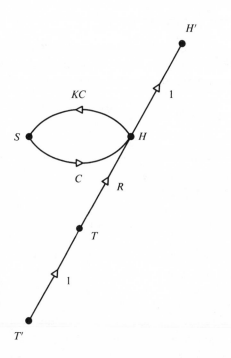

XIV

Absorbing T and S, we obtain Graph **XV**.

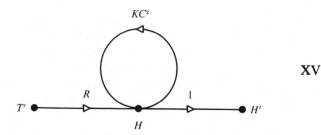

XV

Intuitively we know that the relation between T' and H' must be *reduced* by the loop, or else the functional theory would not make sense. Hence the arrow entering the loop must have the opposite sign from R, which implies that K must be negative. We may choose R negative, in keeping with the conventions adopted above in the chapter.

The loop transmittance of a loop with an operator A may easily be shown to be $1/(1 - A)$.[50] Hence we may always substitute

[50] This is shown in Huggins and Entwisle, *op. cit.,* chapter 2.

for a self-loop of this sort a dummy node which *receives* all influences coming into H, and then transform these by an operator of that form on leaving the dummy node. In our case, this operator would clearly be $1/(1 - KC^2)$. That is, Graphs XVI and XVII below are equivalent to Graph XV.

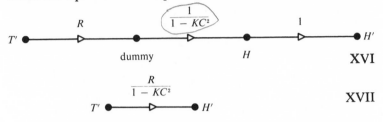

Since K is negative, the denominator increases whenever K is large in absolute value (*i.e.*, whenever H has a strong selective effect), or whenever C is large (*i.e.,* whenever the structure is effective in controlling the homeostatic variable). Hence the transmittance decreases with K larger in absolute value, larger C, and smaller R. What does this mean substantively?

First, the more severe the tension, the more disturbance to the homeostatic variable there will be, even in the presence of functional structures.

But the transmittance will be smaller if K is larger (in absolute value). That is, if a homeostatic variable is one which strongly selects structures according to their consequences, then it will vary much less with external tensions. If there were some way to disturb them "equally," we would expect anxiety about death to be less variable than anxiety about the cleanliness of houses.

The transmittance is also smaller if the structures maintaining it are highly causally effective—that is, if C is larger. The squared C term indicates that this operates two ways. First, causally efficient structures for maintaining H will be selected more strongly than weak ones. Second, the effect of such causal structures on H, leaving selection aside, will be greater. If it is true, for example, that modern navigation reduces anxiety on the high seas more effectively than magic, we will expect (once modern navigation becomes possible) that it will be strongly selected for in preference to magic, and that the amount of anxiety people feel on the high seas will be much less, and much less variable in the presence of storms, than before it became possible.

The Relation Between Tension and Structure Activity

Likewise we may trace out the relations between an exogenously induced increase in tension T and structure activity S. The reductions would be those in Graphs XVIII, XIX, and XX.

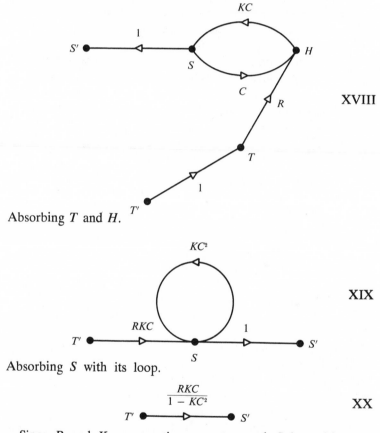

Absorbing T and H.

XVIII

Absorbing S with its loop.

XIX

XX

Since R and K are negative operators and C is positive, we see that the overall sign of the transmittance is positive. Structure activity varies in the same direction as the tension.

However, the relation is not nearly so strong as would be predicted from straightforward causation of the form of Graph XXI.

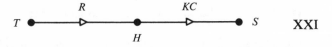

That is, if we take account only of the selective effects of H, we will overestimate the relation between tension and structure activity. We will overestimate because the functional effects of structure actitvity reduce the variations of H and do not allow the full selective effects to get through the graph.

This result is extremely important for social theory, because it shows why there are so many functional alternatives. Let us consider the graph which would represent the situation in which S_1 exists and responds easily to maintain H. Then consider the selective effect of H on S_2, which might also serve the function of maintaining H.

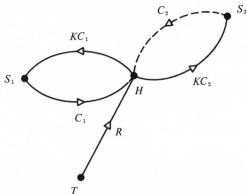

Here we have drawn the consequences of structure activity S_2 *if it existed* with a dotted line, to indicate that at present S_2 has no consequences. Now the graph transmittance from T' to S_2' is given by Graph XXIII (we omit the steps of the reduction).

$$\frac{RKC_2}{1 - KC_1^2}$$

XXIII

$$T' \bullet\!\!\longrightarrow\!\!\!\rhd\!\!\longrightarrow\!\!\bullet S_2'$$

That is, the selective effect in favor of S_2 is multiplied by a factor

$$\frac{1}{1 - KC_1^2}$$

which will be smaller, the more effective S_1 already is in controlling the effects of the tension. This effect of one functional alternative reducing the selective causal force tending to produce other functional alternatives is a crucial distinctive feature of functional causal structures and explains the important role that functional alternatives play in functional theory.[51]

A Formal Representation of Marxian Functionalism

Let us consider from this point of view the analysis of Marxian functionalism given above. The analysis may be represented by the Graph XXIV, which is equivalent to Figure 3.8.

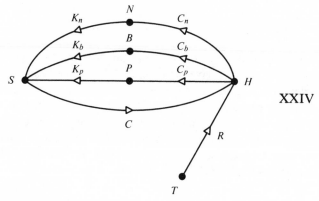

XXIV

The nodes are:

    S, T, and H as before
    N = nobles
    B = bourgeoisie
    P = proletariat

The operators are:

    C_n = the effect of maintaining H on the nobles
    C_b = the effect of maintaining H on the bourgeoisie

[51] See Robert K. Merton, *op. cit.*, and the discussion of the functional form of historicist explanation in the text of this chapter.

C_p = the effect of maintaining H on the proletariat
K_n = the capacity of the nobles to affect structures (power)
K_b = the capacity of the bourgeoisie to affect structures
K_p = the capacity of the proletariat to affect structures
C and R as before

By the additive and commutative properties of such operators, we absorb the nodes N, B, and P to get Graph XXV.

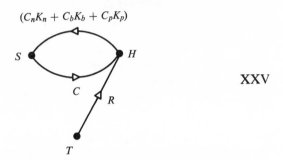

XXV

This is equivalent to the previous analysis of other functional theories except that it gives an explicit differentiated expression for the selective effect, in terms of the interests of the different classes in H and their social power. That is, "touching loops" may be reduced to a single loop at their point of contact by simply combining their effects. As before, the relations between an exogenous change in tensions to the variable H and to structure activity S may be written out as in Graphs **XXVI** and **XXVII**.

$$\frac{R}{1 - C(C_nK_n + C_bK_b + C_pK_p)}$$

XXVI

T' •————————▷————————• H'

$$\frac{R(C_nK_n + C_bK_b + C_pK_p)}{1 - C(C_nK_n + C_bK_b + C_pK_p)}$$

XXVII

T' •————————▷————————• S'

Clearly if the signs of the C_i are different, a change in the relative social powers of the social classes (the K_i) could change the sign of the relations between T and S. In other words, changing powers of classes can change the overall process from one which selects *for* a given structure to one which selects *against* that structure. The larger the tensions tending to disturb H, the faster the selection in either direction.[52]

Loops Not Touching the Causal Path

Let us add to the above considerations the fact that structure activity has *costs* or negative effects. Costs imply another causal branch out of S in the graph for functional theories, corresponding to the costs it generates. Presumably people are motivated to avoid such costs (in other words, negative consequences of S are generally selected against). Consequently the higher the costs, the greater the causal force suppressing structure activity. This may be represented by Graph XVIII.

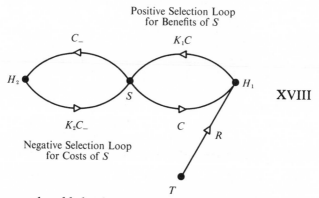

Positive Selection Loop
for Benefits of S

C_- K_1C

H_2 S H_1 XVIII

K_2C_- C R

Negative Selection Loop
for Costs of S

T

We have merely added a loop representing the negative consequences of S (represented by an operator, C_-, which is *not* the negative of C) for other homeostatic variables H_2 which also tend to be maintained by a selective force. The selective force of the maintenance of H_2 we name K_2. If we first eliminate the "outside" loop, we get a "cost-corrected" functional graph of the form of Graph XXIX.

[52] For in that case R would be larger. At this point we can connect many of the results of ordinary functional theories involving exogenous tensions to Marxian political analysis. Marx's analysis of economic instabilities and pressures in capitalist organization are examples of "tensions" that are exogenous to the class conflict as such but that hasten the adaptation of capitalism to the new power of the proletariat.

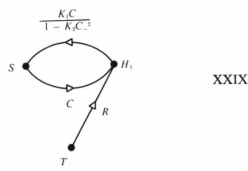

XXIX

That is, the selective effect of H_1 is multiplied by a factor which decreases (the denominator increases, since K_2 is negative) as the *size* of S's negative effects increase (C_- larger) and as the *selective importance* of the variables it damages increases (K_2 larger in absolute size). Adding appropriate exogenous branches, and absorbing H and T, we get Graph **XXX**.

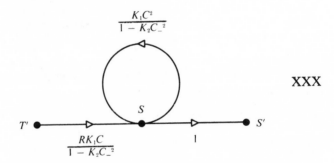

XXX

Reducing the remaining loop, and absorbing S, after algebraic reduction, we obtain the graph transmittance from T to S.

$$\frac{RK_1C}{1 - K_2C_-^2 - K_1C^2}$$

$$T' \bullet \!\!-\!\!\!\rhd\!\!-\!\! \bullet S'$$

XXXI

This expression is the same as the expression in Graph **XX** for the effect of an induced tension on structure activity, except that a term $-K_2C_-^2$ has been added to the denominator. Since this term is positive (K_2 being negative), the denominator is larger, and hence the transmittance for an increase in tension to structure activity is smaller. If the costs are very high ($-K_2C_-^2$ being very large), then there will be a very small selective effect in favor of S. Otherwise all the previous relations hold.

This means that "expensive" devices to reach homeostasis will be used only when the tension is large, when the variable that the structure maintains is very important, and when the effects of the structure on H_1 are strong. Inexpensive social or physiological structures will be used whenever possible. Fevers are more expensive ways of controlling infection than white blood cells, so people are always characterized by high levels of white blood cells but rarely (except when the tension is great) by fevers.

The same sort of principle clearly applies to social life. Usually people can adopt religious or magical beliefs to relieve their anxieties fairly "cheaply." Religion and magic do not have many negative effects. Hence religion and magic are fairly constant features of societies. On the other hand, purges are fairly "expensive" ways of controlling social tensions, so that we less commonly find societies with constant blood-letting.

Both these examples suggest a very interesting kind of alternative formulation of the evolutionary problem, which unfortunately takes us into nonlinear systems of causation. For there would be a selective effect in favor of an adjustive structure which provided high fever only when the tension of infection was very great and otherwise left the body at the normal temperature. A temperature high enough to kill germs is also high enough to run the risk of cooking the brain cells, so one would not want to use it unless the risk of death from infection was very great. On the other hand, one would want to use it under those conditions of high tension from infection. If we could somehow select for *a high correlation between infection and fever,* that would be better than selecting either for constant fever or constant normal temperature. As we all know, exactly such selection for a high correlation between infection and fever has taken place in mammals and other higher animals. Likewise if societies could select for purges only when the danger to society was very great (*i.e.,* if societies could select in favor of systems of justice which purge exactly the right people), such systems would be better than no purges or constant unselective purges. We know that most societies have selected out patterns of behavior which purge people more, the more severely they disturb the social order. That is, there is selection for servo-mechanism type structures, or negative feedback structures, which use "expensive" control mechanisms only when they are needed.

Similar reduction of the cost-corrected functional graph (Graph XXIX) to get the transmittance from tension to homeostatic variables gives Graph XXXII.

$$\frac{R(1 - K_2 C_-^2)}{1 - K_2 C_-^2 - K_1 C^2}$$

$$T' \bullet \longrightarrow \bullet H' \qquad \text{XXXII}$$

Inspection of this expression indicates that there are somewhat compensating effects. There is an increase in the numerator, and an increase in the denominator. The increase in the numerator corresponds to the reduction of structure activity (which, without the costs, would control H better). The increase in the denominator corresponds to something quite similar to what we noted before in the case of the cost-free functional structure (see Graph XXII and the discussion of it). The causal effect of tensions working to select a functional alternative was *decreased*, because one functional alternative was already in the society. But in this case, we have suppressed that structure activity by taking account of its costs. Such suppression means that whatever selective pressure the tension creates operates nearer its full strength, and that there is constant pressure to select for S because the tension is not being relieved too well by the structure whose activity is being suppressed by its costs. When functional alternatives are suppressed by their costs, we would expect there to be a strong selective pressure for any really cheap alternative, one without negative consequences, for H_1 is not being very well controlled—control being too expensive.

The argument above gives rise to another very important result for social theory. It is the nearly cost-free functional alternatives (such as magic and religion) that are least likely to be replaced by other functional alternatives with lower costs. Hence it is in such cost-free institutions as religion where we would expect historicist-functional explanations to be most relevant. The function of sunk costs, discussed in the chapter, is exactly to turn a costly alternative into a nearly cost-free one, to make it more similar to religion or magic.

The General Solution for Graph Transmittance

The reader may have noticed in the treatment of loop graphs that the denominator of the expressions for transmittance through the graph was the same for the relation between tensions and either structure or homeostasis. If he will calculate by absorption, as above, other transmittances (*e.g.,* in Graph XXVIII, the transmittance between T and H_2), he will find that on appropriate manipulation the same denominator appears. A very elegant result in the theory of linear graphs allows the writing down of graph transmittances by inspection—in particular, writing down the denominator of all transmittances in the graph by inspection of the loop structure.

The denominator is calculated as follows. Write down all the transmittances around loops in a linear graph. Then write down the product of all *nontouching pairs* of loop transmittances (a loop "touches" another if the two have a node in common). Then write down the product of all *nontouching triplets* of loops. And so forth. Then the denominator may be written as

$$\Delta = 1 - [(L_1 + L_2 + \ldots) - (L_1L_2 + L_1L_3 \ldots) \\ + (L_1L_2L_3 + L_1L_2L_4 \ldots) - \ldots]^* \quad (9)$$

where the asterisk means that all products of touching loops are eliminated. Thus the denominator of Graph XXVII with two loops is

$$\Delta = 1 - (L_1 + L_2) = 1 - K_1C^2 - K_2C_-^2 \quad (10)$$

because there are no nontouching pairs of loops.

The numerator is calculated in an equally easy fashion. First we calculate the direct transmittance along the direct paths from the source to the observation. For instance, in Graph XXVIII, the only direct path from T' to H' has transmittance R. The direct path from T' to S' has transmittance RK_1C. Then for each of these direct paths, eliminate all loops which touch it. In this graph with eliminated loops, calculate Δ_p just as in the denominator. Multiply the direct transmittance by Δ_p. Do the same for the other direct paths, and sum. This is the numerator. Thus in Graph XXVIII, the direct path from T' to S' touches all the loops, $\Delta_p = 1$, and the numerator is simply RK_1C. But the path from T' to H' does not touch the negative-consequences loop. Hence the numerator there is $R(1 - K_2C_-{}^2)$. The proof of this marvelous theorem is not presented here.[53]

Conclusion

Using the intuitively appealing representation of causal theories by linear graphs, we have easily derived some rather subtle and interesting results. For instance, we have shown why there are likely to be functional alternatives to a given functional structure which are not in evidence, and we have shown that the historical persistence of functional alternatives is especially likely if they have few negative consequences. Hence, whatever functions religions serve, it is in such cheap structures and practices (without negative consequences) that we will expect great variety among societies and intense traditionalism within them. These results were intuitively clear to, and implicit in the writings of, the main functional theorists.[54] But explicit knowledge accessible to intelligent beginners is obviously more efficient for a science than knowledge perceived by the intuition of its geniuses.

With the tools of this section, the student should be able to derive interesting results from complex causal theories without much difficulty by representing the theory as a linear graph. With some practice, this skill can be developed by using the outline diagrams presented in the chapter. Causal loops in general are hard for most people to treat intuitively. This intuitive difficulty is one of the reasons that, up to now, there has been a strong tendency for empirical research to be done on trivial one-step causal hypotheses, rather than on the interesting theories that tell us something about how societies work.

[53] See Huggins and Entwisle, *op. cit.*, chapter 2, especially appendix 2A. The source given for the proof is Samuel J. Mason and Henry J. Zimmerman, *Electronic Circuits, Signals, and Systems* (New York: Wiley, 1960).

[54] See especially Merton, *op. cit.*

CHAPTER FOUR

The Conceptualization of Power
Phenomena

One of the primary skills that a sociologist needs in order to generate theories is the capacity to conceptualize *structural phenomena* in societies. Structural phenomena are characteristics of a system of social relations and groups which cause differences in the way interactions among people affect these people. That is, often a person's behavior cannot be predicted without predicting the actions of other people, whose actions in turn can be predicted only by predicting the actions of still others. *Structural phenomena* are phenomena which determine the form and substance of such systems of interaction. One important type of structural phenomenon is what is generally called *power*. The relation between my action and someone else's action quite often cannot be predicted without knowing whether the other person has power over me. This power is generally determined by his place in society.

In this chapter we will develop a series of concepts dealing with power phenomena. Our aim will be, as with all conceptual work, to locate with our concepts those phenomena which cause variations in people's behavior or which describe phenomena with a unique set of causes.

First we will develop a distinction which has been fundamental in legal thought for many years. This is a distinction between two main kinds of power, which may be called "control over resources" *vs.* "control over people," or "rights in things" *vs.* "rights in persons," or "property" *vs.* "authority."

A right in things is the right to make certain decisions about how something will be used, with the correlative right to keep other people from interfering with such uses. If someone else owns the piece of land next to mine, he can use that land for anything permitted in the zoning code and other applicable laws, and he can petition for an exception to the zoning code. Unless this damages me in certain legally and politically defined ways, I can do nothing about it. Even if I feel that he ought not use his property in a certain way, he still has the power to do so.

A right in persons is a right to have someone do something for me. These two kinds of rights or powers have quite different problems of legitimacy, particularly since legitimacy in the eyes of subordinates is largely irrelevant for the first kind. Moreover, these two kinds of rights give rise to quite different kinds of capacity to control the world.

Then we will turn to the problem of the legitimacy of each of these kinds of power. It has been often observed that the stability of power depends on legitimacy, and that power created by naked force is, in the long run, precarious. That is, of course, just as true of the powers of property as it is of authority, as the movements to nationalize foreign corporations in many poorer countries clearly show.

By analyzing in a few cases *who* has to believe in the legitimacy of a power for it to be stable, we will see that the person *over whom power is exercised* is not usually as important as *other power-holders*. If the criminal does not believe his arrest is legitimate, he can, in the classic phrase, "tell it to the judge." If the judge supports him rather than the policeman, the policeman's power comes effectively to an end. A casual examination of policemen's complaints about the inadequacy of their authority will show that they are much more worried about their legitimacy in front of judges than in front of criminals. The judge's power in turn depends on the legitimacy of judicial decisions among political officials. One need only recall

Andrew Jackson's famous statement about a decision of the Supreme Court, "Let them enforce it." The Court's decision was without effect because it was not legitimate *among other powers,* and not because it was not accepted in good grace by the losing party to the case.

A concept of legitimacy is developed on this basis which shows one basic procedure for constructing structural concepts: concepts of structure may be built from ideas about *chains of contingent activities,* in which how one interaction comes out is influenced by the probabilities of third parties intervening in case of need.

A second major style of concept construction is illustrated if we consider the relation of power to the information-bearing capacity of channels of communication. Any detailed control by a power-holder will depend on the detail of his knowledge of what the person he is controlling is up to. And unless the person controlled can find out in detail what the power-holder demands, he will not be able to obey. An American tourist who talks loudly and angrily to a foreign servant and succeeds only in getting the servant to run about doing everything he can think of that the tourist might want is a type case of powerful impotence getting ineffective obedience.

Most power on a large scale is exercised at a distance, with multiple communications links between policy-makers and the people whom the policy is supposed to control. This communications structure is the administrative apparatus of the system of power. The power exercised from policy-making centers can be only as effective as the structure of communication between the behavior-controlled and the policy-making power-holders. This is why authority on a large scale is always embedded in an administrative apparatus.

By analyzing the characteristics of a very efficient communications system, the pricing system of a market, we can get clues to the sources of information-bearing efficiency. By applying variables extracted from this analysis, we can outline conditions under which power-holders can control the behavior of subordinates precisely and conditions under which their power will be an empty show. Many rulers with great power to reward and punish are in the situation of the American tourist: they would have great power in actual control of behavior if they could find out what was going on.

This illustrates the general strategy of treating a system of links among people from an information-theory or cybernetic point of view. The relation between control and information in a physical system was first worked out in rigorous form in the study of electrical systems and computers. This rigor is not very useful to us. But the basic notion that control can be no greater than the quantity of information received and transmitted by the control mechanisms can be generalized to systems consisting of links among people. Power concepts based on the notion of *the quantity of information* are very useful in analyzing administrative systems.

The third section of this chapter looks at this relation between power and communication the other way around. We will be interested in the communication of demands for changes in policy in a political system.

We may presume that in an area which is sufficiently militarily vulnerable (see Chapter Five), a "government" will exist. The question we then want to ask is under what conditions will this power be accessible to people within the state. There are various devices by which citizens call upon the power of the state, such as court procedures and appeals to executive organs. But one device of fundamental significance in most modern states is the right to make laws—that is, to set the terms on which the power of the state will be generally available. A common type of institution for making laws is a parliament or a congress.

We will therefore develop a concept of *the degree of political access* of a person or group in parliamentary systems. Three elements will go into the construction of this concept: (1) the powers of parliament, or the capacity of parliament to set the terms on which the force of the state is available, (2) the capacity of groups of parliamentary deputies to enter into majorities, or the capacity of given deputies to make use of the powers of parliament, and (3) the capacity of a group of citizens to elect parliamentary deputies. The idea is that in order to set the terms on which governmental power will be available, a group must be able to communicate its preferences among deputies, the deputies in turn must have a real possibility of gaining control over parliament, and parliament must have the effective power to control governmental action.

Political access will serve as an example of a third general strategy of constructing structural concepts, that of a channel of (legitimate) communication. Such channels are described, as far as their causal significance is concerned in this case, by the probability that a message of a certain kind will remain intact (and legitimate) at the end of the channel. This probability in turn is thought to affect the political behavior of the groups; consequently it is a structural phenomenon. Here we describe the probability by means of estimates or indices of the probabilities that, say, a worker's petition will be represented by his deputy in parliament (whether the worker is enfranchised or not), the probability that the deputy's communication will be taken into consideration by the parliamentary majority, and the probability that a message of the relevant kind by a parliamentary majority would in fact be communicated effectively to the organs of government. As discussed more completely below, the overall estimate of such a probability for a single channel is a product of the probabilities in the sections of the channel, and the concept is constructed with the appropriate multiplicative form.

Then we turn to the fundamental problem of the stability of the relation between power and values, or the problem of *institutions*. When we say that a certain value or practice is *institutionalized* in a society, we mean that the powers of that society are distributed in such a way as to exert a continuous force in favor of the value or practice. Thus the rules of civil liberty are institutionalized in the United States, because legitimate powers to interfere with a man's speech are distributed in such a way that the people who have such powers use them only in extreme cases. This distribution is achieved by concentrating power over such matters in the courts, which in turn are heavily committed to maintaining the values embodied in the Bill of Rights. In this case, then, *power to interfere with a man's speech is highly correlated with the value of civil liberty.*

Such a correlation makes the preservation of that value in daily practice much more likely than it would be if all elected officials or all citizens had the power to stop a man from speaking, for belief in this value is not nearly so great among the population as it is among judges. Thus the institutionalization of a value or a practice can be fruitfully defined as a correlation of power with commitment to that value or practice, so that the more powerful a man is, the more likely he is to hold the value. Since the probability that an interaction will be governed by such a value is heavily determined by the correlation between power and that value in the society at large, such a correlation is a structural property of that society.

Then the degree of *institutional integration* of a society can be defined as the degree to which the same broad values are correlated with power in different institutional areas.

Such a conceptualization illustrates the procedure of forming structural concepts by using the *degree of correlation* between two variables as a basis for concept formation. As is explained below, such a strategy is generally useful when there are important interaction effects of two variables.

The final conceptual exercise treats the problem of creating new concentrations of power for specific purposes, or *the creation of organizations*. Organizations are decision-making systems to which a defined group of powers have been entrusted so they can achieve certain purposes. The problem of creating organizations is thus, in part, the problem of collecting together the necessary powers to achieve a given end, on the basis of a theory about how such powers can be used to achieve that end. "Projects" (or plans, or theories) on the basis of which organizations are created describe the powers required to execute the projects. Then we can analyze the distribution of these powers in the society. The powers required by projects and the distribution of those powers jointly determine the *possible organizations* or *possible organization-forming coalitions*. Then the process of bringing such possible coalitions into being is the process of creating organizations (or of "entrepreneurship" or "investment").

Such a conceptualization illustrates the procedure of forming structural concepts by the construction of *feasible sets of alternative actions or groups*. In this case, the combination of the power requirements of projects with the historically given distribution of those powers determines the feasible set of coalitions. The feasible sets would change if the distribution of powers were different, or if new projects were invented and became generally known. The actions of entrepreneurs in setting up coalitions to undertake a new project are of course determined in part by what feasible coalitions there are, and consequently this feasible set of coalitions is a structural property of the system of social relations.

Our purpose in this analysis of different power phenomena is not so much to teach how power phenomena should be conceptualized.

For many purposes other concepts will be appropriate, because not all things that vary with variations in power structures vary with those aspects we will conceptualize here. And no doubt causal investigation using concepts developed here would show, in the long run, that the phenomena identified by these concepts are not exactly the ones that have unique effects and unique causes.

Our purpose is rather to illustrate the usefulness of a number of general strategies of constructing structural concepts in such a way that they can be used in causal explanation and can be empirically studied. The general strategies illustrated are: (1) concepts based on the idea of a chain of contingent action, in which the potential reaction of other people (if a given action departs from a certain path) is part of the constitution of an act (in the analysis of legitimacy), (2) information concepts, in which the degree of control of an action by a power-holder depends on the information-bearing capacity of the channels of communication, (3) communications channel concepts, in which the effect is determined by the probability of communications of different kinds getting through the whole channel (in the analysis of political access), (4) correlation concepts, in which a structure is described by the correlation of two or more variables within it, such as power and a certain value (in the analysis of institutions), and (5) feasible sets of actions and feasible sets of people to carry them out (in the analysis of the formation of organizations).

I / RIGHTS IN THINGS AND RIGHTS IN PERSONS

Individual Powers

By a property right we usually mean a right to make certain decisions concerning the way a certain resource will be used. For any given resource, such as a piece of land, there is a range of things for which the resource might legitimately be used. In the United States, for example, no piece of land may be used to grow marijuana for free sale, and many pieces of land are subject to zoning regulations that prohibit certain uses of the land—building glue factories in residential areas, for instance.

But within the range of permitted uses of the land, the owner has the right to choose. He can sell his right to decide on the use of the land, either forever or for a period of years (by leasing the land). After the lease is signed, two people own property rights in the land, for some decisions are at the discretion of the lessee during a specified period, and others at the discretion of the lessor, especially those on the disposal of the land after the end of the lease.

In particular, if I am an owner's neighbor and I have a drugstore, and if he decides to lease his land to a drugstore chain, I have no recourse. His decision will, of course, damage my business very greatly. He is exercising his property right in such a way as to damage me. I may feel that he has acted immorally in damaging a friend and neighbor to such an extent, and that his action is clearly illegitimate. But insofar as his property right is legitimate in the sense discussed in the following section, I can do nothing about it. We would say that he has a "liberty" to decide on the use of his property, and I am "exposed" to the consequences of whatever decision he decides to take. Being able to expose me to such consequences is, of course, a power over me.[1]

A quite different kind of right is a right to demand a certain kind of behavior from someone else. If I have hired a man, for instance, then a labor contract exists which obliges him to do certain agreed kinds of work and to accept agreed kinds of orders. If he does not, he loses his rights under the contract. Or if I have married a woman, a marriage contract exists which gives me (and her) certain rights to have her do things for me (care for the children, for instance) and vice versa (support, for instance). These rights can be enforced both legally and morally, and I can make my employee or my wife suffer certain consequences if they do not live up to their obligations. These kinds of rights are called "rights in the person" in classical legal language, and "legitimate expectations" in current sociological theory. If rights in things can be described as a system of liberties and exposures, then rights in persons can be described as systems of rights and duties.[2]

---

[1] See John R. Commons, *The Legal Foundations of Capitalism* (New York: Macmillan, 1924), pp. 47–65.
[2] Commons, *ibid.*, pp. 65–142. See also A. Radcliffe-Brown, *Structure and Function in Primitive Society* (Glencoe, Ill.: Free Press, 1952), pp. 32–48 (*jus in rem vs. jus in personam*).

Just as the range of legitimate uses of a property right is more or less limited, so the range of activities one can ask by virtue of a right in the person is also limited by rules and norms. The range within which one can determine the activity of another person in such a situation has been called a "zone of indifference," on the ground that as far as the social relation is concerned, the person to whom orders are given will be (effectively) indifferent to which of the activities within the legitimate range he does.[3]

Either kind of right gives a person a capacity to do more different things. The general definition of "power" is "a capacity to get things done." [4] Either resources (rights in things) or authority (rights in persons) increases the ability of a person to do what he decides to do. What he will actually manage to get done depends on how well he uses his opportunities. He may fail to use them out of ignorance, or lack of motivation, or moral scruples.

Corporate Powers

Up to this point we have been talking as if powers were usually concentrated in a single man. In modern societies the most important powers are very rarely held by individuals. Rather, they are held by *social decision-making apparatuses*. The stockholders of General Motors cannot prevent the sale of the Buick plant if that has been agreed to by the board of directors, nor can a stockholder give an order to a worker in the Buick plant. It is the corporation as a legal personality, as a duly constituted decision-making apparatus, which owns the Buick plant and has a labor contract with the Buick worker. What the stockholder owns is a general claim on the *fund of resources* and on income from the use of that fund by

[3] Originally proposed by Chester Barnard, *The Functions of the Executive* (Cambridge, Mass.: Harvard University Press, 1954), pp. 167–70. For an elegant discussion of this in the employment relation, see Herbert Simon, "A Formal Theory of the Employment Relation," in *Models of Man: Social and Rational* (New York: Wiley, 1957), pp. 183–95.

[4] This type of definition has been argued in the recent literature, especially by Talcott Parsons. See "Authority, Legitimation and Political Action," in *Structure and Process in Modern Societies* (Glencoe, Ill.: Free Press, 1960), pp. 170–98, especially pp. 181–83.

the corporation, a right to vote for directors, and certain legal rights to protect these other two (such as rights to information).[5]

Obviously no person has the legitimate power to pass a law in the United States. Rather, a decision-making apparatus consisting of majorities in the relevant committees in the House and Senate, majorities in the two houses themselves, the president, and in some instances the Supreme Court, holds that power. The resources collected by taxation, the authority to raise an army and to oblige men to obey military orders, the right to take away a man's property by due process of law, and similar powers are not held by individuals in the United States.

When we speak of an individual's power in modern societies, we usually mean his personal capacity to affect the decision that will be the product of some decision-making apparatus. In general, we are interested only in decision-making apparatuses which are small enough for a single man's influence to be of significant size, such as corporations or the governments of small communities. We rarely ask who has more power to pass a national law.

Thus most problems of legitimacy in modern societies are problems concerning the legitimacy of some decision-making apparatus, some socially instituted manner of deciding how resources and authority are to be used. These problems are usually quite different for rights in things and rights in persons. We turn now to the problem of conceptualizing legitimacy, keeping in mind the two kinds of power whose legitimacy we have to analyze.

II / LEGITIMACY OF POWERS

The Nesting of Power

Let us first consider what is likely to happen if I object to a chain drugstore's leasing the property next to my drugstore in the United States and using it to open a competing drugstore. If I try to interfere directly with the activity of that drugstore—for instance,

[5] A corporation is a legal device for separating "ownership" from "control" over assets; corporations developed partly out of the law of trusts in inheritance which had this explicit purpose. If the much discussed "separation of ownership from control" were reformulated as "the corporation as a legal device works as it is supposed to," it might not seem so exciting.

by hiring thugs to keep people off the property—my competitor can call on the police and the courts to stop me and very likely to put me in prison. In the exercise of his property rights free of interference, he has not only his personal powers but, if he needs it, the power to put me in prison.

If on the other hand I object on the grounds that certain activities he carries out are beyond the liberties he enjoys (for example, if he sells narcotics without a prescription), or that he has not met some of the legal requirements for operating a drugstore (for instance, if he does not have licensed pharmacists to dispense drugs), then I can call on the state to stop him. If he is within his liberties as presently defined, I can try to get a new licensing law passed in the local government which will make his location illegitimate (e.g., one providing that a business can have only one drugstore license), or perhaps I can try to get the land next door condemned to be used as a park. If he is not politically able to stop such a movement, he may have to close down. Or he may appeal to higher authority in the courts, arguing that such a licensing law is an illegal restraint of trade. If he wins, then he can call on higher governmental powers to oppose the powers of the local government.

In other words, the capacity of my competitor to exercise his property right is dependent not so much on his personal power as on the way in which he can call upon the powers of the government to keep me from interfering. Whether or not I think he is "unfairly competing" with me, he can go ahead and expose me to the rigors of competition so long as he can call up massive governmental powers to support himself. If I can figure out a way to keep him from calling upon these governmental powers, he cannot exercise his rights. It is thus the legitimacy of his claim *in the centers of power* which is crucial, and not its legitimacy *among people who must take the consequences.*

If we consider on the other hand a criminal caught by the police and arrested, we have a problem of a policeman's right to demand a certain behavior (going to jail) from another person. In order to put the person in jail if he objects, the policeman may have to call other policemen, or even in extreme instances (e.g., for crimes in riots) have the governor call out the National Guard. It is mainly his instant capacity to call on other policemen which makes a policeman able to make arrests.

In order to keep the presumed criminal in jail, he must be indicted—for serious crimes, generally by a grand jury. If the policeman cannot justify the arrest to the grand jury, the man goes free. After the grand jury, a decision-making apparatus (a trial) must be set up, with certain socially instituted characteristics, and the policeman's arrest must be considered legitimate "beyond all reasonable doubt" before the man can be kept in jail.

A policeman thus has power to jail a man who objects to the degree that, when he has difficulty taking him to jail, other policemen or the governor and the National Guard regard the arrest as legitimate. And the man stays arrested only if a grand jury and a petit jury can be convinced of the legitimacy of the arrest. The reason a policeman's authority comes to an end if the man is not indicted or is not convicted is that the policeman can no longer call on anyone to back him up when the man wants to leave jail. In fact, the man himself can call on the power of the state to force the policeman to let him go. The "authority" of the policeman thus consists of the probability that his action will be backed up by other concentrations of power, and it is limited because the conditions under which others will back him up are limited.

One can find many other cases in which governments which were quite *unpopular* in an area were quite stable because they were *legitimate,* in the sense of being able to call upon centers of power, especially the armed forces. On the other hand, popular governments have often fallen because they were not legitimate in strategic centers of power. The communist government of Hungary in the 1950's is an example of the former; the Peronist government in Argentina in the same period is an example of the latter.

Very often, then, an exercise of a liberty or of authority would not be possible against people who object unless certain other strategic centers of power recognize the right as legitimate. A legitimate right or authority is backed by a *nesting of reserve sources of power* set up in such a fashion that the power can always overcome opposition.

Doctrines of Legitimacy

The crucial function of *doctrines of legitimacy* and norms derived from them is to create a readiness in other centers of power to back up the actions of a person with a certain right. Doctrines of legitimacy serve the crucial function of setting up that nesting of powers which usually makes appeals to physical force unnecessary. In many societies these general doctrines are further specified in laws which state precisely the conditions under which some rights will be backed up by other powers. Such laws may or may not reflect very exactly what will actually happen. In many Latin-American countries, for example, the constitution states that the president will be commander in chief of the armed forces, but in many cases that does not mean that the army will actually back up the president's decisions.

One of the reserve sources of power is public opinion; another is the willing obedience of subordinates. If a right is popular, and if it is accepted by subordinates, the holder of the right will have much less reason to call on other centers of power to back him up. In some kinds of activity, such as learning, which require the active cooperation of the subordinate, the legitimacy of power among subordinates may be very important. But power based *only* on the shifting sands of public opinion and willing obedience is inherently unstable.[6]

---

[6] Max Weber, who is the source of much of the current theorizing about the legitimacy of power, seems to be ambivalent on this point. On the one hand, he defines legitimacy of power (which makes "power" into "authority") in terms of the acceptance by subordinates of the rights of superiors to control them. Theoretically he does not talk about the legitimacy of property rights, though in practice he is extremely interested in the topic. On the other hand, one of the identifying features of "charismatic" authority in Weber is that it is not supported by a stable system for mobilizing other powers in its support, especially economic goods, and is therefore peculiarly dependent on the current state of opinion among subordinates. Weber makes much of the instability of charismatic authority, though it is not very clear whether he means that it is evanescent or that it tends to change into other kinds. I think he has both things in mind. He discusses the "routinization of charisma" as the specification of the terms on which authority and resources will be used according to stable norms.

In his concrete analyses of power phenomena, Weber was very little concerned with any estimations of the state of public opinion or of the ideological enthusiasm of subordinates and subjects. Rather, he analyzed the reactions of other centers of power. I think Weber's instinct in the analysis of concrete cases was right, and that his own theoretical analysis of charisma and its differences from other forms of authority should have led him to see that his definition of legitimacy would not work properly. For the definition of power, authority, and legitimacy, see *The Theory of Social and Economic Organization*, translated by A. M. Henderson and Tal-

Examples of doctrines of legitimacy are the liberal doctrine of free use of property and the legal arrangements for the defense of property which embody it, the doctrine of hereditary monarchy and the arrangements of vassalage for giving the king certain resources and authority, and doctrines of national sovereignty in the control of defined territory and the procedures for "recognizing" governments which embody it.

A Concept of Legitimacy

With this analysis of the causal significance of legitimacy, we can attempt to define the concept. *A power is legitimate to the degree that, by virtue of the doctrines and norms by which it is justified, the power-holder can call upon sufficient other centers of power, as reserves in case of need, to make his power effective.* Some of these reserves may, or may not, be the popularity of a man's powers in public opinion or the acceptance of a doctrine of legitimacy of his powers among subordinates. The doctrine of legitimacy limits a power insofar as the exercise of the power is dependent on its being backed up, for this backing will be available only on terms accepted in other centers of power. The chief significance of the legitimacy of powers for the social system as a whole is that it makes the powers available to a decision-making apparatus predictable, in spite of any opposition the exercise of power might run into. This stability in turn means that a given amount of physical force can guarantee far more powers, and it allows these powers to be used for long-term projects. In unstable power systems most energy is devoted to defending powers rather than to using them usefully.

cott Parsons (Glencoe, Ill.: Free Press, 1957), pp. 124 and 152–53. On charismatic authority see *ibid.,* pp. 358–63, especially on the points above, pp. 187–88 (irregularity of budgeting) and p. 266n (routinization). For examples of Weber's concrete analyses of power systems which suggest a different idea, see especially *passim* in *Max Weber on Law in Economy and Society,* translated by Edward Shils and Max Rheinstein (Cambridge, Mass.: Harvard University Press, 1954), or *passim* in *The City,* translated by Don Martindale and Gertrude Neuwirth (Glencoe, Ill.: Free Press, 1958) or his studies of the power situation in Germany east of the Elbe, summarized by Reinhard Bendix, *Max Weber: An Intellectual Portrait* (Garden City, N.Y.: Doubleday, 1960), pp. 38–70.

It will be useful to examine the structure of this definition in more detail, since our primary purpose in this chapter is not merely to give new definitions to concepts but to analyze the logical elements involved in them. We recall that the causal processes we wanted to catch with the concept took the following form: if a man's power is interfered with, he can call on much greater powers in his defense only if he can show the holders of such powers that his claim is legitimate. His use of his property, or his giving an order of arrest, has a different probability of being effective because of this contingency reserve. If this reserve exists —that is, if the exercise of power is legitimate—it very likely will not have to be called upon because the neighbor or the criminal will know that he would lose in the long run. Thus we want to define a variable which differentiates exercises of power according to a criterion of "what would happen if . . . ?"

Many of the effects of social structure on individual acts take on this causal form. An act of a person is reacted to differently by another, if some of these reactions would set still other people in motion—for instance, to punish the other for interfering with the person's rights. Only in this way can we explain, for example, how the law of contracts governs the millions of contracts made each year which never get into court. The variable we want to define does *not* involve the *action* of third parties as a causal variable, but rather the *probability* of action of third parties in given contingencies. "Legitimacy" as we defined it above is exactly such a concept; it tries to locate the causal significance of the contingent probabilities of actions of other power centers. Such concepts are very common among social theorists who deal with structural processes.

III / AN INFORMATION CONCEPTION OF POWER

Decisions and Information

By the power represented in some decision unit (an individual, a firm, a nation), we mean the *causal effectiveness* of the decisions of that unit. If my decision "yes" is a necessary and sufficient cause for the result to be "yes," and if my decision is not predetermined by my conditions of action, then I have complete power over that result. This definition corresponds to the intuitive notion we have of power, and it fits in well with our use of that concept in the outline of Marxian functionalism in Chapter Three.

It is convenient for certain problems of analysis to formulate this intuitive notion in a slightly different way, as suggested by cybernetic theory. We can say that a decision unit's power is the *amount of information added* about what is going to happen by knowing the decision of that unit.

Let us imagine an observer of some variable, say the price of a commodity. If the observer knows all the causal influences on the price of that commodity, he can use economic theory to predict its price. Suppose that he does not know the decision of a particular firm about what to ask. If the firm is a wheat farm in competition with millions of other wheat farms, the observer can predict with certainty the top price the firm can get. But if the firm is one of three major automobile producers, the observer can only predict a range within which the price will fall.[7] After he knows the decision, he knows the price much better.

Thus more information is added by knowing the decision of the oligopolistic automobile firm than by knowing the decision of the wheat farmer. This is because the decision of the automobile firm is a much more important cause of the price level than is the decision of the wheat farm. This difference in information of the observer, before and after he knows the decision, is thus a measure of the power of the firm.

The chief advantage of such a formulation is that it suggests the relation between power phenomena and administrative phenomena. Administration is above all information-processing. A decision unit can be an effective cause of some characteristics of an activity only if it can adjust its decision to that activity. It needs information to do that.

Imagine a Man in a Box

A fictional example may make this connection clearer. Imagine a man in a box, on the wall of which is a button he can push to

---

[7] He will probably give the prediction in the form of a probability distribution of prices.

electrocute a man outside the box. But suppose there is no communication about what the man outside is doing, and no way for the man inside to get evidence on what he is doing. The only information he has inside is whether or not he has pushed the electrocution button.

The most power that the man in the box can have is "one bit," the control over whether the man outside is dead or alive. If he had any information about how the man outside was behaving and could communicate a certain amount to that man, he could probably control his behavior very well. Fear of death is an efficient cause of the behavior of the man outside.

If we add another button inside which flashes a light outside saying "Sit down" and "Stand up," and a light inside that goes on when the man outside sits down, the man inside can control one decision of the man outside, besides controlling his life and death. We might say he has "two bits" of power.

As the communications channels from inside to outside increase in capacity to discriminate among orders, and as those from outside to inside carry more information about the outside man's behavior, the degree of control by the man inside increases. (If, however, the man outside has suicidal impulses, the inside man's control decreases because the signals are no longer effective causes.)

The power of the man in the box, given his control over the motivations of the man outside, is directly proportional to the information-carrying capacity of the channels between him and the man outside.

Even in the presence of complete power to punish, then, the amount of power of a man over someone's behavior can be no greater than the amount of information that can be transmitted between them. The intimate interrelation between administration and power-wielding derives from this fundamental fact.

Prices in Markets as Information

Let us consider from this point of view a case of an "administrative system" which has been thoroughly analyzed theoretically—namely, the market. In a perfectly competitive market for factors of production (labor, capital, raw materials) at equilibrium, each firm will use enough of each factor of production to bring the (marginal) *revenue created* by that use equal to its *price*. Hence the price of that factor in the market at equilibrium tells everyone how valuable that factor is for producing the next unit of product, in *all* the alternative uses which that factor has.

Instead of having to collect thousands of pieces of information about how productive these factors would be in each industry, an individual needs only to find their price. If he can figure out a use for more of a factor which will give more value than its price, he knows that this will be a more productive use than any other. Judgments about usefulness are made by experts closely attending to particular productive problems. But the results of those judgments are transmitted through the mechanism of market prices throughout the society.

Commercial activity, quoting prices for thousands of goods and services, is thus essentially administrative activity for the economy as a whole. By considering this case, we can see some of the crucial features of administrative systems in relation to power structures.

Features of Price Systems

First we note the tremendous degree of *abstraction* that this system involves. We have thousands of engineers, accountants, and market analysts throughout the society trying to figure out the concrete revenue productivity of some new use of a given quantity of a factor of production. All the concrete grease and grime of this evaluation results in a little nudge on the price of the factor. This little nudge is all the other people in the society want to know about that process. If they knew more, it would only confuse them. In general, then, the information capacity of a channel is increased, from a practical point of view, if the essential information is radically abstracted from all irrelevancy.

Thus we will expect usually that power over large sets of social activity will be associated with a high degree of abstraction in communications behavior. Men who decide about dollars are likely to be more generally powerful than men who decide about machines.

A second characteristic is suggested by the location of the original information in a market. The reason that price is such an adequate indicator of productivity in alternative uses is that the judgments that influence it are made by the men most likely to know productivities. Distortions of price systems as criteria for economic allocation are generally associated with price-setting by men far from the productive system (*e.g.*, public officials).

Thus we will expect men to have more power, the more accurate the inputs of information in the system. Much of the *de facto* liberty of the population in traditional dictatorships is due to the capacity of the population to deceive, avoid, or buy off the administration's local data source. Lack of local data reduces the power of traditional dictators.

A third characteristic of power in administrative systems is the converse of the second. Institutions of privacy (*e.g.*, the law of search and seizure) are significant mainly because they deny access to information to the holders of sanctions. The American government has all the capacity of the man with the electrocution button. But if it cannot get much information on my behavior at home, it cannot control my behavior very well.

A fourth characteristic of power exercise is suggested if we examine the way motivation is handled in the market. A key characteristic of money is that it is a reward as well as a carrier of information. That is, the reward itself carries a high amount of information. Money profit rewards much more productive uses of factors by a much higher profit. It rewards small increases in revenue product with small profits.

The degree of discrimination in the reward system itself—that is, the amount of information in the flow of rewards for behavior —thus increases power. If the man in the box has to electrocute the man outside every time the outsider misbehaves a little, he cannot afford to get unhappy over trivial misbehavior. Thus fine-grained control of behavior depends on fine divisibility of rewards and punishments. Those men who control fine-grained punishment and rewards are likely to have more power for the same total sanctioning capacity. This is one reason why most complex administrative systems use monetary controls, for a money payment can carry a great deal of information along with the reward.[8]

A fifth aspect of power in relation to information is not suggested

[8] It has the added advantage that when a communication is backed with money, one knows that the communicator really means it.

by the market but is a commonplace in industrial practice. We know from statistics that a sample often has most of the information in it that a complete measurement of a population would have. The knowledge of the relation between samples and populations is the fundamental basis of statistical quality control in industry. The measured quality of a sample of a production run often has most of the information in it that a complete inspection would produce.

Power-wielding by men of general influence is often based on sampling measurements. Fiscal and monetary policy to control unemployment is usually based on sample measurements of unemployment. Evaluation of the effectiveness of a program to help clients is often carried out by studying a sample.

In fact, a sample may have more information in it than a complete census. If in order to take a complete census, one has to use less skilled measurement (*e.g.,* less skilled interviewers), then one may gain more by accurate measurement in a sample than one loses by sampling variations. It is particularly true of censuses in underdeveloped countries that sample studies give more accurate information than the complete enumerations.

Thus we will expect power in an administrative system to be greater (a) when the degree of abstraction of information flows is carefully planned—usually greater power will be associated with more abstraction, (b) when the inputs of information are more accurate, (c) when information about men's behavior is not protected by institutions of privacy, (d) when the reward system is highly differentiated and flexible and carries much information, and (e) when extensive use is made of relatively cheap sampling devices for collecting information to guide general policies.

In analyzing concrete power systems we need to pay great attention to these administrative information-processing aspects of social systems. Many times real power is located in quite a different place than the formal authority hierarchy would imply, because the formally powerful official can only press the electrocution button.[9]

---

[9] Two excellent studies are Richard McCleery, "Communication Patterns as Bases of Systems of Authority and Power," in Social Science Research Council, *Theoretical Studies in the Social Organization of the Prison*

Situational Variations in Power

Let us consider in this context the variations in social relations and in situations which give rise to different amounts of information about an individual's actions.

In Table 4.1, I have attempted to describe the typical information situation of people in authority with respect to actions differently situated. The stub of the table consists of a list of variables which tend to increase the amount of information. I have rather arbitrarily divided these into "situational" and "relational" variables—those that vary most with the situation in which the action is done, and those that vary most with the relation between people.

First, a few comments about some of these variables. Physical visibility obviously is mainly determined, in modern societies, by walls and doors—and hence by one's status, which permits him to be inside or leaves him outside a given door. Thus in fact it is very much a relational matter: I see my wife a lot because we live in the same house, but I live in the same house because we are married. The imposition of measurement on some aspect of activities is also very much relational: I cannot give tests to students who do not sign up for my course. Norms of privacy prevent some people from collecting information on others but permit other people to do so. The law of search and seizure does not protect an adolescent from his mother's going through his chest of drawers. Exactly *because* access to situations of action is so important in establishing and governing social relations, physical and information access is much affected by social relations.

The relational variables of long acquaintance and acquaintance in many areas of life are mainly the residue of past situational access. I can guess more about my wife's behavior and attitudes from small signs because I know her better. But I know her better because I have been physically present in many situations with her

---

(Pamphlet 15: March, 1950), pp. 49–77 (reprinted in the Bobbs-Merrill reprint series), and M. D. Feld, "Information and Authority: The Structure of Military Organization," *American Sociological Review,* Vol. 24 (1959), pp. 15–22.

TABLE 4.1

Information analysis of situations

	Family members with respect to acts at home	Family members with respect to acts at school	Family members with respect to acts on dates	Police with respect to acts at home	Police with respect to acts at school	Police with respect to acts on street	Foreman with respect to acts at work	Foreman with respect to acts at home
SITUATIONAL VARIABLES								
Physical visibility of action	yes	no	no	no	no	yes	yes	no
Measurability of output or other features of action	no	yes	no	no	yes	no	yes	no
Socially instituted measurement procedures	no	yes	no	no	yes	no	yes	no
Lack of norms protecting privacy	yes	yes	no	no	yes	yes	yes	no
RELATIONAL VARIABLES								
Long length of acquaintance	yes	yes	yes	no	no	no	no	no
Great scope of areas of life in which acquainted	yes	yes	yes	no	no	no	no	no
Solidarity with other observers of actions (or conversely, lack of solidarity between observers and observed)	yes	yes	no	no	yes	?	?	no

in which she was not protected by strong norms of privacy. Because I have a better general understanding of her behavior than I have of most other people's, a given amount of information provides a better basis for control.

The web of social control in modern society bears with greater or lesser effect on activities, depending on where they stand in the information flow to potential sanctioning authorities. Men at conventions are less controlled by family norms than at home; men's private lives may undermine productivity at the plant, without being controllable in any detail by the management; much of the physical violence and assault of society takes place in the family and seldom appears in crime statistics; prostitution, abortion, and other illegitimate businesses depend on the cooperation of the client in not betraying the "crime." [10]

The Logical Structure of Information Concepts

For our purposes, the most convenient way to conceive of *relevant information* is the *degree of covariation* between the signal received by the power-holder and the variable he wants to control. When the real productivity of a section of a plant decreases, the costs measured by cost accounts should increase. If the measured costs fluctuate for other reasons, or if the power-holder's accountants bury productivity information in all sorts of irrelevant numbers, the power-holder gets less relevant information.

This covariation between the signal received and the variable to be controlled may be decreased by:

1. Irrelevant information coded and transmitted from the source.

2. Bias in the encoding process.

3. Bias or adding irrelevant information in the channel from source to receiver.

4. Failure of the channel to filter out noise and irrelevant information.

5. Failure of the receiver to decode the information correctly,

---

[10] Cf. Robert K. Merton, "Problem 5. Observability or Visibility . . . ," in *Social Theory and Social Structure*, 2nd ed. (Glencoe, Ill.: Free Press, 1957), pp. 336–57.

so that he misinterprets the meaning of the communication received.

These same sorts of distortion of messages may decrease the amount of communication from the power-wielder to the variables he wants to control. He may:

1. Give orders irrelevant to the control of the variable.

2. Bias his orders (often because his information is inadequate).

3. Have his orders biased in their transmission to acting people, or have irrelevant orders added.

4. Have irrelevant characteristics of his orders transmitted without filtering (*e.g.*, his private emotional reactions).

5. Fail to have his correctly transmitted orders effectively translated into activities by operating people.

All these processes decrease the covariation between the controlling signal system's activities and what is needed for control of the relevant variables. They are sources of "noise" in the communications system on which a system of power rests.

Most of the cybernetic theory of information is based on the fact that covariation with a controlled variable will tend to be nonrandom. The variation in signals caused by other variables in most electrical systems tends to be random, because it is the product of independent small causes. Hence the *degree of nonrandomness* is taken as a measure of the amount of information in a signal. If other causes intervene in the encoding, transmission, or decoding of a signal, they tend to decrease the nonrandomness of the signal—to make it more nearly random. Thus "static" is more nearly random than voices.

For many purposes the definition of information as nonrandomness is a very useful simplification of the problem and provides an easy way to measure the amount of information in a channel. It is a particular case of a more general definition of the amount of information: the degree to which a signal departs from what would be predicted on the basis of other knowledge of the communications system, not including the variations in the source. The more a signal, upon a change in the variable to be controlled, differs from what it would have been with no variation, the more information that signal carries.

IV / POLITICAL INCORPORATION

Political Isolation and Incorporation

One of the central ideas in the study of the politics of developing areas is "political incorporation." When a group is "politically incorporated," it has a chance to influence public policy and also the government has the capacity to mobilize the loyalty of that group in times of crisis. For instance, one of the recurrent themes in the explanation of why the German Social Democratic Party remained relatively ideological and oriented to Marxist theory is that the party was "politically isolated" up to the First World War. To take another example, the hypothesis has been advanced that whenever millennial religious movements become a mass phenomenon, more than a lunatic fringe as they are in England or the United States, the followers have been recruited from the "prepolitical strata" of the population.[11] Or there is a similar interpretation of why socialism never made much headway in the United States. Unlike most European systems, suffrage for men appeared in the United States before industrialization rather than as a result of it. Therefore the first movements of the developing proletariat were rapidly incorporated into an ongoing political structure.

In these interpretations, the terms "political isolation," "prepolitical strata," and the concrete indicator of universal suffrage seem to refer to the same sort of variable—namely, the degree of responsiveness of the political system to the grievances of workers, or peasants, or other groups. The same sort of conceptual apparatus appears, in quite different language to be sure, in Oscar Jászi's explanation of why the Hapsburg monarchy failed to elicit the loyalty of minority ethnic groups, so that with the end of the First World War most of them opted for autonomy.[12]

[11] See Eric John Hobsbawm, *Primitive Rebels* (Manchester: English University Press, 1959). See also Guenther Roth, *The Social Democrats in Imperial Germany* (Totowa, N.J.: Bedminster, 1963).
[12] Oscar Jászi, *The Dissolution of the Hapsburg Monarchy* (Chicago: University of Chicago Press, 1929) (also in paperback). Jászi uses the term "citizenship" to denote political access.

The Components of Political Access

Here we will develop only those measures which apply to democratic development, in order to indicate the degree to which various groups in the population are incorporated into the national political system.

First, let us consider the implicitly general concept from Marxist political sociology—namely, the "bourgeois revolution," or, as it is sometimes called, the "bourgeois-democratic revolution." The Marxists implicitly maintain that this is a cross-cultural concept, that one can locate countries in which it has happened and those in which it has not, and that a different political system exists afterward than existed before.

The central issue in bourgeois-democratic revolutions seems to be the powers of parliament. In particular, parliaments may or may not have the exclusive power to levy taxes and validate the budget of the executive (particularly important seems to be the validation of the budget of the military). Another power in dispute is whether parliament—or parliamentary bodies—have control over the determination of suffrage regulations for their own election. They may or may not be able to certify the election of their own members. When parliament makes the budget and certifies its own elections, the executive is more or less responsible to parliament and reports to parliament on governmental policy at least at the time of budget approval. Who the government is responsible to is not determined by the government itself but by the legislative body.

For instance, conflict in the period of the Civil War and the Glorious Revolution in England (1640–88) revolved around the powers of parliament. The American Revolution revolved around the questions of American suffrage in the English Parliament and more particularly the powers of American colonial parliaments. In both revolutions parliaments arrogated to themselves the right to certify the election of their own members (in the American case, also, to certify elections to the national government).

On the other hand, the weakness of the bourgeois revolution in Imperial Germany is clearly indicated by the lack of the requirement that the military budget be approved in parliament, and also by the fact that the emperor and the aristocracy in fact controlled the suffrage regulations for at least substantial parts of the electorate. Likewise the setting of election certification and suffrage laws by the tsar rather than the Duma in prerevolutionary Russia is a sure indication that the bourgeois-democratic revolution had not taken place in Russia.

The relevance of the bourgeois revolution to the concept of political incorporation is obvious if we recall that the Marxists are interested in it because it reflects the incorporation of the bourgeoisie into the ruling class. It makes the government into "the executive committee of the bourgeoisie as a whole." The first requirement of political incorporation, then, is that some body have power to control the acts of government, and that the members not be dependent on the government for their membership in that body.

Second, given the existence of some such body with formal powers, people or groups in the population may be excluded from the body politic by either of two devices: either they may not be permitted to influence the composition of the body, perhaps because they are excluded from suffrage, or they may not be permitted to form coalitions within the body which can ever give them control over the formal powers of that body. To illustrate: before the reform of the suffrage in England in late nineteenth and early twentieth century, propertyless people could not vote and hence were incapable of influencing the policy of Parliament through legitimate channels. In quite a different way, much of the proletariat and a fairly large proportion of the peasantry of poorer areas in France and Italy are incapable of influencing how parliament uses its powers, because there is no practically conceivable governing coalition which includes the Communist Party, the party for which many of them vote. Such workers and peasants are more incorporated in Chile, where several governments have been constituted by coalitions including the Communists, and there are prospects of future governing coalitions that will include them.

What we can suggest, then, is that in normal democratic development there are three fundamental elements of political incorporation: the arrogation of powers by a body that certifies its own election, the extension of suffrage, and the possibility of entering into a governing coalition. In order for a citizen to be politically incorporated, he has to be capable of influencing the election of another man, and that man has to have some chance of entering into a majority coalition on at least some of the issues of most importance to the citizen, and that majority must be able to control the government.

The Incorporation of the German Proletariat

To make this more meaningful, perhaps we could return to the statement of analysts explaining the persistence of revolutionary Marxist ideology in the German socialist party. In what sense could we make the statement that the German labor movement was less politically incorporated than, say, the American, and perhaps more than, say, the Russian? In the first place, in Imperial Germany the parliament did not have as much control either over its own membership or over government policy as did the American Congress. Bismarck did at one time dissolve the Socialist party and by law prevent its candidates from being elected, an extreme indication of the government's determining whom it would be responsible to. Secondly, when suffrage was extended and socialists were permitted to be elected, none or only a very few of the other parties would form coalitions with the socialists. In a multiparty parliament, this unwillingness to form coalitions meant that the socialists could never by compromise get into the governing coalition.

Their presence did, however, influence government policy. Bismarck made every effort to incorporate all the other parties into the majority and to satisfy their most insistent demands, so that they would not be tempted into a coalition with the socialists. And he tried to compete with the socialists on their own grounds—for instance, by passing social security legislation—so that they would not get a majority. Workers who voted for the other parties were fairly sure to get into a majority, and hence some of their demands would be transmitted to the executive. Further, the socialists' votes increased fairly steadily throughout the period, so they foresaw that they might some day be able to form a government themselves (they did in fact after the First World War).

None of these conditions held for the Russian working class before the First World War. Members of that class generally could not vote, and when they could they could not form majorities, or if they got into majorities the tsar dissolved the Duma.

In the United States, in contrast, the labor movement was granted suffrage before it ever started. Laborers found many opportunities to make coalitions with Populists and the Democratic party, and both of these parties had some chance of forming a governing coalition. If they formed a coalition that could win, they could control taxes and the budget.

Thus it seems that such a concept of political incorporation locates the same phenomena as the impressionistic concepts mentioned at the beginning of this section. The degree of radicalism and the ideological character of the labor movements in the three countries seem to correspond to the prediction from the implicit theories mentioned above. Such a definition of the concept allows us to make further predictions. For instance, the higher political incorporation of Chilean Communists as compared to French and Italian should result in the Chilean Communists' being less revolutionary, less ideological (more "revisionist," as the Marxists say, to refer to Marxists who follow parliamentary roads to power), less influenced by the more revolutionary Chinese faction, and so forth.[13]

The Construction of a Concept of Incorporation

We could construct an index of the political incorporation of a group as a multiplicative function of (1) the proportion of the group with suffrage, (2) the chance that the parties the group votes for have of getting into majority coalitions, and (3) the powers of parliament.

We will ignore the problem of unequal suffrage (which one does at his peril, for instance, in England before 1832). The first

[13] An interesting study would be to compare the coalition including Communists in Chile, which allowed itself to be voted out of power peacefully (1938–48), and the one in Czechoslovakia which did not and which undermined the constituted government. The very existence of the Chilean case seems to be unknown in the United States, while Czechoslovakia forms a basic part of our conception of communists.

element could be merely the proportion of a class with the legal right to vote. This would range between 0 and 1.

Then we could construct a majority-forming-capacity index by taking for each party the proportion of the time during the last 20 years that it has been in a governing coalition, or a consensus of informed opinion on the probability of its entering the majority coalition during the next 20 years (the figure of 20 years is arbitrary; it seems about right, because I think practical politicians can think that far back or ahead). These indices for each party then would range between 0 and 1. To get the overall probability that the party voted for by a random man from a group has of getting into the majority, we would multiply the proportions of the group voting for the different parties by the majority-forming capacity and sum them. This estimated probability is $\sum_{i} W_i P_i$: W_i is the majority-forming capacity of party i; P_i is the proportion of the group voting for party i; the sum is over all parties. This sum then would be the vote of the group weighted by the probability that the vote would do any good in parliament. This element would also range between 0 and 1.

Then perhaps we could construct a rough index of the powers of parliament by listing the powers of the British Parliament and ranking parliaments by the proportion of these powers they have. One might want to weight control of the budget and taxes and control of certification of members more heavily than, say, the power to demand that kings doff their swords when addressing parliament. This proportion, weighted or not, would then range between 0 and 1.

The product of these three indices then would range also between 0 and 1, unless one made adjustments for unequal suffrage or for parliaments more powerful than the British.

Such an index could also be constructed on the same basis for the whole population of a country and could be used as a measure of the incorporativeness of the whole political system.

Some Difficulties

The index would be a relatively valid measure of the likelihood that the demands of specific groups, or the demands of the "masses" in the political system as a whole, will be effectively communicated to the governmental apparatus. But there are still some problems I would like to mention.

The main ones derive from the fact that all the construction of the index is predicated on a single electoral system. If there are multiple political units, such as states and the federal government, this means that each individual or each group would have different indices in different systems. For instance, Catholics were highly politically incorporated in Boston before they were in Massachusetts, and in Massachusetts before they were in the federal government. Negroes were incorporated in the federal government before they were in the state legislatures in the South. And so on. But it is quite unlikely that the psychological and ideological consequences of incorporation and nonincorporation are so finely differentiated, so that one has a revolutionary ideology toward the national government and a moderate one toward the local government. For instance, it seems that the high political incorporation of socialists in the Milwaukee city government in the first part of this century greatly affected the *national* political ideology of socialists from Milwaukee, making them the mainstay of the "right wing." (The left wing called them, among other things, "municipal socialists.")

Even more serious are the complications introduced by multiple electoral systems for the same level of government—for instance, presidential *vs.* senatorial *vs.* house electoral systems in the United States. One could easily weight an index for local and federal government by the proportion of tax money spent by each, but one cannot weight the tax money spent respectively by the president and the Congress, since they spend the same money. Presumably people are differentially incorporated by the definition above in different ones of these systems at the same governmental level.

The likelihood of being able to construct such an index in any precise fashion in the immediate future is almost nil. Subjective estimates of the components may serve to give rough estimates when the differences are large, but the meaningfulness of the concept for current empirical work is quite doubtful. What is interesting for us here is the conceptual structure. In this case we have a causal theory which holds that people's reactions to a system differ according to the probability that their demands will be reflected in government policy. We conceive that there are three main stages in the communication of a man's petition before it becomes public policy in a parliamentary system. These are communication (by means of a vote) to congressmen or deputies, communication from the deputy to a parliamentary majority, and communication from a parliamentary majority to the centers of power in the government.

The Logical Structure of the Concept

When we have a causal force which is a function of the probability that a given message will get through a single-path communications channel, this force will be a function of the *product* of the probabilities of its getting through the discrete parts of the channel. The concept of political incorporation was constructed with this product form in mind. The proportion of a class voting is a rough estimate of the probability that a given petition from that class will be received in parliament. The probability that the parties for which the class votes will be in the majority (or the proportion of time they are in a majority coalition) is then an estimate of the probability of the message's getting out of parliament on the "laws passed" channel. The index of the powers of parliament is a rough estimate of the probability that a "laws passed" message will be received where the power lies. Such multiplicative probability models are very generally useful when the causal force is conceived of as a function of the total effectiveness of a communications channel.

The difficulties with the concept are quite typical of the difficulties with all such concepts. When different messages go over different channels, as when some petitions in the United States go into state political systems, some into the federal government, then the overall probability of a message's arriving in either of the two different systems cannot be computed from the analysis of only one channel in the two systems.

Likewise when the basic structure of two communications channels differ, as they do between the Soviet Union and England, then the external indices which are good estimates of the probability of a message's arriving in one kind of channel are not good estimates of the probability of its arriving in the other. If we use such indices for the Soviet Union as the number of political associations with paid leadership, the apparent responsiveness of the Soviet government to ancient petitions of minority ethnic groups, the volume of complaint letters in the Soviet press and the apparent responsiveness of the government to them, it appears that the level of access is higher in the Soviet Union than it was in the Russian Empire, but lower than it is in England. But, since all Soviet citizens vote for a party which is always in the majority, obviously an index constructed as above would not work.

However, such an analysis serves two functions. In the first place, it points to the kind of phenomena that we think are causally operative, the structure of legitimate political communications. Second, it allows us, within a subfield of the universe of political systems (unified parliamentary governments), to make rough estimates of the size of the relevant causal force. Then we can see if the dependent variables we hope to explain, such as revolutionary ideologies or loyalties of ethnic groups in wartime, seem to be explained by this structural variable. If the causal theory seems to work in this subfield, then investment in the development of comparable indices in other political systems will be rational. We would also start with simpler communications systems if we were electrical engineers studying the effects on messages of communications channels made of wire.

V / INSTITUTIONS AND INSTITUTIONAL INTEGRATION

Values and Power

If we look around us at the decision-making apparatuses which control substantial resources and exercise substantial authority, we notice that each seems to have a distinct set of values, a distinct institutional attitude. For instance, Johns Hopkins University seems to devote the largest part of its resources to education and advancing knowledge, the United States Army to defending national interests, General Motors to efficiency in producing and selling automobiles, and so forth. Though I as an individual am interested in advancing knowledge, the defense of at least some national interests, and cheap cars, I am not likely to be as single-minded in pursuit of these goals as these organizations are. What does this specialization of the values or attitudes of such organizations have to do with the way society works? It surely must be of fundamental significance that large concentrations of property and authority are associated with distinctive value criteria.

One way to approach this problem is to consider that the more power that is used in the service of a given value or attitude, the more social effect that value or attitude will have. Thus the concentration of power in the hands of Johns Hopkins University rather than in my personal hands makes it more likely that the power will be used to educate and to advance knowledge. And given that the decision-making apparatus of Johns Hopkins University is heavily committed to education and scholarship, the social influence of that commitment is magnified by the resources and authority of the University.

Thus we see that the social effect in the direction of a given value is a product of the depth of the commitment to the value by a decision-making apparatus and the resources and authority that apparatus controls. The significance of such value specialization of organizations with great powers, then, is that it allows society's resources to be devoted to important values in a systematic way. Put another way, it multiplies the high commitment to certain values in some decision-making apparatus by concentrating power in these same apparatuses. This concentration makes such high points of commitment much more influential in determining the course of social action than the low-commitment decision centers. Such a device for backing values with power is commonly called an "institution" in the sociological literature.[14]

A Correlation Concept of Institutions

Another way of saying what we have just said is that the influence of a value in social life can be considered as an *interaction effect*, in which variations in the degree of commitment to a value have different effects, depending on the relative amounts of power held by deeply and shallowly committed decision-makers. As we mentioned briefly in Chapter Two, one of the mathematical func-

[14] This type of formulation of institutions was suggested by Philip Selznick in *Leadership in Administration: A Sociological Interpretation* (Evanston, Ill.: Row, Peterson, 1957), pp. 16–17. See the comment in footnote 35 in Chapter Three.

tions often useful in discussing interaction effects in two variables is the *product* of the values of those two variables.

The common statistic which is based on the product of two variables is, as is well known, the correlation coefficient. It is based on the cross-products of the deviations from the mean and on the standard deviations of the two variables. If the average intensity of commitment to a value is the same in two societies, and if there is about the same amount of variation in the amount of power and in the intensity of commitment, then the above statements are equivalent to saying that *a value will have more effect in a society, the higher the correlation between power and commitment to the value in that society.* Thus, given our picture of the causal efficacy of institutions, it is logical to define *the degree of institutionalization of a value* as *the correlation between commitment to that value and power.* The correlation coefficient would be ideally computed over decision-making units (rather than persons), and a measure of the amount of power *of the kind useful* for achieving the value would be most convenient.

This definition has the advantage of isolating the effects of institutionalization from the effect of commitment to and consensus on the value in the population. Average commitment to the value would be measured by the mean commitment, and consensus by the standard deviation of commitment, both of which are standardized in computing the correlation coefficient. Our statistical experience with the effects on a correlation coefficient of limiting the variance on a variable suggests a very important derivative proposition: that the relative effects of consensus and institutionalization will vary according to the degree of inequality of power. This derivative proposition means that the influence of values in simple societies without great concentrations of power will usually be determined largely by average value commitment, while in modern societies the values embodied in institutions are much more important.[15]

---

[15] More exactly, the total product sum of the two variables (if we were to choose that as a measure of effect) is the sum of N times the product of their means and the covariance:

$$\Sigma XY = N\overline{X}\,\overline{Y} + \Sigma(X - \overline{X})(Y - \overline{Y})$$

Let us ignore the variations in the mean power of societies, arbitrarily setting this equal to 1, so that the total product of analytical concern to

Then we could define "institutions" as the values and norms which have a high correlation with power (which seems to be Parsons' preference), or as the concentrations of power specially devoted to some value (as seems to be the tendency of common speech).

Institutional Areas and Rank-related Power

As a practical matter, it is difficult to measure the values of organizations and other decision-making apparatuses.[16] Power in a

---

us is a sum of N times the mean value of commitment and N times the covariance of the two variables. This covariance will tend to be lower as compared to the mean when the variations in either of the variables are restricted. This implies that in the total product of analytical concern, the mean commitment to the value (the first term) will in general be more important either if there is restriction of variance of power, as just mentioned, or if there is a high degree of consensus on the value and consequently a low variation on commitment, for both these conditions reduce the last term. Thus the corollary of the above proposition is that if there is a high degree of consensus on a value, its social effect will not be much influenced by its institutionalization. This seems to me a trivial result. The correlation coefficient is the covariance (the last term over N) divided by the product of the standard deviations of X and Y.

[16] We get evidence of such attitudes from how they spend their resources, especially money in the organizational budget or time in the organizational schedule. It appears that the purposes to which organizational time and money are put are much more stable than are the budgets or schedules of individuals, which would indicate that in the real world the values of organizations are more stable than the values of individuals.

Some people, especially economists, regard it as philosophically preferable to regard values as characteristics only of persons and refuse to make the "interpersonal comparisons of utility" involved in conceiving of the values of decision-making apparatuses. I am unable to see why it is any more likely that a person will have a stable preference function than that a social structure will have one, and it seems to me that the facts speak against it. As a practical man I will certainly try to put a central value like justice in the hands of a social pattern (the trial) rather than in the hands of a man with a strong sense of justice, because I think that the social pattern has a more stable and controllable preference function than any individual.

In sum, I think that many economists have got themselves into a muddle by an irrelevant philosophical individualism, or by what my friend Philip Slater calls the error of reification of the human personality. That is, it is no more likely that an integrated pattern of behavior will come out of a bunch of cells that happen to be a person than that an integrated pattern will come out of a bunch of people who happen to be an organization. On the determinants of such organizational preference functions, see Selznick, op. cit.

modern society is conveniently broken up into institutional areas: military institutions, educational institutions, productive institutions, judicial institutions, elective political institutions, and so forth. Consequently it is more convenient empirically to talk about *the values institutionalized in different institutional areas.* We do this by asking: What is the correlation (over individuals) between values or attitudes and personal power in different institutional areas? Do we find within judicial institutions that the man with little or no power (the man in the street) has much less respect for due process of law than the justice of the peace and the policeman, and that in turn judges of more important cases have even more commitment, while appellate judges and the Supreme Court have even stronger respect? If that is true, then we would say that the value of due process of law was institutionalized in the judicial system. We would, of course, expect that this concentration of power in the hands of those highly committed to the value would make it much more likely that the value would govern decisions in the society. Such a criterion of institutionalization has the advantage that personal power in an institutional area can be approximately measured by the simple criterion of rank.

In general, in each institutional area a somewhat different set of values is correlated with power. In educational institutions the value of accepting the evidence of well-established facts is well institutionalized. By and large, students feel less obliged to decide a question on the basis of the facts (*e.g.,* instead of what the examining professor is known to think on the question) than do teachers; the writers of textbooks and those who train teachers in university graduate schools feel even stronger obligations. In the armed forces, on the other hand, rank is generally correlated with a sense of obligation to fight to defend national interests. When these values come into conflict, as they might over such questions as the historical justice of our national territorial claims, it is quite usual to find belief in the justice of the claim correlated with power in the military, and to find doubt correlated with power in academia.

On an impressionistic basis we can say that the following values are institutionalized, in the sense just defined, in American education: nonreligious criteria of truth; belief in civil liberty; internationalism in politics and culture; liking of complex forms of art ("classical" literature and music, ballet, etc.); appreciation of wide knowledge, especially of foreign languages; the value of fundamental scientific advance whether or not it has immediate benefits; equalitarianism in politics; the superior value of reading nonfiction as compared to fiction (this shows up especially in the large subsidies of university presses for nonfiction, but the small subsidies or no subsidies at all for fiction); and so forth. In the United States military it appears that some of the following values are especially strongly institutionalized: the sacredness of national territory; the value of devotion to duty as opposed to seeking personal gain; anticommunism in international politics; physical courage; civil direction of the military establishment; and so forth. In American economic institutions some of the values associated with power are: efficiency; "free enterprise" or capitalism; the high evaluation of seeking personal advantage; Republicanism in domestic national politics and nonpartisanism in local politics; mass production and mass sales; favorable attitudes toward banks; and so forth. In the judicial system a group of procedural values on "due process of law" and belief in civil liberty are institutionalized. In American medical institutions values correlated with power include: scientific procedures for assessing the value of treatments; the sacredness of human life and its primacy over all other considerations; fee-for-service professional practice; and so forth. Each of these values has more influence in social life than it would have if it were not correlated with power in the relevant institutional area.

Institutional Conflict

A very interesting set of problems arises when we consider the possibility of opposed values being correlated with power in different institutional areas. It appears, for example, that in many countries values of political order, clear government policy, military autonomy from civilian interference, and noncorruption are strongly correlated with power within military institutions, while values of free play of interests, compromise in government policy, civil supremacy, and "practicality" on the question of rewarding political loyalties are correlated with elective civil political power. We would say in such a situation that the society is "confronted with a problem of institutional integration." We expect in such circumstances that civil government will be unstable, because it is not backed up by the military powers. In other words, such a situation produces a "crisis of legitimacy" (with legitimacy used as it was defined above).

In general, then, by institutional integration we mean that the *same* values tend to be correlated with power in different institutional areas. One of the few values for which we have evidence on such correlations in different institutional areas is that of civil liberty in the United States.[17] Stouffer showed that all kinds of community leaders, including leaders of the Daughters of the American Revolution and the American Legion, are much more likely to hold values in favor of civil liberty than are people in general. That is, all kinds of community power in the United States tend to be correlated with belief in civil liberty. Even though perhaps the correlation is higher in the judicial institutions than in others, the stability of judicial influence in this respect no doubt depends on the general consent of all major power groups to this value.

Such a concept helps us to suggest an explanation of why communist governments of less developed countries seem to be far more stable than noncommunist governments of countries at the same level of development. To take an extreme example, Argentina in the 1960's has almost the same level of per capita income as the Soviet Union, but it has had a much less stable government. If we compare the single occurrence of a major revolution in communist countries (in Hungary in 1956) and a possible revolution (in China in 1966–67) with the average frequency of revolutions in Africa, Latin America, and South Asia, we cannot help being struck with the strength of the relation between communism and government stability.

An examination of communist elite practice suggests that the key is the high degree of institutional integration in communist societies. By a series of devices, many of them quite unsavory, the

---

[17] See Samuel Stouffer, *Communism, Conformity, and Civil Liberties: A Cross Section of the Nation Speaks Its Mind* (Garden City, N.Y.: Doubleday, 1955), especially pp. 26–57. Evidence on the positive correlation between status and belief in civil liberty in the academic community is presented in Paul Lazarsfeld and Wagner Thielens, Jr., *The Academic Mind: Social Scientists in a Time of Crisis* (Glencoe, Ill.: Free Press, 1958), pp. 144–46.

communists manage to make the correlation between commitment to communist ideology on the one hand and power on the other highly positive in all institutional areas.

The Logical Structure of the Concept of Institutions

In summary, we can define the degree of institutionalization of a value in a society by the correlation between commitment to that value and power. Apparently, in order to have any appreciable effect on social functioning, the correlation has to be quite high, so that empirical analysis can use quite crude measures of the strength of commitment and of power and come to clear results.[18] Institutional integration may then be defined by the degree to which opposed values are correlated with power in different institutional areas.

Such a formulation is useful because we conceive that the causal significance of power for social life depends on what values it is associated with; conversely, the significance of a value for social life depends on whether it is associated with power or not. In general, when we conceive that the total effect on a social group depends not only on the values of variables but also on their inter-action, then the correlation (and related product statistics) of those variables in the society is a relevant structural property of that society. The use of correlation coefficients as causal variables, and the use of concepts derived from correlation coefficients such as the concept of institutionalization, are called for whenever the total effect we want to theorize about has an important interaction component among its causes.

VI / THE CREATION OF ORGANIZATIONS

The Dispersion of Powers Needed by Projects

Edward Banfield's book, *Political Influence*,[19] contains conceptions on how large-scale projects involving the use of public powers

---

[18] The relation found by Stouffer was very strong, compared with the correlations he found with other social variables. The theory of how correlations between power and values come to be so high in such cases is very underdeveloped.

[19] Edward Banfield, *Political Influence* (Glencoe, Ill.: Free Press, 1961).

come about. Though the book itself happens to study projects in which a government, the Chicago city government, had a large part, the conceptual apparatus is applicable more generally to all kinds of large-scale projects. This section is directed at generalizing and formalizing this conceptual apparatus to make it more accessible for use in the analysis of entrepreneurship. We will also discuss briefly the creation of organizations to execute projects.

Banfield's image is that in order to carry out various kinds of projects, a *set of distinct powers* must be brought into play. For example, in order to construct an exhibition hall in Chicago, several millions of capital investment were necessary, a piece of land near downtown had to be devoted to the purpose, and in the circumstances this required the diversion of public land to the project, some kind of subsidy had to be worked out (because the total cost and value of the project to the community were supposed to be greater than its potential revenue), and for a subsidy a certain amount of taxing power was necessary, and getting taxing power in turn required favorable publicity and influence on the state government.

Each project or proposal can be described by the combination of powers it takes to make the proposal into a going concern that will yield the benefits it is supposed to yield in a regular fashion. A project is *politically feasible* only if those powers can be mobilized and committed to it. These powers are, in Chicago, dispersed in the community among various elites. The problem of entrepreneurship is to assemble these powers and commit them to the project. Assembly involves on the one hand negotiation with the elites who hold the powers and on the other the modification of the proposal until its power requirements can be assembled.

Proposals and the Assembly of Powers

We can then conceive of a set of proposals, each one of which has its distinctive set of power requirements. We can organize our thinking by setting up a table in which distinct kinds of powers are listed across the top, and projects are listed down the sides. For instance, we might specify the powers of eminent domain, of ownership of a particular suitable site (*e.g.,* a railroad almost invariably requires the former, a factory the latter), the capacity to get a bond issue through an election, favorable publicity, money, license to operate, tariff advantages, and so on.

The exhibition hall may require a suitable site (which might be bought by adding more money to the capital requirements), $26 million, which cannot be obtained without governmental guarantee and so requires a bond issue, and favorable publicity to the tune of 100,000 exposures strategically placed. A new department store, on the other hand, may require only a suitable site, an investment of $5 million, and easily obtainable licenses. A watch factory needs tariff protection of 70 per cent ad valorem, perhaps, besides the business requirements. Two alternative freeway plans, one of which is more expensive but avoids a well-organized neighborhood, another which is cheaper but goes through the neighborhood, have a different pattern of requirements. These power requirements are represented in Table 4.2.

Banfield came upon this way of describing projects because he was interested in describing who participated in decision-making and not because he was interested in the analysis of proposals. Various specialized elites of Chicago participated in getting various proposals adopted. Banfield observed that in a city like Chicago the various powers necessary to carry out particular projects were dispersed among various elites. Only the *Chicago Tribune* could deliver publicity downstate and could indirectly secure (by influence with the state government) the necessary taxing power for the exhibition hall. Only the city government had a suitable site which would not push the capital requirements out of sight. Only insurance companies could give that much credit on the necessary terms. Thus in order for the project to take place, a number of distinct elites with distinct powers had to come together to form a coalition around the project.

Thus elites, or organizational leaderships, are related to projects in the first instance by having different quantities of the necessary powers. This can be represented by a table similar to Table 4.2, except that elites (or organizations) are described in terms of the distinct combinations of usable powers they have. For a relatively wild guess about the power distribution among various groups appearing in Banfield's analysis of city politics, see Table 4.3.

TABLE 4.2

The power requirements of projects

Projects	Eminent domain	Suitable site	Bond issue (millions of dollars)	Publicity (circulation in thousands)	Money (millions of dollars)	Taxing power	License	Tariff advantages (in per cent ad valorem)
Exhibition hall	X	X	26	26	100	X		
Department store		X		5			X	
Watch factory		X		15				70
Renewal project	X		100	100	400	X		
Federally supported freeway	X		40	400	100	X		
Federal freeway alternate	X		30	300	500	X		

TABLE 4.3

The (disposable) power resources of elites

Elites	Eminent domain	Suitable sites	Bond issue (millions of dollars)	Publicity (circulation in thousands)	Money (millions of dollars)	Taxing power	Licenses	Tariff privileges, etc.
Downtown business		X		50	400		X	
Uptown business		X		50	100		X	
City machine	X		200	200	10		X	
State government	X		50	200	20	X	X	
Good-government crowd			50	100				
Federal government	X			100	500	X		
Chicago Tribune			200	1,000	1			X

The first thing to notice is that some projects can be carried out within a single elite. The department store is feasible for the downtown businessmen alone (an alternate project involving more capital and no site would be feasible for uptown small businessmen). On the other hand, no one elite could build the exhibition hall or the watch factory as those projects are described. There are some projects which do not involve coalitions among elites and organizations, and others which do. Banfield, being interested precisely in the interrelation of elites, does not emphasize the degenerate case of the project that can be carried out alone by one elite. The entrepreneurial-theory people have generally considered *only* the degenerate case, where no (unbuyable) political powers were needed to cause the project to go through. Consequently neither Banfield nor the entrepreneurial-theory people have realized that they are talking about the same thing.

Feasible Coalitions

The point of all this is what we have now described the coalitions which, given the inherent nature of the projects, *could* carry out those projects. That is, there is now a limited number of combinations of projects and coalitions which are possible, given the inherent nature of the projects and the distribution of powers, taken together. These are a *feasible set* of coalitions, not in the sense that anyone could build them in fact but in the sense that, unless some of them are built, none of the projects will be carried out because they are not possible in any other way. This feasible set is a structural property of the system, since on the one hand it limits the coalitions to possible coalitions and on the other it depends on the power arrangements in the society as a whole. If the information in Tables 4.2 and 4.3 were complete and accurate, we could specify all the projects which are feasible, and all the possible coalitions for which each is feasible, given the technical characteristics of the projects and the distribution of powers.

Not all these coalitions are, however, *politically* feasible. Some of these generally feasible coalitions will not form because no one, or no one with the relevant powers, is in favor of the project. Some others will not form because some other projects are more valuable for all the participants. Presumably a third matrix giving utilities of all the proposals to all elites could be constructed, and game theory could be applied to give a normatively best solution for each participant. However, this would involve describing not only all technical proposals but also all possible ways of distributing the benefits of each technical proposal. And game theory would probably not give unique solutions; nor does it seem to represent what goes on.

Forming Coalitions

Instead, a tentative proposal draws a preliminary nucleus of support, generally from among those to whom the proposal has the highest utility. The nucleus is often not yet a feasible coalition. Then the project is modified toward what will be acceptable to, and feasible to, a coalition which "appears on the horizon." For coalition involving a large number or a variety of powers, a broker, or a holding company, or a politicians' politician is needed. In order to carry such a coalition to fruition, the trust of a large number of people and knowledge of their resources have to be concentrated in a man or a committee. Thus this kind of entrepreneurship is preeminently a political phenomenon—a fiduciary-brokerage function in a network of influence. But it is also a creative phenomenon, creating and modifying proposals so that they can be the basis of a coalition.

Once a feasible coalition is hit upon, the relevant elites actually have to commit the resources they have said they would. Most resources will have been tentatively promised on the condition that a workable coalition is set up. When the coalition is negotiated, then actual commitments of powers have to be made to the project. In general, this involves setting up an organization.

By an organization we mean, as usual, a set of powers—money, land, legal powers, licenses, and so forth—committed to a single decision-making apparatus with a relatively narrow purpose. A "project" forms an "organizational goal" when the organization is set up. In the United States, organization-creation often involves creating a new legal personality, a corporation, though it may involve only a reallocation of powers already held by an umbrella organization like Congress or General Motors.

For convenience, we might call this set of powers, committed to a single decision-making apparatus, the *legal personality aspect* of an organization, whether or not the decision apparatus and its fund of resources have a separate existence in the civil courts. All that exists at the end of the coalition-formation process is the legal personality aspect of the organization and a set of promises (the "project") specifying what it will aim at.

We may briefly outline some ideas on the general kind of process that goes on in the choice among feasible coalitions, not in order to form separate concepts in this field but merely in order to indicate that it is a different kind of process from that which determines the set of feasible coalitions.

A proposal is a theory of what the environment is, and will be, like. It is a specialized technical-economic theory of what will happen if certain powers are used in certain ways. In the first place, the theory has to be accepted before the payoffs of the proposal can be accepted as the basis of a coalition. A coalition is thus, in a special sense, an "ideological" group which shares a set of beliefs about the project.

There are several kinds of elements in the theory involved in a project: (1) There is a theory of the personal competence of coalition members, a theory that when problems come up someone in the coalition will be able to solve them. (2) There is an environmental, or engineering, theory which says that the environment can be manipulated in such and such a way to yield such and such results, and a corollary accounting theory which says that this manipulation will cost about so much. (3) There is a market theory which says that the ultimate recipients of the benefits (if different from the coalition members, which is the general case)—voters or customers—will provide enough return to the entrepreneurial coalition. (4) There is finally a theory of who will be able to collect what out of the benefits created: a theory that the government will not take it all, that the promoter will not abscond with the funds, that the contracts will be enforceable in the courts, that the board of directors will vote in keeping with the needs of maintaining a going concern rather than to line their own pockets, and so forth.

These are the legal and ethical prerequisites of such an entrepreneurial coalition; they are treated at length by Max Weber and John R. Commons.[20]

In the search process for an originating coalition, several kinds of activities are usually crucial. We can list some of these as follows: (1) An "insurance" function, in which a trusted leader guarantees to each potential coalition member that the others will do their part, and that as far as his expert judgment is concerned the coalition is feasible. The recruitment of business statesmen to boards of directors often seems to serve this function.[21] (2) A "brokerage" function, which puts the members of a feasible coalition into communication with one another. (3) A persuasive function, which ensures that belief in the theory will be general in the group of people who would make up a feasible coalition if they believed the theory. A large part of the persuasive function may be a "research" function, in which the truth of the theory is tentatively tested (especially by consultation with experts) and the proposal accordingly modified. (4) An energizing function, which keeps the proposal active. During the process of forming a group, a small difference in the amount of effort a potential member puts into exploring possibilities may make a large difference in the amount of resources the coalition can start with.

The Logical Structure of Feasible Sets

In this conceptual scheme we run into a type of causal problem that is very common in the social sciences. We conceive that there

[20] See Max Weber, *Law in Economy and Society, passim,* and John R. Commons, *op. cit., passim.* The notion in general that a formal organization is a theory of the environment is due to William Starbuck, "Organizational Growth and Development," in James March (ed.), *Handbook of Organizations* (Chicago: Rand McNally, 1965), pp. 451–534. The elements of the necessary theory are, of course, Parsons' functional problems. Personnel corresponds to latent pattern maintenance, engineering to adaptation, market to goal attainment, and distribution of benefits to the integrative problem. If Parsons is right about the requirements for a social system to function, and if coalition members are smart enough to know these requirements, then they will not enter the coalition until they are satisfied that the system requirements will be met. I think they generally are that smart.

[21] See especially Thorstein Veblen, *The Theory of Business Enterprise* (New York: Scribner's, 1904), for this point and for some deviations it gives rise to.

are two very different types of causal processes operating to produce the end result. One type of process *limits the alternatives* to some *feasible set*. The other causal process selects among the alternatives. We want to conceive the forces in such a way as to separate these two causal processes. For instance, in many modern investment problems in underdeveloped areas we want to study the implication of the following fact: in some countries investment powers are all concentrated in the government (socialist countries) while in others they are split between the government and private elites (capitalist countries). The investment process is presumably quite different in the Soviet Union from what it is in Argentina. The feasible coalitions for many projects will be the government alone in the Soviet Union, various coalitions in Argentina. And we want to separate this problem of different distribution of powers from such problems as the level of technical expertise, the probability of development of different proposals, and so forth, which determine which projects will in fact be adopted out of the feasible set.

The classic instance of such a theoretical scheme is the analysis of consumer behavior in economics. In economics we conceive that the budget of the consumer limits the alternative sets of goods he could buy—he cannot buy any combination of goods that costs more than his income. But within the range of his budget, his decisions on what to buy are determined by his preferences. We think that the causal processes which operate to change a man's level of income are quite different from the causal processes which operate to change his preferences. The set of goods he will buy is determined by which set of goods he most prefers, *among* those made feasible by his income.

In Chicago likewise we believe there are two different causal processes operating. One is that the inherent character of projects makes them require relatively specific combinations of powers. Since some of these powers are likely to be governmental, or otherwise not for sale, large-scale entrepreneurship cannot usually be undertaken by just any coalition; rather, there is a limited number of practical coalitions. Thus one causal process is the inherent limitations of possible coalitions imposed by the specific nature of the project and by the historically given distribution of powers at the time the project is thought of. The second causal process is quite different. It consists of a pattern of social action in which the members of a potential coalition become convinced of the theory involved in the project and of their getting advantages of some kind from it. This process explains which of the feasible coalitions in fact comes into being.

Whenever one has a causal imagery of this kind, the general conception of a *feasible set of alternatives* among which some other causal process *makes a choice* is a convenient conceptual device. If we are fortunate enough to be able to define a single variable (such as utility or money return) for each of the alternatives in the feasible set, and if we believe that a causal process tends to choose that alternative which maximizes or minimizes this variable, then economic theory or linear programming theory (or, more generally, the theory of convex sets) will be useful.

VII / CONCLUSIONS

In this chapter we have taken the particular substantive area of power phenomena to illustrate strategies of concept construction, particularly of social structural variables. In each case the first problem is to locate tentatively the causal process we think might be operating. Thus in the discussion of legitimacy, we noted a number of cases in which the results of an action depended on the implicit possibility of calling on institutionalized reserve sources of power, especially the government. The determinant of this capacity to call on reserves of power seemed to be the acceptance of the legitimacy of the action in other centers of power. Thus we define a variable along which powers vary, which we called "legitimacy" because it seems most similar to that traditional concept. This concept tries to catch this causal phenomenon. Legitimacy was defined as the likelihood that the exercise of a liberty or of authority would be protected by further powers if necessary, by virtue of its quality of being validated by some doctrine of legitimacy or some set of norms.

The armory of a sociological theorist thus consists first of all of causal ideas. If it should turn out that belief in legitimacy by subordinates is causally far more important than belief in other centers of power, and also that authority, rather than property, is the only kind of power for which legitimacy makes a difference, then the results of actions do not in fact vary with their recognition in other centers of power. In that case, we will prefer Weber's conception of legitimacy to the one developed here. Conceptual advance thus depends on the advance of causal theory. When causal investigations show that a conceptual variable does not in fact explain anything, it should be discarded.

Thus an economist might very well show that variation in the historical distribution of powers and the social patterns for creating entrepreneurial coalitions are of very little value in explaining which projects get embodied in organizations. He could try to show that the rate of social return from different projects determines whether investments will seem valuable, that in fact money can usually buy the necessary powers or that government decision-making is generally determined by the social utility of projects (somehow measured), and that therefore the assembly of the relevant powers can almost always be worked out if the project is of great value. If the economist should turn out to be right, the relevant variables would be only the rate of saving in the economy, the scale of the enterprises in terms of money (defining a feasible set), and the relative rates of return. All effort in describing the concrete processes by which such powers are assembled is scientifically irrelevant, and the concepts developed above should be discarded because they distinguish things that ought not to be distinguished.

A second weapon in the theorist's armory is a set of patterns or models of concepts which are useful in different kinds of causal situations. We have selected conceptual developments here primarily to illustrate a variety of such patterns. The concept of legitimacy was defined by the probabilities of certain reactions (backing up a right) in certain contingencies (the right was challenged). The concept of information was defined by the covariation between a signal and the variable which a power-holder wanted to control. The concept of political access was defined in multiplicative terms suggested by the model of a communications channel, of the probability that a message with a given origin or of a given kind will get through the channel. The concept of institutionalization, because of our causal idea of the interaction effects of power and commitment to values, was defined in terms of the correlation between two variables. The conceptualization of the entrepreneurial process involved describing the feasible sets of coalitions which could carry out a project and suggesting the causal processes by which some of such feasible coalitions are actualized. There are other models of concepts, such as the predispositional concept, which could likewise be applied to structural problems.[22]

[22] See Gilbert Ryle, *The Concept of Mind* (New York: Barnes and Noble, 1949). As briefly mentioned above, I am convinced that decision-making apparatuses have predispositions or attitudes just as stable as, or more stable than, individuals' predispositions. I suspect, for instance, that the nationalism of a system of public opinion is quite a stable characteristic of countries, which can be conceived and measured in the same way as an attitude can. It might be defined as the correlation between what the diplomatic corps conceives of as in the national interest with what the public believes ought to be done in international affairs. For one of the few formulations of such a structural predispositional concept in the sociological literature, see Hans Speier, "Militarism," in *Social Order and the Risks of War: Papers in Political Sociology* (New York: Stewart, 1952).

CHAPTER FIVE

The Conceptualization of Environmental Effects

A great many sociological explanations take the form of "environmental effects." The behavior attached to some *element* (an individual, a point in space, a group) is explained by the characteristics of its *environment* (the group culture, the opportunities confronting the element, the characteristics of nearby points in space). Such environmental or contextual explanations involve forming concepts of the relations between elements and the environment.

In this chapter we will treat the logical structure of a number of such conceptions. First we will treat the basic elementary logical structure at the level of the individual element. The specification involves the specification of two components of environmental concepts: a variable characterizing the environment, and a variable characterizing the relation of the element to that environment.

Then we will treat conceptions of the psychological influence of group membership and group participation on individuals. In explaining, for example, the influence of the Catholic Church's birth control policy on contraceptive practice, we use an environmental measure of the policy of the Church, combined with a measure of

201

the individual's relation (membership, degree of activity) to that environment. The policy of the Church has little effect on non-members. But if the policy of the Church were to change, this environmental variation would also change individual behavior.

A second substantive kind of environmental explanation has to do with the concept of *opportunity*. Occupational chances, for example, are determined both by the numbers of positions open in various occupations and by the characteristics of an individual which enable him to take advantage of them. Thus any behavior (such as training for a position) which is explained by opportunities will vary both with environment (there is little training of carriage-makers) and with individual characteristics (people of low academic abilities rarely train for the professions).

We will treat the demography of opportunity in a closed system —as, for example, a bureaucracy that promotes from within. Then we will treat the more difficult problem of the subjective aspiration of individuals for higher positions. The training requirements of positions influence only those who aspire to them.

In a third substantive area, we will discuss points in space as elements. In particular, we will ask what determines the military vulnerability of points in space. The military vulnerability of a point is determined by the amount of military resources (men, fire power) which can be concentrated there. The amount depends on the military resources available elsewhere and on the cost of movement. This analysis introduces the general concept of the "potential" at a point. Several classical geopolitical concepts can be defined in terms of these simple causal conceptions.

I / THE BASIC LOGICAL FORM OF ENVIRONMENTAL EXPLANATIONS

An Example: Elections and Consensus

Consider the following explanation for the lower degree of consensus behind the policies of governments in France (a multiparty system) and the United States.

There are two distinct political functions of the party system and its associated institutions: the articulation of interests, and the aggregation of interests. By *articulation* of interests we mean formulating the problems of a group of individuals (an "interest group") as a collective demand to institute a certain policy in the government. By *aggregation* of interests we mean working these various group demands into a proposed program of government and getting commitment to that program from the government.[1]

In France, the articulation of group interests is undertaken by parties. The aggregation of interests is carried out within parliament in forming a governing coalition. The key characteristic of this system is that no party runs *in the election* on the program of government carried out by the coalition. Hence the Radicals, for instance, do not try to sell their followers the elements of the program of government which come from the other members of the coalition. Instead, they articulate only those programs which appeal to their special electorate.

In the United States, interests are articulated by interest groups and are worked into a program of government in the party platform committee. Then *in the election,* the presidential candidate tries to sell civil rights in the South as well as in the North, union rights to farmers as well as to workers, and so forth. Thus the Democratic voter is propagandized by his own standard-bearer in favor of the central interests of all the interest groups in the coalition (*i.e.,* party).

We would expect, then, the American voter to be more likely to support all the elements of the aggregated program of government than the French voter, who will favor only his own party's elements. Thus we would predict that the consensus behind the policy of government in France would be weaker than that in the United States.[2]

If we examine the logical structure of this explanation, we see

[1] See Gabriel Almond, Chapter 1 in Almond and J. S. Coleman (eds.), *The Politics of Developing Areas* (Princeton, N.J.: Princeton University Press, 1960), pp. 3–64.

[2] I think I have taken this explanation from some suggestions of Duncan MacRae, Jr., but I cannot now remember when or where. See his *Parliament, Parties and Society in France, 1946–1958* (New York: St. Martin's, 1967).

that it has two basic components. The first is a theory about differences in the programs which parties will try to sell to the electorate. The second is a theory suggesting that individuals learn attitudes about other people's interests only by listening to their own candidate.

We can formulate this general structure as follows. There is a variation in an *environmental* variable—namely, the character of the program which parties are advocating. This variable is presumed, in the explanation above, to be the degree to which the program of a party already includes the interest of groups which will make up the governing coalition. This degree of inclusiveness of the program is thought to be higher in the United States. Then there is an *attachment* of individuals to this environmental variable through their loyalty to the party for which they vote. Since this attachment varies from one person to another and "maps" the environmental variable onto the individual, we will call it a "mapping variable."

A Formal Statement of Environmental Effects

The general logical form behind this explanation may be set out as follows:

$$f_i = Km_iE \qquad (1)$$

where f_i is the causal force bearing on individual i (here, support for a coalition program), K is some constant, m_i is the "mapping variable" (here, attachment to the party), and E is the "environmental variable" (here, inclusiveness of the electoral program of the party).[3]

The overall consensus effect of the supposed higher level of inclusiveness of American parties would be obtained by taking the mean of f_i for each country:

[3] The function may have some other mathematical form than the simple product form we have used. The multiplicative form is easiest to handle of the various forms of interaction effects which give rise to partial monotonic relations. Other forms can usually be transformed into it by appropriate redefinition of variables. Hence we will base our reasoning on this special form, with very little loss of generality and much gain of simplicity.

$$\overline{f}_i = \frac{KE \sum\limits_{i=1}^{n} m_i}{n} \tag{2}$$

If the environmental variable, the inclusiveness of the program of parties, is higher in the United States, then the mean consensus-forming force will be higher unless people are more attached to their parties in France. This possibility cannot be dismissed out of hand, and not only because of the folklore about the political passion of the French. Cognitive dissonance theory would predict that attachments to parties will be lower when they advocate more inclusive programs, since some of the elements of programs will be distasteful to parts of the electorate.[4]

II / ENVIRONMENTAL PSYCHOLOGICAL EFFECTS

Group Culture and Individual Attitudes

Perhaps the simplest and most common type of environmental explanation in social theory is that which involves group culture as an environmental variable and membership as a mapping variable. When we cross-tabulate group membership against some attitude or behavior, we usually think that there is a group culture which influences those people who are members.

Membership is, then, a mapping variable which has the values 0 and 1. Its causal force is usually conceived of as exposure to the group culture, or embedding in a set of social relations with people who reward attachment to group values.

Thus when we explain higher Catholic birth rates by Catholic policy on birth control, we presume that some extra-individual process (in Rome) determines the position of the Church on birth control. This position is not a general causal force operating on everyone; rather, it operates only on those who are exposed

[4] But for contrary evidence, see Philip Converse and Georges Dupeaux, "Politicalization of the Electorate in France and the United States," *Public Opinion Quarterly*, Vol. 26, No. 1 (Spring, 1962), pp. 1–23. It seems that in fact the French are less attached to their parties, because party allegiance is not a family tradition there as often.

to socialization into that policy or who are embedded in a social network that supports the policy. To get the causal force bearing on the individual, we must multiply his membership variable by the measure of the policy of the Church.

Thus the analysis has the same form as before:

$$f_i = K m_i E \tag{3}$$

E is a variable measuring the commitment of the Church to birth-control policies. This variable is changed by such processes as take place in ecumenical councils or in the socialization and election of popes. $m_i = 1$ if a person is a member of the Church, 0 if he is not. The value of m_i is determined by such processes as birth into a Catholic family, conversion, or apostasy. Either apostasy, or a change in Church policy, could reduce the causal force to zero.[5]

Refining the Mapping Variable

But if the mapping variable's causal influence is conceived of as exposure or embedding, then we can ask how good membership is as a measure of exposure. The answer is that it is usually easy to improve on membership as a mapping variable by moving to a more powerful measurement of exposure or embedding. The effect of Church policy on the contraceptive practices of devout Catholics will ordinarily be greater than the effect on nominal Catholics.

[5] Often cross-tabulations take the form of classifying people by mutually exclusive group memberships. This may conveniently be represented in vector terms. The mapping variable, m_i, would be a vector with an element for each group (e.g., Protestant, Catholic, Jew; or working class, middle class, upper class; etc.). Only one of these elements will be 1, the others 0. For instance, a Protestant, Catholic, Jew vector would read (1, 0, 0) for a Protestant, (0, 1, 0) for a Catholic, and (0, 0, 1) for a Jew. Then the environmental variable is also a vector, $E = (E_p, E_c, E_j)$, with E_p being the relevant measure for Protestantism, E_c for Catholicism, and E_j for Judaism. The causal force, then, corresponds to the product of these two vectors obtained by multiplying corresponding elements and adding. For a Protestant this would be E_p, for a Catholic E_c, and for a Jew E_j. All further developments in this section can be reformulated easily in such vector terms for the case of multiple groups. We will treat only the one-group case in the text, leaving the generalization to the reader.

Consider, for example, the very interesting result obtained by Lenski.[6] Lenski found that Catholics generally voted more Democratic than Protestants, as had been found many times before. But then he classified Catholics according to two different mapping variables: (1) their social embedding in the Catholic community, by friendship criteria, and (2) their devoutness in the religion, by religious practice criteria. He found that the more *socially incorporated* a Catholic was, the more often he voted Democratic. But the more *devout* he was, the more Republican he voted.

That is, by specifying *different* mapping variables of greater efficiency, he uncovered a very important characteristic of the political culture of the Catholic community in the United States. The purely religious part of Catholic community culture apparently carries elements that predispose their adherents to vote Republican (Lenski suggests moralistic elements). The social part of Catholic community culture (presumably mainly of ethnic content) predisposes toward a Democratic vote.

Thus the pure membership mapping variable, by mixing up the religious and ethnic components of the Catholic subculture in the United States, leads us astray in analyzing Catholic religious influence on politics. Only by greater precision of measurement can we discern that there are really two separate environmental variables, the religious culture and the ethnic culture, with opposite causal influence.

Identifying Group Cultures

This example suggests the other main use of such environmental forms of explanation: to describe group culture. By equation (1) or (3), any variable E which describes group culture will cause a correlation between a mapping variable which measures exposure to that culture and the causal force on the left. Hence whenever f_i and m_i are highly correlated, we infer that the group culture, to which m_i measures exposure, has a causal force in the direction of f_i. Thus we are inclined to weight the beliefs of the priests and the

[6] Gerhard Lenski, *The Religious Factor* (Garden City, N.Y.: Doubleday Anchor, 1963), pp. 35–60 and especially 174–84.

devout more heavily than those of nominal church members in diagnosing the nature of a religious culture.[7]

Another broad type of prediction can be made if there are differences in the aggregate level of the mapping variable m_i between groups. Consider for example the following explanation of a problem in maintaining internal democracy in trade unions.[8] Trade unions are generally identified with the working class and hence tend to be equalitarian in policy. More conservative members of the union, who might form an opposition, tend to have little attachment to their unions since they find the general atmosphere offensive. Only when their attachment is maintained and politically activated by intensive friendship nets or many intra-union associations will they participate sufficiently to maintain an opposition.

Here the causal force of interest is pressure toward participation. It is thought to depend on attachment to the union. But attachment in turn depends on general political attitudes, the *same* attitudes which determine whether a man will be in the conservative party. Hence the mean causal force toward activity will be depressed among conservatives as compared to liberals.

This may be expressed as follows. E is a measure of the radicalism of the policy of the union. The more attached a conservative is to the union, the more he will be stimulated to opposition activity by this radical policy. If we consider now two unions with an equally radical policy, $E_1 = E_2 = E$, the strength of the opposition

---

[7] At first it would seem that we could merely divide through equation (1) by Km_i,

$$\frac{f_i}{Km_i} = E$$

Then if we had a measure of the causal force (*e.g.*, proportion Democratic) and a measure of attachment (*e.g.*, degree of devoutness), we could estimate E. But m_i is often zero. Also there are problems in dimensionalizing m_i and f_i so as to get a meaningful concept of E. Consequently the safer procedure is to use the correlation of f_i and m_i as a qualitative measure of the content of E. The size of the correlation will give an ordinal measure of the importance of the element in the culture represented by E. Those f_i highly correlated with m_i evidently indicate a central component; those little correlated indicate a peripheral component; those not correlated are no part of the culture.

[8] Modified from S. M. Lipset, M. Trow, and J. S. Coleman, *Union Democracy* (Glencoe, Ill.: Free Press, 1956), pp. 92–102, especially pp. 99–100.

will be proportional to the mean impulse toward opposition activity, which for both will be

$$\bar{f}_i = \frac{\sum_{i=1}^{n} Km_iE}{n} = \frac{KE \sum_{i=1}^{n} m_i}{n} \tag{4}$$

Here m_i is the attachment of conservatives to the union, and f_i is the force toward opposition activity. If one union has a low degree of attachment of conservatives through friendship and association, then the mean attachment

$$\frac{\sum_{i=1}^{n} m_i}{n}$$

will be lower, and opposition activity will be less by equation (4).[9] The possibility of a two-party system in unions is thus undermined by the lower attachment of conservatives to their unions.

III / THE DEMOGRAPHY OF OPPORTUNITY

The Structural Determinants of Vacant Positions

In many kinds of social systems, the number of positions of a certain kind is determined by structural forces. For instance, the number of good-quality houses in a central city in any given year is (now that new houses are built in suburbs) determined by the

---

[9] If the attachment of conservative members to the union then declines further in the union with a weak opposition, because the unopposed radical policy offends them further, then an "outvoting" process takes place. This is exactly analogous to that described by William N. McPhee in "When Culture Becomes a Business," in J. Berger, M. Zelditch, Jr., and B. Anderson (eds.), *Sociological Theories in Progress,* Vol. 1 (Boston: Houghton Mifflin, 1966), pp. 227–43. McPhee formulates a simple mathematical model in which each consumer's weight in the mass-medium market is determined by his enthusiasm. His enthusiasm is determined by the proportion of program material presented to his taste. The proportion presented to his taste is determined by his aggregated weight in the market. It is easy to show that some slight disadvantage of a genre at the beginning leads to a progressive exclusion of material in that genre, leading to progressive disenchantment of the audience with the medium.

housing market of the past. The number of professional jobs in a city is determined primarily by its industrial base. This base in turn is determined by historical and ecological forces. Whenever the number of positions is structurally determined, then all variables related to individual opportunity will be determined by a combined effect of objective opportunities and of the relation of the individual to them.

First we will consider a closed system in which recruitment rates for positions are also structural facts. That is, if there is a given number of good houses in a city, then we will consider that the proportion of them open to Negro occupancy is determined by structurally enforced discrimination. Or if a given number of executive positions is open, we will assume that the proportion filled from within the company is determined by a general company philosophy. To simplify matters, we will not consider that the rate for filling positions responds to the availability of people to fill them.[10]

The Opportunity of Individuals

If this structural policy of discrimination is followed, then the number of positions open to a group i is a function only of the number of vacancies in a given time period and the proportion of those vacancies filled from group i. The overall opportunity per time period of the "average" person in group i would be the number of vacancies open to group i divided by the number of people in group i. We can write this as:

$$O_i = \frac{1}{n_i} p_i V \tag{5}$$

---

[10] Nonresponsiveness seems to apply approximately to some important cases. For instance, overcrowding in ghettos is greater where the rate of Negro in-migration is greater. This correlation suggests that there is something like an invariant proportion of white housing opened each year to Negro occupancy. See Karl and Alma Taeuber, *Negroes in Cities* (Chicago: Aldine Publishing Company, 1965), pp. 166–69. Also, there is very little mobility of high executives among companies, suggesting that most companies have a policy of promotion from within. See David R. Roberts, "A General Theory of Executive Compensation Based on Statistically Tested Propositions," *Quarterly Journal of Economics,* Vol. 70 (1956), pp. 270–94.

Here O_i stands for the average opportunity of a member of group i; n_i the number of people in group i; p_i the proportion of vacancies filled from group i; and V the number of vacancies. If we let V be the environmental variable E, and let p_i/n_i (the *relative* discrimination for group i) be m_i, and let O_i equal f_i, we see that equation (5) has the same form as equation (1). The relative discrimination for a man's group is thus a mapping variable which translates the number of vacancies in the environment into a causal force of opportunity bearing on the individual.

We would therefore expect that any effect of opportunity in a closed system would increase both with the number of vacancies and with a decline in relative discrimination. Relative discrimination for a group, p_i/n_i, under our assumptions, can decrease (discrimination against the group can increase) if the number of people in group i increases, or if the rate of filling vacancies from group i decreases. Thus if overcrowding in a ghetto is a response to lack of opportunity to move out of the ghetto, overcrowding should increase as the number of Negroes increases and should decrease as a larger proportion of white vacancies becomes open to Negroes. High in-migration of Negroes would be expected to increase Negro overcrowding in the ghetto, while suburban building would be expected to increase the availability of formerly white housing to Negroes and thus to decrease overcrowding.

Opportunity in Bureaucracies

Likewise let us suppose that commitment to a job is a function of opportunity, and that companies recruit higher executives from within. Then the propensity for lower-level white-collar people to leave their jobs should be less either when (1) the company is expanding the number of top-level positions, or (2) when there are relatively few lower-level positions.

Let us compare, for example, the situation of workers in a pilot plant and in the full-scale plant that develops from it. A pilot plant, because it needs much administrative attention to work the bugs out of a process, tends to have a large number of supervisory positions. Because the scale of the plant is small, it tends to have fewer workers. Hence the ratio of supervisors to workers is greater.

Further, it is usually anticipated that a pilot plant will grow into a regular plant, entailing a still further expansion of the supervisory force.

After a full production plant is brought into being, there is a large complement of workers, and the ratio of supervisory positions is lower and is not increasing. Hence both the environmental variable of the number of supervisory vacancies and the denominator of the mapping variable (the number of people to fill them) tend to increase the opportunity of a worker in a pilot plant. From these considerations, we would expect the turnover of workers—at the same level of pay and at the same ages—to be smaller in pilot plants. And we would expect that workers in pilot plants would explain their commitment to work more in terms of opportunities and less in terms of current conditions.[11]

Demographic Predictors of Training

But we do not really believe that job opportunities will be distributed equally in group i, regardless of what an individual in that group does. Without sacrificing our assumption that the relative discrimination is fixed by policy, we can assume that people of group i may prepare themselves for vacancies. In general, a prepared man will be preferred to an unprepared man. We can then ask how much motivation there would be to prepare oneself. We can take as a preliminary assumption that the *difference in opportunity* made by preparation will determine motivation.

If we add subscripts T for "trained" and U for "untrained," we can define motivation for training, M_T, in a closed status system as:

[11] There are other variables operating. Usually one purpose of a pilot plant is to train supervisors, and workers with supervisory talents and interests are likely to be recruited. The work is less monotonous. Supervisors in a pilot plant are more likely to formulate orders in terms of objectives to be reached rather than giving orders, because they do not know the best line of action. Hence workers learn more and are supervised in a more satisfying way. See the case described in William Foote Whyte, *Men at Work* (Homewood, Ill.: Richard D. Irwin, Inc., and the Dorsey Press, Inc., 1961), pp. 201–04. This case, and discussions with my brother William Stinchcombe, who worked in a couple of pilot chemical plants, suggested the analysis above.

$$M_T = K(O_{i_T} - O_{i_U}) = K\left(\frac{p_{i_T}}{n_{i_T}} V - \frac{p_{i_U}}{n_{i_U}} V\right)$$
$$= K\left(\frac{p_{i_T}}{n_{i_T}} - \frac{p_{i_U}}{n_{i_U}}\right) V \tag{6}$$

Again this has the form of equation (1), but with

$$\left(\frac{p_{i_T}}{n_{i_T}} - \frac{p_{i_U}}{n_{i_U}}\right)$$

as the mapping variable. This is related to the analysis of the previous section by the fact that $p_{i_T} + p_{i_U} = p_i$, and $n_{i_T} + n_{i_U} = n_i$, but the information has been added that some of the i are trained and some untrained, and that the promotion system favors trained men.

We can ask how this motivational force for training would work if it was due to the causal forces represented in equation (6). We can obtain the following results:

1. If the degree of discrimination in favor of trained men,

$$\left(\frac{p_{i_T}}{n_{i_T}} - \frac{p_{i_U}}{n_{i_U}}\right),$$

remains constant, then the more vacancies (larger V), the more motivation for training.

2. The greater the preference for trained men ($p_{i_T} \gg p_{i_U}$), the greater the motivation for training. In particular, if p_{i_U} is zero, if no untrained men are promoted, equation (6) reduces to the case of the previous section but with reduction of n_i to n_{i_T}.

3. If there is nearly complete discrimination against group i, then both p_{i_T} and p_{i_U} will be very small, and the difference between them cannot be large. Hence there will be low motivation for training.

4. The larger the pool of trained men (larger n_{i_T}), the smaller the motivation for training. The larger the group of untrained men (larger n_{i_U}), the greater the motivation for training. Both of these hold only if the p_{i_T} and p_{i_U} are constant. If, however, the structural discrimination takes the form of direct determination of the *prob-*

ability of promotion to a given open vacancy (*i.e.*, the invariant numbers are p_{i_T}/n_{i_U} and p_{i_U}/n_{i_U}), then the numbers will have no effect except that of the previous section. I suspect that this latter condition is the usual one.

Thus the environmental theory represented in equation (6) gives rise to many common observations: that discrimination against group *i* destroys ambition and self-improvement in the group; that "unfair" promotion systems decrease ambition; that a society with expanding opportunities (large *V*) leads to a vigorous and self-reliant population.[12]

IV / ASPIRATION AS A MAPPING VARIABLE

Sex Variation in Aspirations

In a study to explain the distribution of student rebelliousness in a high school, I obtained the distribution of occupational aspirations and expectations shown in Table 5.1, for boys and for those girls who expected to be working in ten years.[13] The other girls either wanted or expected to be housewives. We find that 33 per cent of the boys want and expect to be manual workers, but only 3 per cent of the girls.

Rebellion and Aspiration

This is of great importance for the problem of rebellion, because the training requirements for middle-class positions include good

---

[12] William Starbuck suggested in correspondence that greater precision in prediction could be obtained if the revenue from promotion and the cost of training were taken into account. If these revenues and costs are constant, all the above results still hold. Some deviant cases from these results might be explained in such terms. For instance, it has been suggested that the Brazilian frontier did not have the same effect on society as the American, because the returns to working in the jungle could only motivate slaves. Hence the jungle frontier did not recruit free men and have a democratic influence in Brazil.

[13] Arthur L. Stinchcombe, *Rebellion in a High School* (Chicago: Quadrangle Books, 1964), p. 61.

TABLE 5.1

Nearly all girls who want and expect to be working in ten years expect white-collar jobs, while many boys expect to be workers. Boys have much more conflict between levels of aspiration and levels they expect to reach.

Aspirations and expectations	Girls	Boys
Upper middle class[a] on both	47%	29%
Lower middle class[b] on both	40	12
Skilled and farm manual on both	3	21
Unskilled on both	—	12
Aspirations higher than expectations	9	22
Expectations higher than aspirations	0[c]	5
Total	99%	101%
Number	233	581

[a] Professional and executive aspirations and expectations.
[b] Clerical, sales, or small business aspirations and expectations.
[c] Less than 0.5.

performance in school. The requirements for working-class positions do not. Thus many of the boys do not aspire to positions which have as requirements good performance and good behavior in school. It turns out that it is largely these boys who account for the greater rebelliousness of boys. Also, the girls who aspire to be housewives are more rebellious than girls whose aspirations lead in the direction of jobs requiring education.

What seems to be happening, then, is that the *requirements of jobs* are mapped onto high school behavior *by way of aspirations.* This suggests that the theory might be formulated as:

$$C_i = Ka_iR \qquad (7)$$

where C_i is the pressure toward conformity in a school for individual i, a_i is his aspiration, and R is the requirement of the job.[14]

[14] See *ibid.*, chapters 3 and 4, pp. 49–102, for the relevant facts. Here the vector notion is almost required. a_i in (7) would be a vector of aspirations for a variety of jobs for individual i, with an entry corresponding to the job he wants, and R the vector of corresponding job requirements. Compare footnote 5.

R is to a considerable extent an environmental variable, the objective requirements of jobs, though it is obviously mediated by the individual's perceptions. It is rather difficult for a student to perceive that one becomes a physician as a drop-out, or that 20 years of education are required for one to become a logger.

Aspirations are determined by a number of causal influences. Some of these have no relation to job educational requirements. For instance, the sexual division of labor in society in fact fills most manual positions with men, most housewife positions with women. Aspirations correspond. Aspirations also vary systematically by the social class of parents.

But aspirations are also heavily determined by experience with the requirements themselves. For instance, boys from the lower middle class who flunk a great many classes give up their middle-class aspirations. They do not, however, resign themselves very well to working-class aspirations.[15]

We would expect, then, that either changes in job requirements, or changes in individual aspiration, would produce variations in the pressure to conform.

V / GEOPOLITICAL CONCEPTS AND MILITARY VULNERABILITY

The Territorial Aspect of Power

The most important ultimate appeal in systems of legitimate power is physical force. In the last analysis, if a government could not win a military encounter with me when I stopped the drug store from opening, the legitimacy which allows my neighbor to call on that government does not do him much good. In 1964, the inability of the United States to win any military encounters in Cuba with the U.S.S.R. and on the Chinese mainland made the illegitimacy of those governments (according to the doctrine accepted in the United States) unimportant. Ultimately systems of

[15] See the section, "The Decision Not to Succeed," *ibid.,* pp. 136–45.

legitimate power are stable only if there is a defined set of circumstances in which they can win military encounters and force obedience.

If we look around the world at the present time, we note that which military forces can effectively control an action depends to a very great degree on the territorial location of that action. This dependence of the military vulnerability of an activity on physical location is so intimate that Max Weber defined a "state" (or "government") as a monopoly of legitimate violence *over a given territory,* rather than over a defined set of actions (which is the crucial point for Weber's theory).[16]

This territorial reference of violence suggests that important concepts in this area should be formulated in geographical terms. The theoretical system of geopolitics attempts to do this. Our purpose here will be to develop concepts which will aid us in formulating the conditions under which a given area will tend to form a "state" or a "government"—in which, in other words, there is likely to be a government to which a defined territory is militarily vulnerable. Only in the very long run will the geographically determined probabilities that a government will win actually determine military control. The genius of a guerrilla leader, his luck in finding out what the enemy is doing, extraordinary tenacity by his troops, and similar concrete military considerations can make an army win or lose when "it really should not."

Likewise such a geographical formulation of military vulnerability will not explain which of the vulnerable points an army will really attempt to govern. Unless it is worth it, the army may not expend the resources. If two points are equally conquerable by a given army, and if one has a diamond mine or a warm-water port while the other does not, we cannot predict which one will be con-

[16] Our conceptualization of legitimacy would make this read, "a monopoly of violent acts which will be backed up by further force if necessary." That is, what distinguishes the criminal gang's violence from police violence is that if the gang loses, it just loses, whereas if the police lose, more forces are called in until they win. This definition makes a good deal more sense than the one that would be implied by Weber's definition of legitimacy, as "a monopoly of that violence accepted by the subordinate population of a territory." Many effectively legitimate violent activities are extremely unpopular.

quered and which will not by an analysis of vulnerability alone. With these cautions about phenomena that the following analysis has no hope of explaining, we can proceed to analyze military vulnerability in general.

The Causes of Vulnerability

The military vulnerability of a point to a prospective government can be formulated as the amount of military resources that could be moved to that point by the government, as compared to the military forces that could be mobilized by other people. We will concentrate first on the movement of military resources to a point.

The amount of military resources that can be moved to a point depends first on how many resources the prospective government has, and second on whether it can move them to that point. Thus it depends on the distribution of military resources in the area of a point. If there are few military resources, or if large resources exist but cannot be moved to the point because they are too far away or because there are geographical barriers, then the point is relatively invulnerable. If large military resources can be moved cheaply to a point, it is highly vulnerable.

Let us assume that the resources that might be devoted to military enterprises in any given small area are proportional to the gross income of the area.[17] This gross income will tend to increase as the density of population increases, or as the per capita income increases. Let us suppose that we can define clearly the boundaries *from which* military resources can be recruited for any given group. We break this up into small areas (say counties, or areas near that size). If we assume that per capita income is approximately evenly distributed within the group, so that areas within the group have approximately equal wealth per capita, then the amount of potential military resources in an area i would be approximately

$$kIp_i \qquad (8)$$

[17] This measure of power for nations as wholes is suggested in Kingsley Davis, "The Demographic Basis of National Power," in Monroe Berger, Theodore Abel, and Charles H. Page (eds.), *Freedom and Control in Modern Society*, (New York: Van Nostrand, 1954).

where k is a constant of proportionality, I is the average per capita income of the group, and p_i is the population of area i.

According to Davis' ideas in "The Demographic Basis of National Power," the total power of the society would be

$$\sum_i kIp_i \tag{9}$$

or proportional to the sum of the gross incomes of all areas in the society, or proportional to the total income. In effect, this assumes that the physical distribution and transportation of resources are irrelevant to the questions he wants to consider.

In order to move this killing power to a point P_o, one has to expend resources. Let us suppose that "distance" in the sense of "difficulty of moving over a piece of terrain at a given stage of transportation technology" is a homogeneous variable directly related to distance in miles, or kilometers, or whatever. (There are in fact important discontinuities in the variable; for instance, the effective distance over a mile of Pyrenees is longer than over a section of plain, which in turn is longer than a mile over ocean for a naval power. We may perhaps better deal with this below.) Distance in miles or kilometers from area i to the point P_o will be called d_i.

For each unit of distance, there will be a cost of transporting killing power. Let us assume for the present that there is a *ratio* of resources used up each mile, or each kilometer, which is a homogeneous variable. That is, to transport a hundred riflemen a mile might cost about the same amount of resources as to equip one rifleman. (The discontinuity mentioned above in connection with the Pyrenees can be taken care of either by stretching the distance scale into a "difficulty of terrain" scale, or by modifying the cost of transportation for different sections of the path from i to P_o. The latter is probably easier.) But we assume temporarily that a constant proportion of the possible killing power has to be diverted from killing to moving the killing power. The cost of transporting killing power declines with historical time, but unevenly, with inventions and civilian investments (in railroads, horses, merchant marine, and so forth) playing an important role. Let us call the proportion of killing power used up for each mile c.

Then after the first mile there are $(1 - c)$ times as many resources as there were at the original point, or $(1 - c)kIp_i$. Then we can assume that only the resources that are left after the first mile have to be transported the second, and so on, giving rise to a function of the form

$$(1 - c)^{d_i}kIp_i \tag{10}$$

for the amount of killing power originating at point i which can reach point P_o. Or we can assume that all the resources that are going to end at point P_o from point i make the complete trip, and do not get used up on the way. The transportation cost, we assume, is the same for each mile,[18] giving rise to a function

$$(1 - cd_i)kIp_i \tag{11}$$

In this expression, we recall, c is a measure of the efficiency of transportation expressed in terms of the proportion of resources used up in each mile or kilometer of transporting the killing power; d_i is the distance from point i to point P_o; k is a proportionality coefficient; I is the per capita income of a group whose capacity to attack point P_o we are evaluating; and p_i is the population of area i within that group.

Note that either expression (10) or expression (11) has the same form as our previous examples of environmental explanation. The environmental variable, E, is kIp_i—that is, the military resources at point i. The mapping variable, m_i, is the function that maps this causal force onto another point, P_o. In expression (10) this is $(1 - c)^{d_i}$; in expression (11) it is $(1 - cd_i)$.

Because in this case our ideas of the *components* of the environmental variable and of the mapping variable are much more explicit, both are expressed in terms of other variables (population and income for the environmental variable; distance and transportation cost for the mapping variable). Thus the fundamental logical structure of environmental influences is the same, although the elements are points and the environment is the characteristics of other points.

[18] Probably the exponential form holds for the part of the path lying beyond the military bases of the country, while the linear form approximately applies for the part lying between i and the bases.

Summed Vulnerability

Summing over all the areas of the group, we get a measure of the amount of killing power the prospective government can concentrate at P_o, which we will call the vulnerability of P_o, or V_o. It takes the form

$$V_o = \sum_i (1 - cd_i)kIp_i \tag{12}$$

This function is defined for all areas, including those within a country. In fact, as will be seen presently, the vulnerability of points within a country to the government of that country gives rise to important geopolitical concepts. Let us examine the computation of this index in a mythical country, using some constant for k.[19] First we will use this computation to define the geopolitical areas in the neighborhood of a mythical country, and then to discuss what would happen when the values of the underlying variables change.

The basic elements of the calculation of this measure are represented in Figure 5.1. The points P_{o_1} and P_{o_2} are equidistant from the center of country A. If we assume that the cost of transportation is relatively large, then V_1 will be different from V_2 if the population of A is concentrated near the western border of A. This can be seen if we imagine that the population is heavily concentrated in areas 4 and 5, or in other words that $p_4 + p_5$ is a large fraction of the total population. Then the killing power of the country has to travel a smaller distance to P_{o_1} than to P_{o_2} from those two areas, and, since they have most of the population, the total resources that can be moved to P_{o_1} will be greater than those that can be moved to P_{o_2}. Hence V_1 will be larger than V_2, or the point to the west will be more vulnerable than the point to the east.

---

[19] A separate theory could be built of the determinants of k, or the efficiency with which income is turned into killing power. Such a theory would have to take into account the capacity of governments to mobilize resources for military purposes, and the technical efficiency of the weapons industry which converts a mobilized resource into killing power.

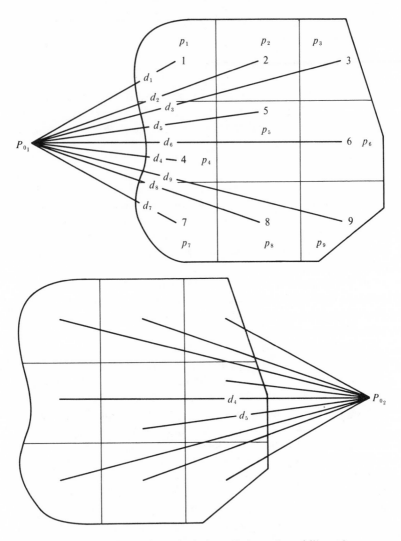

FIGURE 5.1   The calculation of the vulnerability of points to country A. If the population of country A is heavily concentrated in subareas 4 and 5, then V_{o_2} of the second graph will be lower than V_{o_1} in the first, since d_5 is about the same in both cases, but d_4 is much longer in the second case.

Mapping Vulnerabilities

We can, of course, represent the values of this function on a map by means of isolines, in the same way as we do for variables like altitude in a topographic map. An isoline is a line connecting all points that have equal values of some variable. Suppose that areas 4 and 5 are in a river valley, with dense agricultural settlement, surrounded except on the west by hunting and gathering or other nomadic peoples with a very low density. The value of p_i within an area where agriculture is carried on will be much higher, as will the gross income of that area. Such a geographical distribution tends to increase the value of the vulnerability measure within the settled area, which forms a "high" on the isoline map in the area of settlement. The value of the index is also raised for the surrounding areas; the nearer they are to settled areas, the more vulnerable they are. How rapidly this high slopes off depends on the cost of transporting the killing power from the settled lowlands into the bush. In general, c is very much higher in agricultural populations than in industrial populations, and often higher than it is among horse-borne nomads nearby.

Thus the introduction of agriculture into country A in the valleys tends to turn the area from one with vulnerability of all the area at a very low level (in a hunting and gathering economy) to one with highs in and near agricultural areas, sloping off rapidly into relatively invulnerable territory. This "invulnerable territory" is not invulnerable because it is well defended, of course, but because it is hard to move troops into it. Such isolines are represented for our hypothetical country in Figure 5.2, where we have supposed that the equal-valued isolines of country A overlap to a certain extent with country B to the west.

Derived Geopolitical Concepts

Now let us see how more or less traditional geopolitical concepts look in this framework. Let us define the following terms, some traditional, some perhaps a trifle modified.

1. "Potential state area" will be defined as an area in which the

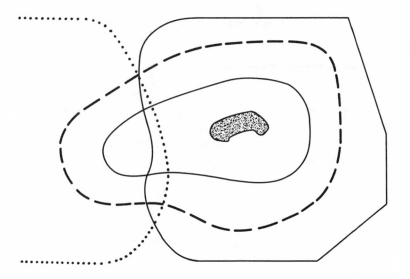

——— Border of potential state territory of A,
or the isoline within which country A
could collect taxes if the army of country B did not interfere

•••••••••• Border of potential state territory of B,
a neighboring country

FIGURE 5.2 Hypothetical isolines of military vulnerability of country A and a neighboring
country B. The patch in the middle
indicates the center of the country's
population, hence the point most vulnerable to the military forces of the
country. (Generally we would say the
"most defensible.")

vulnerability of all points is greater than some critical value to
some possible government. This critical value will be defined as
that vulnerability sufficient to enforce regular payment of taxes
to a central government over local opposition. The defeat of the
Whiskey Rebellion in 1794 in the United States, for example,
shows that western Pennsylvania was potential state area in this
sense just after the founding of the United States. At that time,
much of the Mississippi Valley was not potential state area to
anyone, nor were the mountains and deserts of what is now the
224

western United States. The highlands of Central Mexico and of Peru were potential state area before the arrival of the Spaniards, while very little of the rest of the Americas was. With preindustrial transportation, only agricultural areas of a relatively intensive type seem to be potential state area in this sense. On Figure 5.2 the broken isolines locate the potential state area of countries A and B.

2. A "heartland" may be defined as an area which is a potential state area to only one group. In Figure 5.3 the heartlands of A

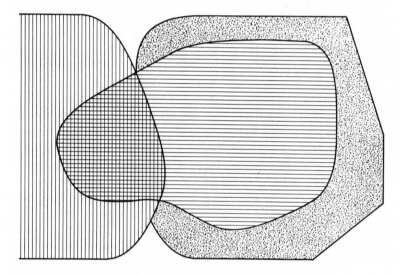

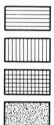

	Heartland of A
	Heartland of B
	Disputed border territory
	Bush claimed by A and not claimed by others

FIGURE 5.3   Geopolitical areas within and in the neighborhood of country A, defined by the values of the vulnerabilities of areas to A and B.

and B are identified. That is, if the value of the vulnerability index reaches the minimum level required to enforce a regular taxation system, but if the value is large for only one group (generally the group settled there or a settling invader), then an effective monopoly of military violence is established for the heartland area. This means that in fact the area can be conquered by an invader only with great difficulty, except for factors of luck or military genius or other nongeographical factors. This does not mean that the area may not be subject to raids for booty by, for instance, surrounding nomadic people, nor that the disaffected elements of the population may not take to the hills and try to raise a rebellion.

Instead, it means that the normal number of governments which could effectively control the area is one. This one may change from time to time, by conquest or revolution. But in the case of conquest or revolution normally one new state is created—perhaps after a more or less extended period of warring states.

3. "Disputed border territory" will be defined as an area which is vulnerable to two or more groups at least to the level required to enforce taxation. We might further specify that the vulnerability not be exceptionally uneven. Suppose, for instance, that the minimum level of vulnerability capable of supporting a taxation system is (by some system of evaluating the parameters) 1,000. Then an area would be disputed border territory if its vulnerability to two groups were respectively 1,500 and 1,700. But it would not be effectively disputed border territory if it were vulnerable to the first at the level 1,500 and to the second at the level 15,000. Such a disputed border territory is crosshatched in Figure 5.3.

4. "Bush" (or "wilderness," or "frontier") would be defined as an area having values of vulnerability too low for regular taxation systems to be built. This may be between two states, or it may be all over some areas which are not settled agricultural areas, or it may be throughout some inaccessible mountain areas. When it is in between two potential state areas, we might call such bush territory "marches," using the medieval English terminology, as in "Lords of the Welsh Marches."

5. A "power vacuum" would be defined as an area which was in fact vulnerable at the level required for becoming state territory, without being at present controlled by any group to which it is

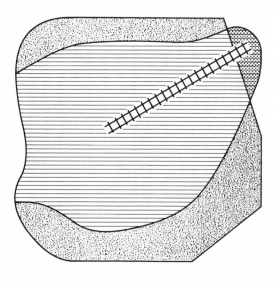

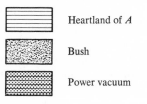

Heartland of *A*

Bush

Power vacuum

FIGURE 5.4   The effect of building a road into the bush on the geopolitical areas in country *A*.

vulnerable. Power vacuums may happen, for example, when an area is disputed border territory and neither side will let the other move in. Or it may happen, as illustrated in Figure 5.4, by a decline in the cost of transporting military power into the bush.

Some Applications of the Conceptual Apparatus

In order to illuminate the nature of the conceptual scheme constructed above, let us consider some cases where the values of the underlying parameters have changed. First, what happens as we allow c (the proportion of killing power used up in transportation) to decline, say because of the development of ocean-going ships or railroads? Then the areas that can be reached by these means of transportation become more vulnerable to any people who can use ships or railroads, if their national income is high enough to mount such military ventures. The most important development for an island nation such as Great Britain (after internal unity was achieved, for which roads were more important) is the development of ships. Ships make ports all over the world more vulnerable. As is well known, the first colonial conquests of the European powers in Asia and Africa were the port areas, the mouths of rivers, the areas up the rivers as far as they were navigable, and other places accessible from the sea. Only much later was colonial hegemony extended into the interior.

A case in which most of the variables changed was the extension of the heartland of the United States into the Southwest during the nineteenth century. The center of gravity of the Mexican population was still, during that century, the ancient agricultural highlands of Central Mexico. Much of the mountain and desert territory that the Mexicans claimed was in fact bush. It actually remained so within parts of Mexico until fairly recently, as is indicated by the impunity with which revolutionary movements flourished in some of these areas up until about 1925. Transportation technology between this central highland and what is now the American Southwest did not improve substantially enough to bring the Southwest into Mexican potential state area.

But with the American settlement of the Great Plains, the transportation development of the Mississippi River system, and the growth of railroads, the vulnerability of the area with respect to the United States changed radically, becoming first what might be called "disputed no-man's land" and then later potential state area for the United States. In this unstable situation, it took only an excuse to transfer nominal sovereignty to the United States. What is more, this nominal sovereignty was rapidly transformed into real sovereignty, and a state "existed" in a sense in which it had never existed before in the Southwest. It was not very long before taxes were collected regularly in this area by the United States in a way quite unknown under Mexican rule.

A third phenomenon which can be analyzed with these concepts is the fact that at the present time in Western Europe and North

America the normal situation is one of clearly defined cultural borders. If one maps a cultural characteristic of the United States which differentiates it from Mexico (for instance, if one makes an isoline map of the proportion speaking English, or of the average per capita income), the map has a very steep gradient around the recognized border. This would not have been the case, for instance, in medieval England as we moved from London toward Wales on the one hand, or toward Scotland on the other. "Sovereignty" extends right up to the border now, and then it stops suddenly while the sovereignty of another country starts, with all the attendant consequences for cultural borders. This is a consequence of the fact that in Western Europe and North America in the nineteenth century (and perhaps a little earlier in some places) all nominal or political borders lay in disputed border territory as defined above. That is, wherever the border is drawn in such territory, each nation can enforce its will over the civilian population right up to the border.[20]

This conceptual system could be developed in several ways. For instance, discontinuities in the cost of transportation over different types of terrain could be taken explicitly into account, as hinted at earlier, to define such concepts as "natural boundaries." These would be areas where the gradient of vulnerability for one group declines very rapidly in one direction and for another group declines very rapidly in the opposite direction. The effects on these gradients of technological revolutions in the transportation of weapons could easily be studied by means of this approach, some-

[20] Sharp cultural borders also seem to depend on the existence of a heartland for each country; at least they have in the past. For instance, because Poland never had a heartland in early modern times, as defined above, it could not prevent pieces from being chopped off and acculturated to various other cultures. The cultural picture of Poland even today shows this sloping off toward the Russian, German, and Balkan cultures, which seems to result from the historical indefensibility of the center of the Polish nation. But at least in this situation, the powers on each side of Poland did have "heartlands" in this sense. How the unity and sovereignty in nations will be preserved when, with the development of cheap delivery of very powerful weapons, all world territory becomes "disputed border territory," I cannot tell. Militarily speaking, the normal number of states in the modern world is one, perhaps after a more or less extended period of warring states.

thing which is difficult if one defines natural boundaries in such purely physical terms as mountain ranges, jungles, bodies of open water, and so on.

The Logic of Potential Concepts

This conceptualization of the vulnerability of a point (and consequently the geopolitical concepts derived from it) illustrates a generally useful strategy in conceptualizing causal forces which we think depend on what can be moved to and from a point. This would apply to housing sites (the number of workers who might move to and from them, from their places of work),[21] the location of stores or warehouses (movements of customers or goods), or similar problems. In these cases the causal force of something located farther away is less than that of the same thing located closer. But also the more of that something there is, the more causal force it has. To conceptualize such causal forces, "potential" concepts are generally useful.[22] These are variables defined in such a way that influence of an area is a declining function of distance and an increasing function of a spatially distributed variable. The exact form of the functions, of course, depends on how one thinks the causal force in fact operates.

There is no theoretical reason why similar concepts could not be defined using "social distance" as the distance variable. For instance, presumably the degree of effect toward voting Democratic of a person's acquaintances depends both on the intensity of *their* Democratic attitude and on how intimately they are related to the person. Thus there is a theoretical possibility of constructing a "Democratic potential" to describe the interpersonal environment of individuals in voting studies. Since it is very difficult to measure interpersonal distance or intensity of attitudes, and since we have little idea of exactly how much a person's influence declines with

---

[21] See Beverly and Otis D. Duncan, "The Measurement of Intra-City Locational and Residential Patterns," *Journal of Regional Science*, Vol. 2, No. 2 (1960).

[22] For a general treatment and empirical applications, see Otis D. Duncan, Ray P. Cuzzort, and Beverly Duncan, *Statistical Geography* (Glencoe, Ill.: Free Press, 1961).

each step of interpersonal distance, we cannot as a practical matter construct such a concept empirically. Such concepts may however be useful in thinking about processes like attitudinal influence.

VI / CONCLUSIONS

In this chapter we have rung variations on a common logical structure rather than presenting a large number of structures as in Chapter Four. This is because many sociological problems take the form of explaining the behavior associated with an element by characteristics of its environment. Many beginning sociologists can conceive of no relation between an element and its environment except that the element is "included" in the environment. Fine-grained analysis of environmental influences requires a great deal more conceptual precision than this. Because the basic logical structure of such explanations has not been made explicit, it is possible to predict with considerable success the logical sloppiness of an explanation by noting how often the words "context" or "environment" appear in it.

The basic logical form of such explanations is that of an interaction effect. A given environmental variable has different effects, depending on the relation of the element to the environment. A given relation to the environment has different effects, depending on what kind of environment it is.

The key to the analysis is the construction of relational or mapping variables characterizing elements. These translate environmental variables into causal forces acting on behavior associated with the element. We have outlined several of these: membership, level of activity or commitment, relative discrimination in opportunity structures, aspiration, and cost of transportation. Others having the same logical form include: needs of the element (environment as resources), capacities of the element (environment as problems), friendship links of the element (environment as distribution of characteristics of friends), causal links between two or more activities (environment as other activities—see Chapter Six), and the like.

Because this logical form of explanation is so simple and flexible, it often occurs as an element in complex theoretical structures. Very often the tension in functional explanations has this form. Tensions vary both with variations in the environmental variable and with variations in the relation between an element and the environment. Hence structures, or structure activity, will vary both among elements and among environments.

Consider for example the discussion in Chapter Three of magic in navigation. Uncertainty varies both with the technical level of the social structure (canoe *vs.* ocean liner) and with the degree of risk in different environments (high seas *vs.* lagoons). We expect to find navigation magic more prevalent (1) at lower technical levels and (2) when people sail the high seas. This interaction between technical capacity of the element (here a society) and characteristics of the environment (weather and distance) is of the same logical form as the concepts of this chapter. It plays the logical role of a tension in the functional analysis of magic. Environmental concepts of tensions are quite frequent, for many tensions come from the environment.

CHAPTER SIX

Concepts about the Structure of Activities

A social scientist confronted with an automobile plant immediately observes that much of the organized social activity has to do with making automobiles. This is perfectly obvious, but by no means trivial for social theory. One may say, if one is so inclined, that a man attaches fenders because his foreman "expects" him to, because he is "rewarded" for it, or because it "fulfills the functional requirements" of an automobile firm's social structure. But he also obviously does it because it is a required activity in making automobiles.

When a cost accountant or an operations researcher analyzes the "social structure" of an automobile plant, he breaks the structure up into component activities and studies various aspects (costs, time, location, tools required, sequence, and the like) of these activities. The units of activities which make up the cost accountant's "cost centers" are components of the social structure of the firm, looked at as a structure of activities. For the cost-accounting system to be efficient, these cost centers need to be relatively causally autonomous subsystems of the firm. The costs of a given activity ought to be allocated to the product to which it is causally connected. If other people's mistakes are charged to a cost center, the cost account is not a good guide to policy-making. The categories to which costs are charged are supposed to correspond to distinct expenditure decisions and also—to be useful in evaluating that decision—to distinct causes of increased value of the product.

Thus the cost accountant of a firm is a special kind of social scientist who analyzes one aspect of the structure of activities of the firm. The fact that cost accounts are useful tells us that activities have an inherent causal structure. Whoever is in a cost center subsystem at a given time, whatever his culture, psychological predispositions, friendships, and enmities, the center remains more or less causally autonomous from other subsystems. If such causal connections between activities were unreliable, cost accounts would produce statistical hash.

Further, within those subunits, the causal interrelation of social activities is moderately stable. When an Italian foreman is succeeded by a Negro foreman, it still is a full-time job to put on fenders. The result of foreman-worker interaction is a set of attached fenders, more or less regardless of the psychological state of the interaction.

This stability of the structure of activities and the distinctness and stability of causal relations among activities are particularly marked in technology. If a society is going to eat wheat, there has to be a certain scheduling of plowing, planting, and harvesting. Social relations have to adapt to this, or else the society will have to do without wheat. A certain number of fenders have to be put on a given number of autos, or else one has to put up with mud all over everything.

But there are other inherent connections among activities besides those created by technical requirements. Some of the most important of these are spatial relations. Whether or not a man hears a conversation or sees a person's face is heavily determined by whether or not he is in the same room. If a man is to spend part of his day in a house and another part elsewhere at work, he has to travel between. If goods are to be got off a ship and onto a train, there must be a place where trains and ships can get close; usually such places are created by the meeting of a large river and an ocean.

These inherent and causally autonomous connections between activities create a need for conceptualization of activity structures. For the inherent relations among activities create relations among the activities of different people. Relations among the activities of different people are the stuff of social structure. The purpose of this chapter, then, is to outline strategies for forming concepts about the structure of activities involving many people. As before, we are interested in locating the causal forces inherent in such structures—the forces that make some man attach fenders whatever the ethnicity of his foreman. The point is that the overall structure of car-making will cause fenders to be attached, one way or another.

We will be cutting people apart into smaller or larger time-segments, much more than in preceding chapters. The thing that makes an automobile firm go is fender-putting-on, not whole men. We will conceive of "groups" made up, not of members, but of time-segments of member activity. We will want to define those time-segments by the inherent relations of the activity done during them to other activities.

Perhaps a further example will make the main point clearer. If we are studying a debate in an organization meeting, we will be interested in that time-segment of each man's activity in which he "has the floor." If it is a real debate, his activity during that time-segment will be largely determined by the previous history of the debate: what motion is being discussed, what the opponents have said, what the supporters have said, what justification the speaker used to be recognized and get the floor, and so forth. Concepts about the structure of debate will be useful in explaining his behavior during that time-segment. Quite different causes might explain what he thought about when wool-gathering while someone dull had the floor, or what he said to the interesting woman sitting next to him during a lull. These causes may have nothing to do with the structure of debate activity.

First we will deal with *attention-related concepts,* since systems of activities have distinct attention structures. An attention structure may be thought of as the arrangement of attention-controlling structural elements which characterize a system of activities. These elements include spatial determinants of attention regulation (who is allowed to enter the scene of attention focus and who is obliged to be there watching); temporal determinants (how much time is spent by people in the particular attention-focusing situation); and procedural determinants (what regulations determine the pattern and duration of attention focus).

The attention structure of a set of activities is of causal importance because the effect of someone else's activity on my actions and attitudes is a function of the probability I will pay attention to it, multiplied by the duration that my attention is focused on it. For this reason, attention structures of the activities of a social institution are often deliberately organized by officials (teachers, foremen, parents) to increase their influence on the actions and attitudes of members.

A second set of conceptions is organized around the notion of the *variability* of causally significant variables. If a variable is causally significant for an activity, then the activity must be adjusted when that variable varies.

This adjustment requires, first, decisions about what to do. Hence the explanation of the social distribution of *amounts* of decision-making activity depends on the variability of variables related to that activity. And since information is useful for making decisions, the amounts of information-processing activity likewise depend on the variability of causally significant variables.

To illustrate the strategy of forming concepts based on variability for this purpose, we will talk about the explanation of commercial activities. Commerce is, on the one hand, an arrangement for making decisions about flows of goods—where they should go, to whom, at what price. It involves a great deal of paper-processing; the papers carry information relevant to the various decisions that have to be made or that have been made.

The key aspect of a flow of goods which produces its *information and decision burden* is its variability on variables relevant to its value, its origin, its destination, and the property rights in it. We will attempt to develop a conception of this information and decision burden of a given quantity of goods, in order to explain the distribution of commercial activity.

Another illustration of a variance-related concept is that of the *rate of social reconstruction* demanded of a given social structure. If the composition of the activities required of a social structure is very different over time, then the structure will have to be reorganized frequently to do the varying activities. Certain common features of capital good industries (construction, ship-building, movie production, machine-tool production, etc.) derive from the high rate of social reconstruction required.

A third illustration is a concept we have used repeatedly: that of uncertainty. We will point out briefly the relation of this concept to the logical structure of variance-related concepts.

A third set of conceptions consists of what are commonly called *ecological* concepts; these are mainly derived from the observation that the causal force of one activity on another declines with distance. In particular, we will discuss various *external effects,* in which location near another activity makes the activity of interest more (or less) efficient. *Transportation networks and their nodes* are related ecological concepts. They concentrate information and decision activities near transportation terminals, because nodes increase the number of options for the path of a particular good, and information and decision activities make sense when there are options. This point is further specified by relating it to the mixing demand of quantities of goods.

Many conceptions related to the structure of activities, besides those of hierarchy and power treated in Chapter Four and conceptions of communications treated in Chapters Four and Five, fall into one of these broad categories. The illustrations of concept-formation given here are, as before, intended to teach the reader strategies for forming his own concepts.

I / THE STRUCTURE OF ATTENTION

Spatial Aspects of Attention Regulation

It is most convenient to begin with the simplest aspect of attention structures, their spatial aspect.[1] Much of the space in which social activity is carried on is systematically divided up by barriers

---

[1] Much of the conceptual foundation of this section is due to Erving Goffman. See especially his *Behavior in Public Places* (New York: Free Press, 1963).

to perception and access, because such barriers are central devices for governing attention. A great deal can be learned about group structure by studying the details of arrangements of rooms, which rooms are divided from which others, the population of rooms at different times, and the devices for admission to these rooms.

We can first consider three spatial aspects of attention regulation: the degree to which there is a *common focus of attention* (almost always clearly indicated by the arrangement of furniture); the arrangements for *access to that focus;* and arrangements for *entering or perceiving into, or leaving and perceiving out of,* the room. We may take as two extremes a theater and a street. In the theater during a performance there is a single legitimate focus of attention; in the street there are many. In the theater the focus of attention is legitimately accessible to only a defined group of people, the actors (indicated by special entrances to the focus); in the street everyone is legitimately equally in and out of the focus. In a theater perceptual barriers are strong, and entering and leaving are highly governed by norms; in the street perceptual barriers fall where they may, windows give onto the street and are not controlled from the street, and people enter and leave through many doors.

The chief causal role of common foci of attention is that of working out and disseminating a *common culture.* Thus schools focus attention systematically on common course subjects so that people will, in common, learn American history, or algebra, or singing, or whatnot. Meetings and congresses develop common norms and policies for a group. Parades and spectacles provide common symbols of emotional loyalties. "Hyde Parks," or places where any speaker can try to get a crowd to listen to him, provide an opportunity for new common cultures and solidarities to emerge from one man's mind into many. Conversely, groups and activities without extensive common foci of attention tend to develop various subcultures or to intensify individual predispositions.

There are two classes of attention structures without common foci. In the first, common foci are positively prohibited, as in libraries, bedrooms, factories, or study halls. Such situations are deliberately arranged so that individual predispositions to read or sleep will not be disturbed, or so that reward systems (wages or grades) bearing on individuals and focusing their attention will

TABLE 6.1

Examples of variations in attention structures

Examples of situations	Common focus	Monopoly of focus	Norms about entering and leaving; perceptual barriers
Theater, lecture hall, concerts, most "churches"	yes	yes	yes
Parades, stadiums, spectacles, night clubs	yes/weak	yes/weak	no
Floor of Congress, meeting halls, Quaker meetings, revival meetings, family dining rooms in the United States	yes	no	yes
Hyde Park and other institutionalized "free speech" areas; many folk-singing sessions	yes	no	no
Factories and work places, laboratory classes, libraries*	no	yes†	yes
Perhaps airline waiting rooms with public address systems; a logically empty class	no	yes	no
Bathrooms, bedrooms, homes in general	no	no	yes
Streets, parks, restaurants, and other "public places"	no	no	no

* Casual observation suggests that in college libraries there are different attention structures for men and women. Women more often look up from their work when someone walks by than men do. I think this is a Good Thing.
† When there are any.

not be disturbed. In the second, there is no established common focus, but one is reasonably free to build one, as in parks or on streets.

Causal Significance of Monopoly of Focus of Attention

The causal role of monopoly of access to foci is closely related to the role of common foci. The existence of a common focus of attention means that a common culture can be worked out and disseminated. The existence of a monopoly of access to the focus of attention determines the direction of cultural influence.

In a school, where there is a common focus of attention monopolized by the teacher, cultural influences are in the direction chosen by the school's faculty and administration, without respect to the predispositions of the students. In meetings or in Congress, on the other hand, while a common focus exists, no one monopolizes it, and the direction of cultural influence is determined by the balance of group interests and attitudes.

Libraries and factories are examples of situations in which there is no common attention focus, and where the monopoly of access exists for the purpose of denying anyone access to one. These "negative" monopolies are strategically used to intensify selected predispositions or commitments derived elsewhere. Libraries are devoted to the purpose of intensifying people's predispositions to read material of their choice. Factories are devoted to the purpose of facilitating attention-direction by reward systems outside the immediate situation.

Finally, there is a fourth class of activities in which there exist neither common foci nor monopoly. In a park or on a street there is no commitment to the transmission of a common culture nor to the intensification of predispositions; rather, there is expression of natural levels of predispositions.

Norms regulating presence at and departure from the scene of attention foci determine the extent to which an individual will receive whatever causal force is inherent in the attention structure.

The Temporal "Size" of a Group and Group Influence

According to our common-sense causal notions about group influence, the causal forces outlined in Table 6.2 on an individual are proportional to the time spent in these different attention structures. If children spend much time in the street, then the subcultural influence of street-corner gangs becomes stronger relative to that of family or school cultures. If people spend more time in school, they learn more mathematics. If people spend more time in voluntary group activity and meetings, they intensify

TABLE 6.2

Causal impact of groups with different attention structures

GROUPS WITH LARGE TIME-SEGMENTS IN:			CAUSAL IMPACT
Common foci	*Monopolized foci*	*"Coerced" attention*	
yes	yes	yes	Common movement in direction of monopolizing culture, regardless of predispositions (*e.g.*, schools)
yes	yes	no	Common intensification in direction of monopolizing culture, in accordance with predispositions (*e.g.*, entertainments)
yes	no	yes	Common movement in direction of balance of group interests and attitudes, regardless of individual predispositions; "homogenization" (*e.g.*, meetings, congresses)
yes	no	no	Organization of solidary groups of like-minded people, with homogenization inside and differentiation among groups (*e.g.*, Hyde Parks)
no	yes	yes	Intensification of selected predispositions or reward structures for everyone (*e.g.*, libraries)
no	yes	no	Transmission of common information to those inclined to be interested (*e.g.*, airport waiting rooms)
no	no	yes	Intensification of individual, "private" predispositions (*e.g.*, bedrooms)
no	no	no	Expression of natural level of "public" predispositions (*e.g.*, parks)

their commitments to the common values of the group and approach the attitudes of other participants more closely. From the individual point of view, causal influence is proportional to time spent.

From the aggregate point of view, those *groups* which occupy large time-segments will have more causal influence on the culture of their members. The important groups in our society, from this kind of measure, are families (whose cultural influence is often measured by ethnicity, religion, and social class), work groups (measured by industries and occupations), schools (measured by years and subject specialization), and the "informal" (situation 8 in Tables 6.1 and 6.2) groups physically associated with these large occupiers of time. This is why questions on family background, schooling, occupation, and industry always appear on well-designed survey questionnaires. Since these groups are the chief focusers of attention, they are the chief determiners of culture, attitudes, and views of the world.

Aggregate Effects of Group Activity on the Environment

Above the main focus of our discussion was the effect of groups on individuals who paid attention to group-organized foci of attention. The primary function of many groups is not the transmission of culture to their members. Men organize factories to produce goods, not to produce trade union members. They organize political parties and associations to influence public policy, not (usually) primarily to intensify the commitments of members. By and large, the causal influence of a particular kind of activity on the environment is proportional to the time devoted to that activity. Hence, we are generally interested in the aggregate time devoted to group purposes as a measure of the effect of group activity in inducing changes in the environment.

There are two components of the aggregate time spent in group activity. The first is the proportion of each day that the members or workers devote to group activity. The second is the number of men so involved. When Lenin said that the Communist party could not win with weekend revolutionaries, and when Max Weber chose as a crucial characteristic of bureaucratic (as opposed to feudal) government administration that the workers be full-time, they were both pointing to the proportion of the day factor in aggregate effectiveness. Weber held that the causal impact of government policy throughout the realm was much greater with full-time workers than with part-time workers. Lenin held that the causal impact of a revolutionary party ideology would be proportional to the number of full-time revolutionaries.

Likewise it is clear that, controlling for the size of each man's time commitment, the number of men determines the causal impact. Among research universities (*i.e.,* those with large time-segments devoted to the advancement of knowledge), the causal impact of big universities on disciplines is much greater than the influence of small ones. U.S. Steel is at the center of the American economy, while Jantzen Sportswear is peripheral, largely because U.S. Steel is so much bigger.

In general, then, the appropriate measure of the size or volume of a group is the aggregate sum of man-hours devoted to it.

The Schedule and Agenda of Group Attention

In addition to the spatial and temporal components of attention regulation, procedural components are causally significant. Procedural components determine the content or subject that will occupy the focus of attention and the duration of its occupancy. The scheduling of materials for the foci of attention through the drawing up of agendas is a central determinant of the causal impact of a group, both on its members and on the environment. This is why fights for the control of the House of Representatives so often focus on the Rules Committee, which does the scheduling.[2] The same applies to control of the agenda in voluntary associations. Teachers control classroom interaction by controlling the agenda (in schools it is called the curriculum). The supervision of work in factories mainly involves controlling what people are paying attention to.

Agenda formation involves two rather distinct processes. One is

[2] See Robert Peabody, "The Enlarged Rules Committee," in Peabody and Nelson Polsby (eds.), *New Perspectives on the House of Representatives* (Chicago: Rand McNally, 1963), pp. 129–64.

the scheduling of meetings, work, classes, meals, sleep, and so forth—allocating time to group activities. The second is the control of the specific content to be put into the focus of attention. For convenience, we will call the allocation of time-in-rooms "scheduling," and the control of the content during scheduled times "agenda formation." Thus the curriculum of a school consists of two components: the schedule of class hours-in-rooms and the syllabus of each course. The organization of a factory in its temporal aspect consists of the division between time-at-work and leisure, and the substantive production schedule. The temporal organization of a voluntary association consists of scheduled meeting times and the agenda for those meetings: the issues discussed.

Power and Agenda-making in Groups of Different Structure

The variable of "monopoly" in Tables 6.1 and 6.2 is essentially a description of who controls the agenda, in both these aspects. The variable of freedom to leave and enter the room essentially measures the degree to which it is a binding agenda, the degree to which the agenda controls the attention of individuals. Thus in a typical meeting or congress, the agenda can be influenced by all legitimate participants. In a theater or school it cannot be; there it is a monopoly of some defined group.

Let us consider now the relation between agenda formation of a group, and the variation between officials and members in the proportion of the day spent in group activity. Some groups have a relatively narrow variation in time devoted by participants. Bosses do not devote much more time to factories than do workers, and teachers do not devote much more time to schools than do students. On the other hand, associations such as churches or trade unions usually have a very wide variation between full-time clergymen or officials and Sunday-morning Christians or merely dues-paying members.

The amount of variation is crucial to the issue of agenda formation, because in order for a man to focus attention on something he usually has to be there. And he may have to plan the agenda or write the sermon in advance. Differentiation of power over the agenda in groups with narrow variation in amount of time devoted depends on authoritative control over sanctions, usually by legitimate officials such as teachers or foremen. Differentiation in power over agenda in groups with wide variation in time spent does not depend so much on control over sanctions as it does on spending time enough to control the focus.

Hence the causal effect of group activity, both on members and on the environment, depends on different variables in low-variance groups than in high-variance groups. The causal thrust of a revolutionary organization, or a church, or a trade union, or a political party, will be heavily determined by the character of the full-time workers. The causal thrust of a bureaucracy, or a factory, or a school, will be determined more by who controls rewards and punishments, since all spend enough time there to control attention.

In Table 6.3 we have tried to outline the causal impact of groups on their members and on the environment according to two structural characteristics. One is the variance in time devoted to group activity. The other is the degree of institutionalized inequality in sanctioning power (rewards and punishments) by officials.

Full-time hierarchical organizations tend to magnify officially institutionalized policies as a cause of both member behavior and of effects on the environment. Full-time nonhierarchical organizations tend to magnify the effects of consensus on both individuals and on the environment. High-variance organizations (part-time associations, segmentary organizations) with high hierarchical control magnify the causal impact of officially instituted values, policies, or decisions in limited areas of members' lives. High-variance organizations with low hierarchical control tend to magnify the causal impact of beliefs of activists.

The Logical Structure of Attention Concepts

Activities are related to one another when they are in "the same situation." By being in the same situation, we mean that the activities are possible objects of attention for other people in the environment. The significance of such situational relations among activities differs, depending on the normatively enjoined attention structure that pertains to the situation. Because of this potential causal impact of mutually perceivable activities, much of the social

TABLE 6.3

*Variations in the structure of time spent in
hierarchical and nonhierarchical organizations*

Variation in time spent	Control over sanctions by officials	General causal impact	Examples
Low variance (full-time organizations)	High control	Activities highly directed according to institutionalized principles, represented by officials' policies. Movement of individuals toward culture of officials or magnification of officials' impact on environment.	Schools, factories, armies, most bureaucracies
Low variance (full-time)	Low control	Activities highly directed according to group consensus. Movement of individuals toward group culture, and magnification of causal impact of consensus on the environment.	Congress, juries, utopian communities, university faculties, some street-corner gangs
High variance (associations)	High control	High control of limited aspects of men's lives by oligarchs' policies.	Political machines, medieval church, some trade unions with hiring halls
High variance (associations)	Low control	Magnification of the causal impact of activist culture. Leadership of public opinion by "opinion leaders."	Modern churches, most trade unions and most political organizations

structure consists of arrangements of situations so that the attention structure brings about a "proper" relation among activities.

We can imagine a man's day as divided among situations in time-segments. Within any given time-segment, a main determinant of what happens to him and how he responds is what he pays attention to. Attention is particularly crucial for what cultural beliefs and values get into his consciousness. The social psychology of attention is the key link between individuals and cultural systems. Those who want to change cultural systems (agitators) or to transmit received systems (teachers) must be masters of the attention-management aspects of social structure. Agitators and teachers more often fail by failing to get attention than by not having anything worthwhile to fill the focus of attention with.

The impact of a situation on the mind of a man is determined by two broad classes of variables: how the content of his focus of attention is determined, and how long he stays in the situation.

The content is determined first of all by whether the attention focus of the situation is common or splintered, and whether or not it is protected from distractions by careful control of passage across situation boundaries. If it is common and protected, it will tend to have a homogenizing effect. If it is splintered and protected, it will tend to reinforce selectively predispositions derived from elsewhere. If it is splintered and unprotected, it will tend to respond to natural levels of predispositions.

If there is a homogenizing effect, its direction will depend on who controls the agenda. If there is a monopoly over the agenda, the effect will be in the direction of the monopolizing group. In organizations with a high variance in time spent, this group will consist of the activists, who are generally ideologically distinct from the general membership. In organizations with mostly full-time participation, this monopolizing group will generally consist of established hierarchical superiors. If there is no monopoly over the agenda, the homogenizing tendency will tend to be toward a balance of the interests and attitudes of the participants.

The degree of effect on individuals of such common cultural foci will be mapped onto them and will affect their attitudes and behavior in proportion to the time they spend attending to it.

The interdependence of activities of a man who attends to an action with the activities of the man who performs that action is part of the social organization of the situational aspect of activities. In organizations concerned with passing on culture, like schools, the central framework of the social structure is a schedule of situations with defined attention structures. People's roles in the organization are defined by a schedule of situations they are to be in (their course schedule). Deviant behavior of both teachers and students is mainly defined by failure to satisfy the norms of the attention structures of those situations—failure to maintain discipline for teachers, failure of attendance or disruptive behavior for students. These attention requirements of situations remain stable, though students and teachers change.

II /   ACTIVITIES CONCEPTS BUILT ON THE VARIANCE [3]

The Significance of Variability

The causal connection between activities and objectives ("purposes," "return variables," "decision variables," and so forth) makes the *variability* of any causally significant property of activities a crucial consideration. Consider for example the differences in the markets of American Telephone and Telegraph and General Motors. The telephone service market is very stable; the automobile market for any particular firm is very unstable. G.M. therefore has to build mechanisms to adjust its productive activities rapidly to changes in market conditions.[4] A.T.&T. can regard its market as stable and does not need to adjust to it. Much of the administrative apparatus of modern business cannot be attributed to any particular productive or service objective (such as producing cars) because its purpose is to adjust objectives to variability in the environment.

[3] The work on the materials on commerce in this section and the following one was supported by a grant from the National Science Foundation on "The Social Embedding of Industries in the United States." Richard R. Rubin first formulated many of these ideas while working with me on this project.
[4] See especially Alfred D. Chandler, Jr., *Strategy and Structure* (Garden City, N.Y.: Doubleday Anchor, 1966), pp. 174–85, for General Motors' mechanisms for adaptation to the market.

In this section, we want to consider a number of concepts of the structure of systems of activity which are built to take account of variability.[5] These are (1) the variance of characteristics in a lot of goods which creates the *information and decision burden* of a given quantity of goods, (2) the variance of the composition of activities of a given organization over time, producing a high *rate of social reconstruction,* and (3) the variance of causal variables affecting the outcome of activities, producing *uncertainty* about reaching objectives.

As an example of (1), the information and decision burden of a quantity of goods, consider the difference between general cargo *vs.* grain or oil in sea shipping, or between carload lots and less than carload lots in railroad shipping. General cargo and less than carload lots are both heterogeneous, and the total load is made up of many different items with many different destinations. A ship full of general cargo, or a railroad car full of less than carload lots, must carry with it information on the recipients of each piece of goods; it requires multiple decisions on the routing of each lot within the cargo; at the terminal it requires multiple decisions about handling the goods so that they can get to the proper recipients. Grain and oil, or carload lots, need only one piece of information on the recipient, only one routing decision, and only one handling decision at the terminal. This difference in the information and decision burden can conveniently be conceived as measured by the variance of product characteristics; it is closely causally related to the administrative activity generated by the goods.

An illustration of (2), the rate of social reconstruction, is provided by the subcontracting system in the construction industry.[6] By subcontracting for different services at different times, the or-

---

[5] Another set of conceptual tools based on the variance treats variance in quantities of resources, power, privilege, or prestige of individuals or social units in stratification systems. We have treated some of this above in passing, when we discussed how values cannot be highly correlated with power if there is very little variance in power (Chapter Four). For a fuller treatment of variance-related concepts in stratification, see my paper on social stratification in the new edition of the *Encyclopedia of the Social Sciences.*

[6] Arthur L. Stinchcombe, "Bureaucratic and Craft Administration of Production: A Comparative Study," in *Administrative Science Quarterly,* Vol. 4, No. 2 (September, 1959), pp. 168–87. A Bobbs-Merrill reprint.

ganization at a particular site can change the composition of its activities very easily. In building a particular building, the construction problem changes drastically in the social organization (the activities) needed. It goes from the architectural planning phase, to the site-preparation and earth-moving phase, to the shell-construction phase, to the mechanical, electrical, and decorative finishing phase. This rapid rate of change in the activities necessary requires a rapid social reorganization of the work force, which is achieved by the subcontracting system.

Uncertainty (3) of achieving objectives is related to the variance of causal variables, whenever this variability cannot be predicted at the time the activity is carried out. A good example is research, where the results cannot be predicted very well from the amounts of activities of various kinds devoted to it. Another example is the stock market, where speculations, in order to pay off, have to be made *before* changes in stock prices. In both research and the stock market there is much talk of "geniuses," of men with a "specifically extraordinary" talent for dealing with uncertainty. Such magical conceptions are much less common in other fields—we rarely speak of "geniuses" in the distribution of electricity. Magic, extraordinary profits, gross status inequalities, and other important social effects are dependent on the degree of uncertainty in activities. Obviously things cannot be uncertain unless their causes have high variance.

1. The Information and Decision Burden of Goods

Consider the difference between the cargo of an ore boat going from the mines to a steel company (or a banana boat from United Fruit's plantations to their docks in Tampa) and the cargo made up of a variety of goods shipped by exporters in Hamburg to importers in New York. Each piece of ore has the same route: the same origin and the same destination. Each piece has roughly the same physical characteristics: the same fragility, the same perishability, the same density, roughly the same size and shape. Each piece has roughly the same legal and economic status: the same relation to the customs laws of the receiving country, the same value per pound, the same owner before it was loaded and the same owner at the receiving point. That is, the variance of the characteristics of the route, physical characteristics, and legal and economic characteristics is very low. The general cargo from Hamburg, however, will have high variance on all these characteristics. Route: it comes from different producers or commercial houses and will end up with different importers. Physical characteristics: varying fragility, perishability, density, size, and shape. Legal and economic status: varying customs classifications, varying value per pound, varying owners at origin and destination. Thus the variance of general cargo is very high on all these characteristics, compared to the variance of bulk cargo.

What this means is that the whole process of shipping ore (or bananas, or any other bulk cargo) can be highly routinized. Special ore docks, ore boats, and ore-loading equipment can be designed and built. The processing of the cargo through customs can be routinized and simplified. For the ownership of each piece at each point in time to be clearly specified and the risks of transportation to be uniquely determined, the ore or banana boat needs one set of papers. The number of cargo-handling decisions to be made at each end is reduced to one, since the product is homogeneous and is going to a single receiver from a single sender. During the loading and unloading process, the unique identity of each piece does not need to be kept track of, so the piece does not have to be stopped for someone to see what its identity is. There is only one receiver whose receiving schedule must be coordinated with the arrival of the goods, so warehousing and warehouse handling costs are saved. In each of these respects, the general cargo from Hamburg requires more information: to guide more decisions about loading and handling, and to make more special arrangements for distinct packages. It will involve more stopping to inspect and certify, more warehousing and scheduling.

A casual inspection of the work force of all parts of the distributive apparatus shows a high proportion of clerks. Clerks process information. In the United States in 1960, the proportion of clerks in railroads and railway express was 21.5 per cent; for marine transportation it was 13.2 per cent; for wholesale trade it was 22.2 per cent; for warehousing and storage it was 20.7 per cent. This indicates that a main job of the distributive apparatus is to process information about goods, for that is what clerks do.

The gross cost of information-processing forms a large part of the burden of transportation and distribution.

The effect of this burden is indicated by the differences in transportation rates between general cargo and bulk cargo, or between carload lots and less than carload lots. Clearly the information and decision burden of a ton of goods is a consideration for costs in the distributive apparatus, and equally clearly it is closely related to the homogeneity or variance of product characteristics. Let us first consider some of the general sources of variance or product characteristics of cargo, and in each case go on to treat devices for minimizing such variance. Much of the dynamics of the distributive apparatus can be understood in terms of such minimization.

It is convenient to group variables whose variance is important in terms of (a) those affecting *handling costs,* (b) those involving the *preservation of the physical organization of goods in transit,* especially the uniqueness of each unit, and (c) those involving the *distribution of rights and obligations* with respect to pieces of goods.

(a) Terminal costs are a large part of the costs of any transportation system and are much more highly variable with types of goods than the costs of movement of goods. For instance, it has been estimated that in the Port of New York the total cost of handling a ton of general cargo was $17.20 when the cost of handling a ton of oil was $1.00.[7] Switching, unloading, and reloading, storage and notification of receivers, certification that a certain man can pick up certain goods, and physical reorganization of a flow of goods in terminals for further routing take up a large part of transportation time and resources. Some goods require a great deal of special handling of a nonroutine sort, while others require very little.

The main source of such handling costs seems to be the number and variety of shippers and receivers per ton of goods. That is, it is the number and variety of dockside or terminal decisions about

---

[7] John I. Griffin, *The Port of New York* (New York: Atgo Press, 1956), p. 55. This does not include most of the extra legal and commercial paper costs, nor the costs of providing special physical conditions in transport (crating, etc.).

where a good should go, and when, that creates work. Variety of shippers and receivers is also one main source of variety in sizes, shapes, densities, and other physical characteristics, which also present handling problems. For different shippers ship different things, and different receivers need different amounts of those things. This in turn means that information about the disposition of each parcel has to travel with it and has to be hooked by a reliable coding scheme to communications which travel separately to the handlers.

The connection between number of shippers and costs explains why railroads can use the number of shippers and receivers as a principal criterion of transportation charges, which are higher for less-than-carload lots. When carload lots are shipped, special sidings and specialized handling procedures can be designed which drastically reduce terminal costs. The usual practice of most transportation systems of specifying a minimum weight (or volume) below which all shipments cost the same is another indication of the importance of handling costs of individual shipments. Costs of physical transportation vary with weight; evidently below a certain weight, costs of decisions and handling do not vary with weight.

The number of lots (*i.e.,* the number of separate shipper-receiver relations for a given weight) can be reduced by several devices. One is for wholesalers to assemble mixed lots of merchandise for simultaneous shipment, so that a single shipment— though heterogeneous in physical characteristics—is homogeneous in sender and receiver. This assembly generally means that the wholesaler takes title to the goods before shipment, so as to create a mixed inventory out of which larger lots can be shipped.

Another device to reduce the number of shipper-receiver relations is for the producer to set up branch offices, or to hire brokers, at major central nodes of the transportation system. For instance, in citrus fruits, a broker receives carload lots of fruits, which he then sells to local fruit wholesalers or chains, who then construct their own mixes of fruits and vegetables. Brokers tend to be used when there are many relatively small producers (*e.g.,* fruits, apparel); manufacturers' branch offices tend to be used when there are few large producers (*e.g.,* cars, rubber goods, paints, chemicals).

A third device to reduce the number of shipper-receiver relations is the chain retailer, who supplies his many stores from multiple sources. Each order to the producer is, however, large enough to involve a single sender-receiver relation for many tons of goods and hence minimizes the information load per ton. The shipment from the central chain warehouse to a branch store also has a single shipper-receiver relation, since the branch is not buying from multiple wholesalers or producers.

In addition to variance in shippers and receivers, variance in the physical characteristics of the goods affects handling costs. The size, shape, density, and fragility of lots vary. This variation makes it difficult to design handling facilities for maximum efficiency and requires multiple decisions about how to handle each piece of goods. Handling facilities must be designed for the maximum fragility, maximum weight, maximum size, and the most peculiar shape. Hence there is always either a great deal of unused capacity or else great difficulty with the most fragile, heaviest, or most awkward pieces.

These costs are minimized by a number of devices. One is to set limits on fragility, weight, or size. Another is "containerization," the homogenizing of the shipping units by artificial devices for making them the same size and shape, thereby reducing the handling decisions to decisions about each (larger) container rather than each small piece. Another is by previous grading of some kinds of goods into homogeneous subcategories, so that single handling decisions can apply to each category. Grains are generally graded before shipment, so that within a grade one ton is as good as another. Separate lots of grain do not have to travel separately to be graded at the destination.

Most of the devices listed above to reduce the number of shippers and receivers tend to have as a side effect the homogenization of the physical characteristics of each lot and hence tend to reduce handling costs in both ways. For instance, brokers in citrus fruits not only simplify the orchard–New York shipper–receiver relation to one; they also make it possible to send carloads of physically homogeneous oranges rather than a mixture of fruits and vegetables.

(b) Most of the causes affecting handling costs also increase or decrease the costs of preserving the physical organization of goods in transit. The easier it is to treat a shipment as a unit in the terminal, the easier it is to keep the shipment together. For instance, a heterogeneous lot from a wholesaler to a retailer may often be packed together in the same boxes, or in standard-size boxes, and since the order travels together it can be loaded in the same place. Hence most of this subsection can be written by the reader from the section above. Especially important here is grading into homogeneous categories before shipment, as with grains.

But two considerations are especially important in arranging goods for transit, as opposed to handling. These are the fragility and the perishability of goods. Arranging the physical environment of the shipment so that things do not get broken, so that goods do not rot, so that animals do not die, is much more difficult for some goods than for others. It is perhaps stretching things somewhat to call such potential variance of the condition of goods over time a "variance-related concept." But the special physical arrangements for packaging, for refrigeration, or for air supply for animals create special transportation problems. The isolation and homogenization of shipments requiring such special conditions constitute a great economy in transportation costs. It would clearly be ridiculous to ship both furniture and meat in refrigerated railroad cars. Minimizing the variance of shipments along dimensions of conditions required in shipment is the beginning of economy.

The requirement of special conditions is so obvious as to be trivial, but it implies a close relation between the shipper, the transportation system, and the receivers at the other end. Thus we would expect producers of perishable goods (meats, fruits and vegetables, explosives and other unstable chemicals) to be under great pressure to integrate forward into the distribution system, either through dispersed manufacturers' branches (meats and chemicals) or through brokers (fruits and vegetables). The vertically integrated meat-packing houses, the United Fruit Company, the extensive use of brokers by citrus and lettuce growers, all can be considered devices to secure regularity in the flow of goods requiring special physical conditions in transit. That is, they are devices to minimize the number of decisions that must be made about the special conditions needed for each shipment of goods that are perishable or unstable.

(c) A final set of variables whose variance affects transportation costs has to do with the process of changing the legal status of goods in transit. At a rough guess, about a third of "transportation" costs in internal trade, and maybe two-thirds in international trade, are generated by the problem of keeping track of legal obligations on pieces of goods. Commerce requires first of all arranging for property rights to pass from the original holder to the receiver and hence involves sales contracts, credit arrangements, prices, arrangements to pay shipping costs, and other commercial matters. Second, commerce requires the specification of who takes various risks of transportation: risks of damage in transit, risks of delays, risks of loss of market value during the time of transit, and so forth. Finally, commerce requires the arrangements for the actual activity of processing goods through various decisions: getting goods through customs, arranging for insurance, arranging credit, notifying the shipper that the goods have been received and that he ought to collect his bill, and so forth. These legal problems require rapid and complex routine communications.

The number of distinct legal statuses of goods per ton, the number of titles, insurance policies, contracts for transportation, the variety of distinct values of pieces of goods and hence distinct quantities of obligations, the variety of distinct credit relations created by transfers of title, and the scheduling of payment, the number of different national currencies used to pay for distinct obligations, and the variety of exchange regulations to which those currencies are subject, all contribute to the volume of commercial paper that must be related to each ton of goods.

Probably the greatest source of variance here is that between international trade and internal trade, because of the variety of customs, exchange, banking, and contract laws that must be related to each piece of goods in international trade. The overall shipping cost, including all port activity of general cargo in international trade, is probably higher than that of any other kind of "transportation," even though the actual cost of movement per ton-mile is among the lowest. People who can get through this thicket and actually get small quantities of a variety of goods from one country to another usually get rich. But the mixing of lots from many senders to many receivers also tends to create great legal complexity per ton.

This legal complexity of a ton of goods is not, of course, an inherent characteristic of the goods. It is produced by the variation of legal processes and legal statuses that a set of goods moves through during transit. If these legal processes move lock-step, as is usual when a cargo consists of a single lot from a single sender to a single receiver, only one set of decisions has to be made. These decisions may be in a longer chain in international trade than in internal trade, and any one stage may involve many decisions (*e.g.,* a heterogeneous single lot moving through customs) rather than a single one.

But the basic device for reducing legal complexity per ton is to lock legal decision processes together. The locking is usually done by integrating the shipper and integrating the receiver, so that larger lots pass through a single sequence. The basic sources of complexity are the *length* of the sequence of legal statuses or decisions 'and the *variance* of the timing of sequences, of the people involved, and of the relevant commodity characteristics.

A second major device is to simplify each decision by highly formalized and routinized papers or forms of legal conveyance, where only the formal characteristics of the commercial paper enter into the decision. The extraordinary uniformity and formality of commercial papers (*e.g.,* checks) simplify each decision without reducing the number of decisions.

As we move, then, from one cubic foot of space occupied by cargo to another cubic foot, we need to ask three questions: (a) Is there variation between these cubic feet in handling characteristics, especially ultimate destination, size, shape, density, and fragility? (b) Is there variation in the physical environment needed to preserve the goods in transit, especially temperature, urgency or speed of processing, or protection against shocks and blows? and (c) Is there variation in the legal status of goods, especially variation of ownership, liability for damages, obligations under customs laws, and credit arrangements? Such variance in handling characteristics, transit conditions required, or legal status increases the information and decision burden per cubic foot (or per ton) of goods.

The social characteristics of the lines and terminals which handle goods with different information and decision burdens will be sharply affected by such variance in the goods they handle. The higher the burden, the greater the amount of decision work and paper work. The social structure of the distribution apparatus thus depends on the variance structure of the goods flows. "Economies of scale" in distribution come about largely because large size enables firms to reduce the information and decision burden per ton of goods. The larger the total flow, the more easy the segregation of flows so that each flow will be homogeneous in one or all of the above respects. Homogeneous flows allow specialization and routinization of the sending, receiving, and legal transfer of goods and result in great administrative economies.

2. The Rate of Social Reconstruction

A second variance-related causal influence is the rate of change over time of the *content* of activities needed to achieve some objective. In the building-construction industry, the shipbuilding industry, the machine-tool industry, the movie industry, the ladies' garment industry, and research and development activities, the productive problem of a firm shifts rapidly. First one designs a building and then builds it in stages, roughly from the bottom up and from the outside in. One also builds a ship roughly from the bottom up and the outside in. One must write a movie, build sets, film, then cut. In a research project one must alternate thinking and trying, and trying involves stages of design of instruments, data collection, and data analysis.

But the production process of making a car also is a serial combination of different activities. The crucial difference in construction, shipbuilding, machine-tool building, movie production, or research and development is that large chunks of work come into a firm, and a combination of activities has to be set up to do that work. Then later, perhaps, another big chunk of work comes in, requiring a somewhat different combination of activities. Building an office skyscraper does not call for the same set of activities as building a one-story factory building. It is not the same thing to build a nuclear aircraft carrier as to recondition a cargo ship. It is not the same research job to develop a communications satellite as to develop a transmission system for submarine cables.

The shifting productive purpose and the unsteadiness of the flow of projects require a rapid reorganization of the productive apparatus to handle new activities. Insofar as these activities require specialized skills, rapid reorganization implies a rapid turnover of specialized personnel. Engineers and applied scientists would always be in demand *even if* there were no shortage of research personnel, because new talents are required for a new project. The craft hiring halls of the construction and shipbuilding industries, the lending of stars among motion-picture producers, and the recurrent advertisements in industrial centers for tool and die makers, all reflect the rapid reconstruction of social systems in such industries.

There seem to be three main sources of variance in activities which affect the rate of social reconstruction in an industry. The first is the most obvious: variance in the gross workload of the industry.[8] The construction industry, the shipbuilding industry, the machine-tool industry, and research and development are all closely related to the investment process. The market for capital goods (*i.e.,* the rate of investment activity) is much more variable than other markets in gross volume. Further, both building construction and, to a lesser extent, shipbuilding are very dependent on weather. The movie industry would be dependent on weather if it were not located in a desert. This high variability in gross volume implies reorganization of the whole industry.

The second major source of variance in the activities composition of a particular enterprise is the large economic size of an integrated technical unit. That is, ships, buildings, movies, punch presses, and new design principles are all much larger than automobiles, refrigerators, or citrus fruit trees, in the amount of activity needed to produce them.

A third main source of variance is the unpredictability of fashions. In the movie industry and the ladies' garment industry, a shift in fashion may produce a "need" for many spy movies, or many movies with Elizabeth Taylor,[9] or many short skirts. The rapidity and sensitivity with which productive activities must adapt to fashions produce pressure for rapid social reconstruction, even if the overall amount of film used per year, or the amount of cloth on the average woman, remains fairly constant.

[8] See my "Bureaucratic and Craft Administration of Production: A Comparative Study," *loc. cit.,* for evidence on variances in the construction industry.

[9] The fact that in a few years the reader will not know who I am talking about makes the essential point.

These three sources of variance create the need for individual productive operations to be very flexible. A construction enterprise may need to be destroyed each winter and resurrected each spring, because of variations in gross workload. A new order for a large technical unit, say a historical extravaganza in the movie industry, requires both a large increase in the amount of activity in Rome (or somewhere) and special talents for specific roles. A sudden shift in fashions may double the size of an apparel factory which is prepared to make the new product.

In order to average out such variations in large projects, a firm must be gigantic. In the movie industry there are several gigantic firms. Most research and development goes on in gigantic firms. In such cases, the individual "projects" have a high rate of social reconstruction, though the firm itself may be reasonably stable. In most such variable industries, however, firms themselves have high variability in the composition of their activities.

In other words, high variance in the overall workload of an industry (often found in capital goods industries), and high variance for individual firms or departments within a firm caused by a small number of very large projects, tend to produce high rates of social reorganization of the system of activities. We now want to know what *social* consequences are caused by higher or lower rates of social reconstruction in enterprises.

There are three main social requirements that flow from the necessity for high rates of social reconstruction: (a) a *system of performance contracts and subcontracts,* rather than stable employment contracts, for subsets of activities; (b) a system for *transmitting information about performance capacities* of people between productive groups—a system of certification of competence—and (c) a *minimization of the fixed overhead costs,* especially administrative and capital costs. One will, if possible, contract specially for administrative labor, rent equipment rather than buy it, and use the same rock-next-to-a-trail-for-the-hero-to-jump-the-bad-guy-from as was used in a competitor's Western.[10]

---

[10] This may make the trails look pretty heavily traveled for realism, but most Western fans have never seen a desert trail. No doubt there is a selective affinity between a movie industry established in the southern California desert and Westerns as the main standard fare.

(a) When new systems of activities have to be built rapidly, one would rather contract for the activities than for the men. Rather than provide stable job descriptions for permanent roles, one wants to specify the objectives to be reached and let people adapt their own roles to the requirements of the objectives. One requires of the men hired, or their supervisors, that they be able to read blueprints and follow them, rather than that they be able to do specific jobs. This usually means that one requires a larger repertoire of skills in each worker and delegates much more responsibility to him to decide which activity from his repertoire is appropriate. This variety of potential activities and the discretion involved often mean that the man is a "craftsman" rather than an "operative," or a "professional" rather than an "official."

The subcontract with a firm which agrees to provide a certain result for a certain price, and to adapt its skilled work force to the role-requirements involved in getting that result, is a more efficient administrative device than writing job descriptions and devising personnel practices for a shifting work force.

The relation between specifying objectives and high variability should imply, for instance, that if we classified all manual workers and foremen into those who can read blueprints and those who cannot, the average number of distinct employers per decade would be greater for the blueprint-reading group. For blueprints have to be read when one's role is defined in terms of an objective to be reached, rather than in terms of activities to be performed. Such role definition by objectives is more characteristic of industries with rapid social reconstruction.

(b) The requirement of a larger repertoire of skills and a greater degree of discretion in the work force implies that the work force must be highly skilled. But the rapid reconstruction of social systems implies that skill cannot be tested and developed in long employment. This combination requires supra-firm institutions for training and certifying workers as skilled. For manual workers, these institutions are usually craft unions. For engineers and applied scientists, a combination of *résumés* or *vitae* reporting work experience and publications or professional degrees serve this function. For movie actors, there are apparently two main devices. One is, of course, to go see their old movies. Another is a quick test, an audition or a screen test.

(c) A great deal of reduction of fixed administrative overhead is achieved by subcontracting. The usual practice in these industries is to subcontract both for the physical work and *also* for the administration of the work. When one lets a subcontract for certain dies to a job shop, the shop provides both die cutters and foremen, and also payroll clerking work, buying of materials, and so forth. These same functions are performed by subcontractors in construction. Renting required capital equipment (*e.g.,* earth-moving machinery, movie sets, computers for research purposes) also makes it easier to vary overhead costs with variations in the workload.

Thus high variance in the workload of a firm, created by high variance in the gross volume of activity, or by the large size of the technical units, or by highly variable fashions, tends to produce a social system with distinctive features. These distinctive features are due to the requirements of rapid reconstruction of organizations to adjust to radically varying mixes of activities.

3. Uncertainty

We have already considered uncertainty as a causal variable, in the analysis of Malinowski's functional theory of magic in Chapter Three. Our purpose here is to discuss the internal structure of the concept of uncertainty. This is appropriate at this point because things that do not vary do not produce uncertainty. Uncertainty is therefore a variance-related concept.

The distinctive feature of variance in uncertainty is the time order of action and variation. We know what a ship is carrying when we send it off and hence we know how much work there will be in the receiving port. We know, before we construct a set of contracts to build a skyscraper, what kind of skyscraper is wanted. These create no uncertainty. Uncertainty is a crucial variable when action must be taken now, but the causal variables which determine the outcome will vary in an uncontrollable fashion in the future. If we could bet on horses after the race was run, it would not be a gamble. If we could set to sea after we saw whether a storm was coming, we would not ask the gods to protect us from storms.

Uncertainty is a characteristic of an activity to the degree that (a) causal variables affecting the outcome of action have high variance, (b) we cannot, at the time of taking action, predict the value of the causal variable which will have the influence, and (c) we cannot cut the causal connection between this variable and the outcome. Thus when prices are effectively controlled, "speculation" disappears, because the variance which caused uncertainty about the outcome of commercial transactions is reduced. When meteorology became reliable enough to predict the weather, the uncertainty about airplane arrivals decreased. When the "Titanic" was built to resist running into icebergs, it was no longer necessary to furnish lifeboats to provide for the uncertainty about whether it would float or not.

When uncertainty cannot be controlled, it tends to produce magical beliefs and practices. These correspond to the sources of uncertainty outlined above. (a) Magic may involve supernatural coercion of the future—a reduction in future variance of causal variables by supernatural means. (b) Magic may involve "divination," supernatural prediction of the future. Or (c) magic may cut the causal connection between varying conditions and the outcome by supernatural means, by inducing "luck."

Belief in magic, divination, and luck is widely distributed in highly uncertain activities: athletics, the stock exchange, gambling, combat, mining, and fishing. In somewhat more sophisticated uncertain operations such as research or creative art, magical ideas go by different names: "inspiration" and "genius" for supernatural coercion, "intuition" for divination, and "serendipity" for luck.

In modern times and in sophisticated intellectual environments, the main focus of magical thought is about the qualities of individuals. "Talent," "genius," "brilliance," "creativity," all are common parlance in the uncertain environments of the creative arts, research, and advertising. Close analysis of people's linguistic behavior in using these words will show that people generally refuse to identify them with any measurable characteristics of individuals. Instead, people want to wait to see whether a man's work creates box-office receipts, or a redirection of the work of a scientific discipline, or sells Hathaway shirts. If his work brings results, he *had* talent or genius, he *was* creative. If not, he was perhaps a very competent worker.[11]

The Logical Structure of Variance-related Concepts

The overall importance of the variance of variables for the structure of activities is that activities can be routinized if their determinants have low variance. If goods in transit have low variance of origin and destination, of physical characteristics, and of legal characteristics, whole shiploads can be loaded, shipped, and unloaded in a series of routine and repetitive operations. If a steady market for electric power produces a situation in which the same activities can be performed repetitively without adjustment, routinized mass production and bureaucratic administration are possible and economical. If the determinants of the outcome of an action are all known and controlled at the time of action, the intervention of gods, diviners, geniuses, and luck is superfluous. Competent, routine, everyday activity is sufficient.

Hence all kinds of social variables having to do with the routine-nonroutine dimension of activities are most economically explained by using variance-based concepts as causal variables. The amount of information and decision work, to take account of nonroutineness, is one such routine-nonroutine dimension. Hence we find such information and decision work greatly influenced by the variance in cargo characteristics. The rate of social reconstruction, and hence subcontracting, professionalization of labor, and low overhead operations, are other variables on a routin-nonroutine dimension. Hence variance in gross workloads, lumpiness variance of the workload of particular firms, and variance in

[11] Some men may indeed be able to control variables that others cannot, or to "look into the seeds of time and say which grain will grow and which will not." The point is that such "genius" is probably just as common in electric power distribution as in the theater, or science, or advertising. The constant preoccupation with such specifically mysterious qualities and the unwillingness to commit oneself to measures of these qualities are indications of magical thinking. The presupposition of this book is that "genius" in constructing social theories is the result of learned skills and strategies. But these skills and strategies cannot take the uncertainty out of scientific advance. Hence even if the book were successful, we would still expect to hear of genius.

fashions are central to their explanation. Magic, divination, luck, and genius are interventions of nonroutine forces into activities. Their creation is dependent on the psychological reaction to high future variance on variables causally related to outcomes.

One can think of many other systems of activities which vary markedly on a routine-nonroutine dimension. In international relations, diplomacy is more routine than warfare. Probably diplomacy is more prevalent when there is low variance in the relative power positions of nations over time; war is probably more prevalent when there is high variance of relative power positions. Wakefulness in class is produced by nonroutine teaching and is probably related to the variance of such variables as loudness and pitch of teachers' voices, the rate of social reorganization of the classroom, variance in the levels of language used (e.g., obscenities wake classes up), and the uncertainty of examination results.

That is, whenever the dependent variable can be thought of as varying between routine and nonroutine, the variance will be a *causal* variable in explaining it. The higher the variance, the more nonroutine the social response. Both high and low *average* levels of variables may produce equal degrees of routineness in the response, if their variance is low. If their variance is high, then variables with either high or low averages will tend to produce nonroutine responses.

III / SPACE-RELATED CONCEPTS AND THE ECOLOGICAL ANALYSIS OF ACTIVITIES

Space and the Causal Connection Between Activities

We have already noted that the monopolizing of foci of attention, with its consequences for the relation between cultural content and social structure, is intimately related to physical arrangements. But the spatial aspect of systems of activities is not exhausted by barriers of perception that organize attention foci; many causal connections between activities are systematically affected by the spatial distribution of activities. Usually the casual effect of one activity on another declines in a monotonic fashion with the distance between the activities. We have already dealt in Chapter Five with a particular case of such a relation, where the military resources at a certain place decline in military effect with distance from that place, with the steepness of the decline being dependent on transportation technology. And we have shown some consequences of this fact for the evolution of political structures. In this final section of the chapter, we will discuss some space-related concepts which derive their causal importance from the decline in causal relationships among activities with increases in distances between them. But the concepts treated here have more direct relations to activity systems than the highly abstract potential concepts dealt with in Chapter Five, and less psychological focus than the attention-related "room" concepts discussed earlier in this chapter.

First we will discuss the important concept in ecological theory of "external effects." Many activities are more easily carried out, with less expenditure of resources, if they are done near some other activities. At a place at which those other activities are carried out, then, these activities will be facilitated. We say that the presence of those other activities has an "external effect" on the activities in question.

There are four main ways in which being near another activity can cause an activity to be more economical. Nearness (1) facilitates the transmission of information about an activity; hence when activities are causally interdependent, nearness facilitates the adjustment of activities to each other. Offices and businesses dealing with information flows—banks, lawyers, wholesalers, business services, newspapers, post offices, telegraph services, and the like—all create external effects for each other. Nearness (2) facilitates certain activities because of physical connections between the activities, as when one activity uses a product of the other. Nearness (3) facilitates some activities because they are more easily carried out in a traffic stream induced by other activities. A supermarket across the street induces a stream of traffic, a concurrence of people disposed to buy groceries. A specialized food store, or even another supermarket, may have its activities facilitated by traffic disposed to buy groceries more than it is damaged by competition. Finally (4) activities may need to be located near each other because they are done by the same people. Work places and residences need to be located near each other for that reason. The first part of this section, then, will be devoted to the analysis of the concept of external effects, in these various aspects.

The second part of this section will deal with concepts related to nodes in transportation systems, as a particular kind of spatial structure of activities. Above we noted a large number of activities for which being near breaks in the transportation system (harbors, railroad yards, and so on) is an external economy. What is it about the structure of transportation systems that creates terminals? And why are terminals causally crucial?

In order to conceptualize this influence, we must consider the relations between the physical structure of networks and decision-making activities. The key aspect of a node in a network is that the number of options about further paths increases, and decisions have to be made about which option to take. Social activities directed at decision-making therefore congregate about such nodes. Not only do information activities have external effects on each other; their location is intimately dependent on the nodal points of transportation and communication networks. Information is worth something only when it is related to decisions.

One crucial function that takes place at transportation nodes —harbors, railroad yards, truck terminals—is commonly called "breaking bulk." This essentially consists in adding to the information and decision burden per ton of goods. A ton of goods leaving a wholesaler who breaks bulk has had attached to it a great deal of information about the ultimate recipients of the goods and about routes to those recipients. It has often had a good deal of legal information added, about the effects of customs laws of the country on the price of the goods, about property rights in the goods, about credit terms and payment schedules, and the like. It carries a much larger burden of commercial paper with it, sometimes a new physical organization in packages or shipment sizes appropriate to its next transportation phase, a greater amount of temporal organization of its sending and receiving dates, and so forth. This process of changing the information content of physical flows is intimately tied in with terminals. The location of information-adding activities—wholesaling, banking, warehousing, and the like—near terminals is a main source of location dynamics in city-location theory.

A closely related function at nodes is more related to their centrality than to their bulk-breaking characteristics. This is changing the product mix of flows. When a flow of goods leaves a producer, it is organized according to technical interdependence of production. When it arrives in a household, it needs to be organized according to the mix of consumption. At some point in the transportation network, the mix must be changed. When oranges leave Florida, they are unmixed or mixed with other tropical fruits. When they arrive in the home, they need to be mixed with cereals and meat and other fruits and vegetables.

At one extreme, often approximated in poorer countries, retail traders may specialize in goods originating in a distinct productive system, and the combinations are made by long shopping trips by the householder. At the other extreme, approximated perhaps by Sears Roebuck or A&P, the combinations are made by organizations which buy from producers and maintain the mix pretty much intact from that point onward. A central function of merchant wholesalers and of chain stores is to mix commodities in their proper proportions from diverse sources. When the retailer sells a very large proportion of his goods from a single source—as, for instance, new automobile dealers or gas stations—very little specialized mixing has to take place. In such distribution systems, merchant wholesalers and chain stores are quite uncommon. (In automobile parts, in contrast, merchant wholesalers are much more common.) At the other extreme, grocery stores, department stores, and dime stores have very small proportions of goods coming from any one producer, and merchant wholesalers and chain stores are much more prevalent.

This mixing function is intimately dependent on ease of flow from multiple sources to the mixer, and multiple flow from the mixer to the consumers. Hence such mixing activities are located at central nodes. Sears developed in Chicago, Woolworth's in Philadelphia, and wholesaling is highly concentrated in New York. The metropolitan location of mixing relates to the centrality of these cities in the transportation network. By noting the differences in the flows from automobile or gasoline manufacturers to dealers, and from makers of bobby pins or growers of oranges to dealers, we can derive some interesting predictions about the nodalization of different types of commerce.

In one sense, the location of decision activities and mixing activities at nodes is merely another example of external effects. For certain kinds of businesses, nearness to a transportation node is an external economy. But the characteristics of nodes are sharply determined by the overall structure of networks. One can locate lawyers' offices near courts, wherever the courts happen to be. But one cannot locate wholesaling near terminals, wherever terminals happen to be, because terminals do not just happen to be where they are. Why they are where they are depends on the structure of the transportation system.

The General Concept of External Effects

As we defined external effect above, it is a causal relation between two activities which declines with distance and which facilitates one of the activities.[12] Legal advice is facilitated by closeness to courts and law libraries. Banking and other legal information-processing industries are facilitated by being at legal centers and, as hinted above, by being at nodes in transportation networks. Steel-shaping industries are facilitated by being near steel-producing centers. Stores are more effective if they are near traffic flows which bear customers and near parking lots and their associated activities. The writing of newspaper articles is facilitated by being near the President of the United States.

A single exogenous cause of the location of a particular activity can influence the location of a large number of activities, because these activities are tied together with the exogenously located activity by external effects. We will treat one such exogenous force, and a few of the closely linked activities, in the part on networks

---

[12] There is a more general conception of external effects which is not related to space. Mathematical work by a Soviet statistician may be an external effect for, say, formal linguistic analysis in the United States. Kolmogorov may be more *relevant* than anyone in the United States, and with mathematics the cost of transportation is insignificant compared with the cost of irrelevance. Such external effects not dependent on space will not be treated here.

below. Our focus in this first part is on the causal connectedness among activities which tends to group them together into spatial bundles.

Types of External Effects

1. *Information Effects:* If two activities have a high degree of causal interdependence of any kind (physical, legal, temporal), and one of them has a high degree of variability caused by some exogenous variable, then rational planning of the second depends on rapidity and accuracy of information about the first. Amounts of information transmitted between two points tend to be higher, the closer they are together. Whenever information transmission becomes a critical consideration, the location of the points with respect to each other tends to be minimized, and the structure of activities tends to take on a roughly spherical form.

> The skyscraper facilitates personal contacts in a way never possible before. From my office on the twenty-eighth floor of a building in the Times Square district, I can get to practically every person of importance in the architectural and business field in fifteen minutes' time.[13]

Let us consider, then, the general conditions under which activities will have to adjust finely and in detail to each other, and consequently when information external effects are likely to be crucial. Such activities should be concentrated in skyscrapers, or at least in districts with many skyscrapers. Such activities seem to include: (a) coalition formation, for detailed knowledge of the thoughts and commitments of other men to a project are critical (see Chapter Four, above); (b) comparison shopping, in which large quantities of money can be lost or gained by imperfect information; hence exchanges of large legal claims (stock exchanges, futures markets for commodities) and markets for expensive and highly individual goods (jewelry, works of art, new high fashions) have high information external effects; (c) selling organizations for goods with a highly unpredictable market, where adaptation to the market is

[13] Harvey Wiley Corbett, "New Stones for Old," *Saturday Evening Post*, March 27, 1926.

critical for producers (women's apparel, new products, and innovations generally); (d) information-collecting, -distributing, and -selling enterprises (newspapers, wire services, accounting firms); and finally (e) communications nodes which will be used by all of the above, such as cable offices, courier services, consulates, travel agents, central post offices with a variety of special services, and the like.

(a) Coalition formation (underwriting bond issues, forming major corporations, distributing large risks among insurance companies, forming the combination of architectural and financial skills needed to construct a major building, forming receiverships for major bankrupt corporations, and the like) requires accurate and detailed knowledge of the commitments that other people are willing to undertake. These commitments in their turn depend on the commitments that still other people are willing to undertake. There is an intimate interdependency between components of the coalition which requires detailed knowledge of exactly what X means when he says he will do such and such. Knowledge of the current developed of the commitments and knowledge of each other sufficient to form a basis of trust generally depend a great deal on face-to-face interpersonal contact, repeated going back and forth between potential coalition members as the commitments of each move through their stages to final commitment, and a great deal of feedback and sensitivity to changing opinions.

Probably no other enterprise is as dependent on rapid and accurate communication of a developing situation as is coalition formation. This is probably why politics tends to be very highly concentrated at a single point in the governmental unit, and why politicians, to a very high degree, travel to that point to communicate their opinions. It probably accounts for the high concentration of financial activities in a cube formed of skyscrapers in the financial district, and the location of the offices of great coalitions (*e.g.,* corporations) in that same cube. The chances are very high that if a man works in a building with more than twenty floors, his work is directly related to forming coalitions of some kind.

(b) By comparison shopping, we mean two things. First, the buyer is highly motivated to compare the offerings, in price or quality, of a number of sellers; he is sufficiently interested that he will enter a special "buyer role" of collecting information and will spend substantial resources to collect that information. He will, for instance, travel some distance to see what is offered. Second, we mean that the information which he needs to collect (or communicate) cannot be conveniently collected at a distance, either because it involves visual inspection or because the situation changes from hour to hour or minute to minute. The first would be the case with fashion shows; the second with stock markets (with stock markets, the information can be communicated to most individuals by wire, but information on the last bid and offer needs to be physically centralized). When these two things are combined, as with fresh fruit and vegetable markets where goods are highly variable and where speed is very important, there is considerable pressure for centralization even though the commodity takes a great deal of space for its value.

The interdependence in this case, then, is created by relations among sellers and by the rapid information collection which buyers need to carry out in order to take advantage of differences between buyers. The act of another seller can make a buyer's activity in contact with a given seller highly irrational.

(c) Certain kinds of unpredictable markets produce the same sort of high needs for information among producers and sellers. The failure of a jobber in the women's apparel trade to make his decision (on what to contract for) on the basis of the latest information on fashion trends can make his investment very irrational. He needs to adjust his contracts for fashion goods to the latest orders of buyers, who in their turn will have waited as long as possible before buying their inventory to see which way things are developing. Hence he needs to be intimately tied to his buyers (wholesalers), and jobbers will tend to concentrate in places where it is easiest to come into contact at the last minute with as many buyers as possible.

A new product inherently has a highly unpredictable market, because neither the past experience and present feelings of buyers as determined by market research, nor the past experience of the seller of the product, are reliable guides to the size of the market. Also, usually small modifications which had not been thought of before can substantially affect the convenience or salability of a new product; and feedback from the market, indicating what these modifications should be, is highly productive. Hence new products generally are more likely to be concentrated near sources of market information, and new related products will tend to be located near each other.

(d) It hardly needs explaining why information-selling enterprises, especially if timeliness is important, need to be near sources of information.

Finally, it is important to note that much of the necessary information for each of these problems is the same—current knowledge of the market, current knowledge of the commitments of others, current knowledge of changes in world or governmental conditions, and the like. Market information is useful to new enterprises. Market information is very much carried through financial channels. Hence new enterprises need the same information that other users of financial services need. The formation of coalitions to expand the scale of production of a new type of goods is intimately related to the unpredictability of new goods —one would not be forming coalitions at this late date if the market could have been forecast far in advance. Hence these various new enterprises and new coalitions are intimately dependent on each other and on their markets for information. Moreover, all of them are, in particular, dependent on all the kinds of information that are easier to get in downtown Manhattan. In societies in which commercial law is less formalized and stable than in the United States, this whole complex is likely to depend also on rapid knowledge of the latest developments in exchange regulations, or tax liabilities of different parties to a contract, or whatnot. Hence many of them need not only to be near each other, but to be near the centers of government. In societies in development, the law is usually changing rapidly in respects relevant for commercial practice. Hence there are great external effects of information in being located near the central government, near the minister who has charge of new investment regulations, or of price-fixing for particular lines of commodities, or of fixing exchange rates, or of introducing import prohibitions.

Thus the high degree of legal uncertainty of economic life in countries currently undergoing economic development produces great external economies, for all the activities outlined, in the capital city. This is another reason, in addition to the analysis of Chapter Three, why great primate cities tend to grow up in underdeveloped countries. Very generally these great metropolises are also centers of government. Commerce is tied to these centers of government by rapid changes in legal policy with respect to commerce.

In addition, when the government uses its discretionary power to encourage specific enterprises, many of the coalitions that need to be constructed to carry out new enterprises have the government as a central member. Hence the information economies analyzed above for coalition formation generally also explain why much of the coalition-forming activity goes on in the capital.

Thus, aside from the well-known concentration of financial operations, new enterprises, and sophisticated markets near to each other in metropolitan areas, explained by the notion of external effects in information handling, we can derive another empirical result. One could rank countries by the rate of change of commercial policy, by legal uncertainty of commercial relations and obligations, and by the degree of discretion used by the governmental administration in granting certain legal privileges to particular enterprises. One would predict then that the higher the degree of legal uncertainty in commerce and investment, the greater would be the tendency for new economic coalitions to be formed in the capital city, and hence the greater the proportion of all financial activity which would be carried on in the captial city. As an example of countries at approximately the same level of development, one would predict that the banking of Argentina would be more highly concentrated in Buenos Aires than the banking of Italy in Rome.

2. *Physical External Effects:* There seem to be two main forms of physical external effects: (a) those in which the physical state of goods used by two activities changes in a way unfavorable for the second activity if the activities are too separated, and (b) those in which there are transportation economies to be gained by short physical distances.

(a) When a physical good to be used in further activities is produced by an activity in such a form that its physical state is appropriate for the use but changes rapidly from that time on, then the activities tend to be located close to each other and in close temporal interdependence. For example, steel coming out of steel-making furnaces in the form of ingots is in a convenient physical state for its first rolling, because the preserved heat helps keep it at the appropriate consistency. Any long shipment or delay would allow the ingot to cool, and it would have to be reheated. For another example, bread after it is baked is in an appropriate state to be consumed but changes rapidly from that state with time. Hence in both these cases, the rolling of the ingots tends to be done near to steel production, and the baking of bread near the homes where it will be consumed.

If it is possible, this temporal interdependence between activities tends to be dealt with by incorporating the activities within the same organization, as the making of steel and the first rolling tend to be. But even when they are done by the same organization, their external effects are taken into account in the ecological organization of the enterprise.

(b) When a physical good to be used in further activities changes bulk, or changes in information and decision burden during the course of its trip from origin to destination, or changes in fragility, then transportation costs can be minimized by the strategic location of activities with respect to each other. Usually changes in bulk take place early in the trip, because most changes in bulk are reductions. Hence changing bulk early saves transportation costs. An exception, however, is baked goods, which increase in bulk with baking. Usually changes in information and decision burden are increases, and hence they tend to take place near the destination. Many changes in fragility are increases, and hence they also tend to take place near the destination.

Thus by and large, ignoring other influences, processes which decrease bulk (reduction of ores, threshing of agricultural products, extraction of turpentine) tend to be done near the origin of goods, while those few which increase bulk tend to be done near the destination (baking, addition of water to soft drinks). Any activities on a flow of goods which increase the information and decision burden tend to be done near the destination (wholesaling, packaging of individual items), while those few which decrease the information burden tend to be done near the origin ("containeri-zation," grading of grains). Any activities that increase fragility (assembly of machines, baking of china, bottling of beverages) tend to be done near the destination; those few which decrease fragility (canning and freezing of agricultural products, packaging generally) tend to be done near the origin.

This makes either the last activity before the reduction of bulk, information, or fragility, or the first activity after an increase of bulk, information, or fragility, an "external effect" for the activ-ity which produces the change. In the absence of disturbing factors, original production will be an external effect for bulk-, information-, and fragility-reducing activities. Consumption activ-ities will be external economies for bulk-, information-, and fragility-increasing activities.

3. *Traffic Effects:* External effects are also produced by traffic generated by an activity. If many of the wealthiest people in a city come to the center of the city to work, then retail trade in expensive goods will be facilitated by financial districts, legal and governmental centers, and wholesale centers. The evening traffic created by a theater facilitates the operation of other entertain-ment enterprises, other theaters, bars, fancy restaurants, houses of prostitution, and the like. The exact disposition to buy of the traffic created by other activities creates greater or lesser external effects for different enterprises. A bar's activity is more facilitated by the flow of traffic created by a theater than by the flow created by a church. The greater the distance between activities depending on the same sort of traffic flows (and generating such flows for each other), the less each facilitates the activities of the other. Much of the concentration of competing enterprises in a given line of goods near to each other is explained by the fact that they each gain more from the traffic created by the others than they lose from the intensified competition.

4. *Activities Done by the Same People:* Finally, activities which have to be done by the same people are external economies for each other. The most striking case is the relation between activi-ties at work places and activities done at home. The division of labor has not progressed far enough yet to permit some people to work all the time and some people to eat and sleep all the time.

This will no doubt come with further progress, but until then homes will be located near work places.

5. *Economies of Scale:* Many activities can be done more easily if they are done near other concentrations of the *same* activity. The activities can use the same capital equipment, the same administrative and information-processing apparatus, the same skilled workers and managers, the same coalition of capital, and so on. In addition, the larger the flow of goods, either in manufacturing or in commerce, the greater the possibility of routinization, because larger flows are generally less variable. New activities are therefore likely to be located near previous activities of the same kind. (The ecological implications of economies of scale were pointed out to me by Edwin Mills.)

General Concept-forming Strategy for External Effects

The general strategy for forming concepts of external effects, then, is to locate a causal connection between two activities which facilitates at least one of them. Generally, activities will be done under conditions in which they are easiest. Since very many causes decrease in their impact as the distance between the cause and the effect increases, concepts invented with this general strategy will generally be useful in explaining the spatial organization of activities.

Such concepts are also quite often useful for explaining the administrative division of activities—which activities will be done by the same organization and which by different organizations. The closeness of activities to each other facilitates their administrative control from a single center, by reason of the information economies that go with closeness. Also, many such causal connections between activities also have a temporal aspect, so that each being governed by an integrated schedule for both facilitates one of them. Being under the same authority facilitates integration of schedules of interdependent activities.

Causal connections among activities which decline with distance tend to be created whenever information about one activity facilitates rationality in the other, whenever physical changes of state or transportation economies tie together activities operating on the same flow of physical goods, whenever activities make use of the same sort of traffic, whenever activities have to be done by the people who do other activities, or whenever the activities are the same. Many of these causal connections change with the development of the technology with which activities are carried out. The degree to which residence and work create external economies for each other has been greatly reduced by automobiles. The causal connections between agricultural activities and eating activities have been greatly reduced by canning and freezing. Airplanes have greatly decreased the information economies of being in financial centers, for most of those men on airplanes carry briefcases which contain legal and financial information (the airlines' main competition is clearly the telephone rather than other forms of transportation). On the other hand, the general increase in complexity and sophistication of the economy means that there are more relevant facts and ideas to be ignorant of and makes being at information centers more crucial in many lines of activity.

Networks, Nodes, and Commerce: Some Empirical Food for Thought

Let us consider a number of well-known facts about the transportation and distribution system, and about New York City. The reason for treating them together will soon be obvious.

First, both the transportation system *and* the distribution system are, to a large extent, information-processing systems. This is obvious if we examine the proportion of the labor force clerical in the transportation and distributive industries. See Table 6.4. The job of clerical workers is the processing of routine information. If we were to add sales workers, whose main job is to process information to and from customers, the information-processing character of the transportation and distributive industries would be even more marked. In the final panel, we have given the proportion clerical in the financial industries. Clearly the processing of legal information on obligations of clients involves a great deal of clerical work.

Now let us consider, in relation to this knowledge, several peculiarities of New York City. First, it is well known that New York is the great financial center of the United States. It is a chief

TABLE 6.4

*Percentage of the labor force of various industries
who were "clerical and kindred workers" in 1960**

INDUSTRY	PER CENT CLERICAL
Transportation	
Railroads and railway express	21.5
Airlines	30.0
Marine transportation	13.2
Warehousing and storage	20.7
Distributive	
Wholesale trade	22.2
Retail trade	11.8
Financial	
Banking and credit agencies	66.1
Insurance	47.2
Security and commodity brokerage and investment	41.7
Manufacturing	12.8

* Source: U.S. Census of Population, 1960, "Occupation by Industry," U.S. Department of Commerce, Bureau of the Census.

wholesaling center. It has one of the highest proportions of the labor force clerical in the country, and a great many other middle-class workers. That is, it is clearly the greatest center for processing commercial information in the country.[14]

Second, it is also well known that New York is the greatest port in the country. It is not so generally understood exactly where its advantage as a port lies. New York does relatively badly in competition for bulk cargoes: oil, coal, and ore. It does very well in competition for general cargo, especially for highly sophisticated and expensive cargo such as manufactured goods. New York gets some three-quarters of the export cargo of manufacturers who could *save money on transportation charges* by shipping through Boston or Norfolk. In other words, general cargo shippers are *willing to pay extra* transportation costs in order to go through the New York port.

A third feature of New York is not very well known, but it

[14] See O. D. Duncan and others, *Metropolis and Region* (Baltimore: The Johns Hopkins Press, 1960), *passim*.

is of fundamental significance for an understanding of the concentration of information-processing and of the competitive advantage of New York in foreign trade. This is that the volume of *intraport* shipping within the New York harbor area is normally larger than the total New York foreign-trade volume. For example, in 1956 there were 31.7 million tons of imports and 9.2 million tons of exports through the New York port, for a total of 40.9 million tons of foreign trade. In that same year there were 47.9 million tons of local and intraport shipping within the harbor. (Water shipments to and from U.S. points outside the harbor were 66.0 million tons.)[15] This intraport traffic constituted about 80 per cent of all intraport shipping in the United States.[16]

Examination of the physical facilities of the port[17] shows it to be, in essence, an enormous floating railroad yard, with 290 "carfloats" for moving railroad cars, with capacities ranging up to 20 cars per carfloat. Added to this is a barge materials-handling system of great capacity and flexibility. The great capacity to make multiple connections between railroad systems, from railroad systems to docks, and from one dock to another, is the essence of being a *node* in a transportation system, for a node in a network is a place where multiple paths can be taken by a flow of goods or people. This high, discretionary connectivity between lines of transportation allows great flexibility in mixing goods from different flows, assembling them (either by "wholesaling" or by "manufacturing"), and then sending them out in proper mixes along different lines of transportation.

This mixing of goods, changing the composition of flows along communications segments, is a highly information-intensive process. The mixed flows have a higher information content, a higher internal variance of characteristics, as described above. This content is provided by the multiple decisions that take place in mixing the flow of goods. These decisions are based on market information about who needs the goods, legal information about who has

[15] John I. Griffin, *op. cit.*, p. 60.
[16] *Ibid.*, p. 57. Most of this shipping was of fuels and involved the industrial arms of the port rather than the commercial ones. This somewhat undermines the point made below.
[17] See *ibid.*, pp. 28–34.

ordered them, who will pay for them, and when, and transportation information about the cheapest, fastest shipping line.

We may summarize the above facts, and our interpretations of them, as follows:

1. Transportation and distribution are, in general, highly information-intensive operations.

2. New York, the great port in the United States, is also the great center for processing information. Its information-processing superiority is great enough to overcome freight-rate advantages of other ports, especially for information-intensive "general cargo" freight.

3. The great port in the United States is also intensively involved in "nodal activity"—that is, the combination and mixing of flows of goods and their redistribution to various outgoing transportation segments.

Conceptual Formulations of Nodal Concepts

This suggests forming concepts of *nodes, nodal activity, and information and decision processes* so as to formulate the apparent causal connections between them.

Nodes: Our idea of the causal influence of a transportation node is that it is easier at nodes to assemble packets or mixes of goods from a wide variety of sources. That is, the value of the flow of goods coming along a certain transportation line to a wholesaler increases as other flows of goods are combined with it. The value decreases with the amount of mixing to which the goods have already been subjected—that is, the amount of "node activity" that occurs along the transportation line before the goods reach the node of interest.[18]

In order to simplify the problem, let us suppose that all important transportation lines have the same capacities, so that we can merely count transportation lines. Then let us consider a firm which originates a homogeneous flow of goods which has to be

[18] See O. D. Duncan and others, *op. cit.,* p. 128, where it is shown that "metropolitan functions" are less prevalent, the closer a city is to another metropolitan center.

mixed with other goods in order to make up a cargo, or an inventory of a store, or a commodity bundle of a household. In Figure 6.1, this source is labeled "Manufacturer." Suppose the manufacturer has two alternative paths from his plant to a port, to Baltimore and New York, as in Figure 6.1A. New York has a much larger number of other flows coming in from elsewhere, and so it can perform the mixing function much better. Let us define the "mixing demand" of a segment as the difference in heterogeneity of the flow when it enters the node, compared to its heterogeneity on leaving the node; for instance, shipments of nuts come in separate from bolts, but go out as nuts and bolts—"mixing demand" is the difference in heterogeneity attributable to flow originating along the segment. The mixing demand in the segment from manufacturer to New York will be high.

Suppose that, as in Figure 6.1B, the manufacturer has two choices, one of which goes to Baltimore, and one of which goes to New York by way of Philadelphia. Philadelphia, like Baltimore, is something of a node, and some mixing of flows can take place there. The total mixing capacity of the line to New York is much

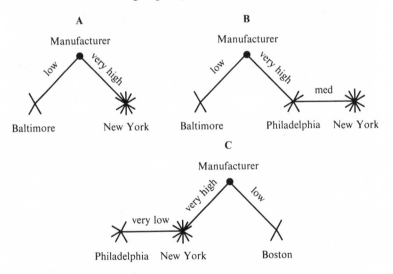

FIGURE 6.1 Evaluation of network segments as generators of mixing demand (see text).

higher than that of the line to Baltimore. On the other hand, the mixing burden on New York will be reduced by the capacity of part of the flow to be mixed in Philadelphia. Hence the mixing demand of the flow as it comes into New York will be lower than in Figure 6.1A but still substantial, because of the lower mixing capacity of Philadelphia.

Consider finally a manufacturer (or other originator of homogeneous goods with high mixing needs) who can go either to Boston, or to New York, or to Philadelphia by way of New York. Boston will not often be chosen for mixing, because New York–Philadelphia has so much more capacity. But once the flow gets to New York, its mixing can conveniently be done there. We would expect very little mixing demand flowing in specialized flows out of New York to be mixed in Philadelphia. Hence the mixing demand on Philadelphia would be small.

The appropriate conceptual scheme, then, would start with a mixing demand at points of origin of goods, measured by the difference between the homogeneity of the flow goods originated at a point and the homogeneity of the packet bought by a retailer or consumer. For instance, small hardware items sold in dime stores have a high mixing demand, while automobiles or coal have a low mixing demand. This mixing demand is *decreased* as the flow of goods passes through nodes in the transportation system. The decrease is proportional to the number of different flows coming into the node, allowing thereby the mixing of the flow with other flows.

Ignoring distance and freight rate problems for the present, we can say that this mixing demand is *channeled* into that transportation segment which has the greatest mixing potential. The attractiveness of segments is proportional to the total number of other transportation lines to which the flow can connect by taking that segment. The greater the mixing demand, the more attractive the highly connected line.

The mixing demand on a particular node would then be an aggregation of the mixing demand flowing into the node along each of the channels leading into it. The greater the number of channels, the fewer and smaller the previous nodes on those channels, and the greater the production of goods with high mixing demand in the hinterland, the greater would be the aggregate mixing demand at a node. Thus we would expect the mixing demand to be highest at nodes in the industrial Northeast, to be reduced by the development of subordinate nodes at the other northeastern ports, and to be greatest at the most connected node in the area.

Such a set of causal ideas would generate the following kinds of patterns:[19]

(a) The greater the mixing demand (*e.g.,* manufactured goods *vs.* coal, oil, and ore), the greater the attractiveness of highly connected nodes (compare the predominance of New York in shipping manufactures with the predominance of Norfolk in shipping coal or of Baltimore in shipping ore).

(b) Hence the greater the mixing demand of the goods, the greater the degree of inequality between nodes. Another way of saying the same thing, in the terminology conventional in geography, is that the hinterland of the most connected node will be larger for manufactured goods than for bulk goods. Further, to the degree that new transportation lines are generated by a mixing demand, then the greater the division of labor and the more sophisticated the production system, the greater the mixing demand at origins. Hence central nodes will be more attractive in advanced economies, and transportation will be more nodalized in sophisticated technologies. Thus we would expect a greater proportion of new transportation lines to finish in a few nodes in more advanced countries.[20]

(c) Highly connected nodes will decrease the mixing or wholesaling function of nearby nodes, even if they are also quite highly connected. Hence the concentration of wholesaling should decline at nodes near greater nodes, compared with that to be found at comparable nodes elsewhere. (See the results of Duncan and others cited above.)

(d) If one were to compare the mixing activities for flows of

---

[19] Recall that mixing demand is a function of the *difference* in heterogeneity of a flow of goods, between origin and destination.

[20] I think this is not true, and hence that it speaks against the theory here. Since our purposes are those of concept formation, this does not matter. This result contradicts the result arrived at in the argument on external effects and legal uncertainty and also that in Chapter Three. Also one could argue that decentralized information is more available in advanced countries, and that this decentralization more than compensates for the above centralizing tendency.

goods coming from one central node to another with flows coming from noncentral nodes (*e.g.,* for Philadelphia, compare flows from New York with flows from points in Pennsylvania), there should be less mixing activity on the receiving end of intermetropolitan flows.

Node Activity: There are two main things that we will expect to happen at nodes: (a) There will be the physical mixing of flows of goods, illustrated by the heavy volume of intraport shipping in the New York harbor. (b) There will be processes of transferring legal responsibility for and ownership of goods, so that the new mixed flow has a legal status appropriate to its new mixture and its new economic function.

(a) What kinds of activities are likely to be incident to the physical mixing of goods? First, there is the physical transfer of goods from one transportation segment to another: switching, repacking, loading and unloading, and other physical acts of reorganizing flows should be more common at nodal points. The number of physical switching activities concentrated at ports or other nodes should be higher for goods (and flows) with a high mixing demand. Second, there is likely to be temporal reorganization of the flows, so that the flow leaving is scheduled in accordance with the needs of the receiver rather than the needs of the producer. Temporal reorganization will tend to produce warehousing and storage activities and the activities of coordinating receiving and shipping schedules, inventory policy-making, and the like. The higher the mixing demand of a flow of goods, the more switching and inventorying activity for that flow will be concentrated at nodes. Coal inventories are likely to be kept at the mines or at the plants which use them. Apparel inventories or machine inventories should be more often concentrated at ports.

(b) The higher the mixing demand of a flow of goods, the more likely is it that legal ownership and responsibility will be transferred at nodes. Oil, coal, ore, or other goods which are bought by the consumer in bulk should less often have transfers of ownership in ports or other nodes. Apparel, hardware, and machinery should more often have transfers of ownership take place at nodes. Thus the amount of legal activity, the amount of ownership of inventory by port-connected movers of goods, and hence the financial and inventory capital intensity of port-connected transfer firms should be higher for flows with high mixing demand. We will expect wholesalers located at nodes to be more likely to take ownership of incoming flows, and to sell the outgoing flows on their own account, for apparel, hardware, and machines than for grain, coal, or oil. The proportion of all the papers that go with a flow of goods which are composed at nodes should be greater for flows with a high mixing demand.

These two taken together imply that firms which combine physical and temporal mixing of goods flows with transfer of ownership functions—especially merchant wholesalers who take title to goods and sell from an inventory—should be especially highly concentrated at nodal points as defined above. Bulk cargo ports, such as Norfolk and Baltimore, should have many fewer wholesalers per ton of goods than does New York.

Thus we would expect a high degree of nodality to be associated with a high degree of nodal activity. These forces will be modified by distance and freight-rate factors. But we will expect that flows with a high degree of mixing demand will be much less affected by direct transportation costs, and much more affected by the nodal properties of the transportation network. Further, we will expect that when freight rates are an insignificant cost relative to the value of goods, the nodal properties of the system will be controlling.

New York competes most effectively for general cargo (high mixture demand) and for the most expensive cargo (low relative transportation costs). This is explained by the principles of the previous paragraph. Nodal concepts should explain very well the shape of the jewelry or fur wholesaling trade, and the location of wholesalers in that trade. They should be nearly irrelevant to the location of the wholesaling of wheat, coal, ore, pig iron, and the like.

Information-Processing Activities: Our causal conceptions imply that nodal activities—the mixing, storing, and legal transfer of goods—generate information needs at nodes. Relatively few of the clerks in the railroad or airline industry travel along with the goods. They are concentrated at terminals. We suspect that the reason international banking is concentrated in New York rather than in Norfolk is that processing legal obligations and guaranteeing payments require more work for a ton of general cargo than for a ton of coal, and that the work is efficiently done in connection with nodal activities. That is, information needs are generated or caused by nodal activities. In turn, the information institutions which grow up around nodes constitute an external effect for mixing activities that take place there. Hence nodal activities would continue to be concentrated at New York even if Norfolk were to become the "natural" node for a new southern industrial region.

Consider, for example, the following advantages listed by a textbook in international trade for locating the export office of a firm in a great port city ("large seaboard city").

1. Better opportunity for making sales to resident and visiting foreign buyers and to export commission houses.

2. Opportunity for close contacts with other export executives, foreign trade organizations, governmental bureaus, and similar sources of up-to-the-minute information.

3. Time and money savings in overseas transportation and communication. Days may be saved in receiving and sending foreign mail, and shipments may be expedited so as to catch certain boats. Frequently, also, money may be saved on transportation costs, because of the company's direct personal contact with the various steamship lines.

4. Greater availability of experienced export personnel, such as assistants, clerks, translators, and so forth.

5. Better opportunity for obtaining credit information, financing sales with large foreign trade banks, hedging exchange, and contacting and entertaining visiting foreigners and returning government officials.[21]

All these advantages are information advantages, but they are listed as advantages of being at a node in the transportation system. The connection between information advantages and nodal location is so obvious to practical men that they advise people to go to ports rather than to international information centers; for all practical purposes, a port is an information center.

The reason for the concentration of information at ports is clearly that each one of the decisions on mixes of flows requires information, and that new information has to be sent out along with the new flow. The main content of the information flow is

---

[21] Paul V. Horn and Henry Garvey, *International Trade Principles and Practices,* 4th ed. (Englewood Cliffs, N.J.: Prentice-Hall, 1958), p. 437.

legal information: offers and orders, letters of credit and applications for exchange permits, manifests for customs inspectors and for insurance companies, receipts and bills of lading for goods received and sent, and the like. Most goods do not flow until someone takes responsibility that they will be paid for at the other end. Information about who will pay, when, where, how, and in what currency, is the main basis for routing and mixing decisions taken at nodes. At the nodes papers will be generated for both senders and receivers of those goods to be mixed at the port: orders and invoices, in all their various legal forms, will be written at ports for goods flows with high mixing demand.

General Strategies for Concepts on Networks

On the basis of this example of concept construction, we can outline the main strategic principles in constructing network-related concepts. First, the flow originating at a certain place is likely to have distinctive characteristics which affect its relation to nodes and nodal activities. The concept of the original mixture demand of a flow, by comparing the homogeneity of the flow at the origin with the mix at the destination, is such an origin variable; it distinguishes, for example, coal from hardware in terms of what happens to them at nodes.

Second, nodes change the origin-determined values of such variables. Such transformations of the origin-determined variables are quite generally proportional to the degree of connectivity, the "order" of the node. That is, the more different segments that meet at a node, the greater its capacity to change the origin-determined value. Thus the mixture demand of a flow from an origin of goods is reduced more by passing through New York than by passing through Philadelphia. The origin variable is thus chosen with respect to what happens to it at nodes, and the "degree of nodality" of the node is measured in terms of the forces thought to transform this variable. If the sizes of the flows are approximately equal, the degree of nodality may be most simply represented by the number of transportation lines that come together at the node.

The conceptions of "nodal activity" are formed by asking what activities concretely have to be performed to change the incoming flows into outgoing flows. In our case these are physical mixing (switching, etc.), temporal reorganization (warehousing, etc.), and legal transfers. These nodal activities should then vary in proportion to (a) the origin-determined value of the variable analyzed, and (b) the "degree of nodality" of the node. The wholesaling, warehousing, and switching activity of a node should, in our case, be greater for goods flows with a high mixing demand, and greater at the great node of New York than at minor nodes like Baltimore.

The information activities of a node will be proportional to the number of separate decisions that have to be made in carrying out the nodal activities. Since in general nodes will be decision-points about paths of goods, information activities will be generally concentrated at nodes. But the number of decisions involved in mixing flows is greater than the number involved in switching one flow to a single corresponding outflow. Hence informational density, especially of a legal and financial sort, will tend to be greatest at nodal points.

The key to the productive use of network-structure variables for explaining social phenomena, then, is the analysis of the network in relation to the activities involved in flows along networks. The main insight to look for is the variable characterizing flows which is most influenced by the degree of nodality or order of a node. This then gives the key to formulating origin-determined variables in the most fruitful way. It also suggests what nodal activities must be involved in changing such a variable. This in turn leads immediately to the kinds of decisions that need to be made and the kinds of information institutions which will be demanded for rationality in such decisions.[22]

---

[22] Because a graph or map of a transportation system is so elegantly simple, and the "order" of nodes so obviously related to activities, there is an intuitive temptation to treat networks by graph theory. This is unsatisfactory because usual graphical properties do not correspond to transformative activity. By the usual graph-theoretical treatment of networks, for instance, a node's being near another node *increases* its connectivity. But in fact it *decreases* its functions as a node, because more of the inputs to it are already transformed. Network properties derive their importance in sociology from their significance for structures of activities, and hence conceptions of network properties (*e.g.,* nodality) should correspond to the sources of activities and not necessarily to formal graphical properties. We lose mathematical elegance but gain theoretical economy by following the strategy outlined above rather than a graph-theory strategy.

Concluding Comments

Abstractly, we can conceive of three main kinds of causal connection between an activity and a place which are likely to have economic consequences: (1) An activity may have a causal connection to inherent characteristics of the place. (Mining is more efficiently carried out in a place with coal deposits; contacts with the deity are easier to carry out in Rome or Mecca.) Such characteristics of a place are usually called resources. (2) An activity may have a causal relation to another activity being carried on in the same place which may facilitate the carrying out of the first or interfere with the carrying out of the first. Such relations are usually called "external effects." (3) An activity may have a causal relation to other activities carried on elsewhere, such that access to the place where the other activity is carried out is a requirement for the place at which the first is carried out (e.g., wholesaling has to have access to manufacturing). We talk about the "accessibility" of a place in this case.

Each of these kinds of causal relations between activities and geography creates ecological causal forces, because any optimizing behavior with respect to activities having such causal relations to places will result in systematic spatial structuring of activities. It is for this reason that spatial concepts of the structure of activities tend to be related to one or another of these abstract forms. The main factors in location theory are resources, external economies, and transportation structure or access. This is because each concept corresponds to a logical form of causal relations between activities and places.

For sociological concept formation, the inherent characteristics of places which bear causal relations to activities (resources) are of little interest. They are the subject matter of the theories of other disciplines, such as geography, or religious history, or technology. Many important ecological processes, however, have to be explained in terms of the development of resources. A good example of a concept related to resources is that of a "frontier in land." A frontier in land is a place which, because of the development of the arts, of transportation, or of markets, has become profitable to exploit with a much more labor-intensive technology than previously. This raises the rate of return on labor on the frontier relative to the older areas of dense settlement, which tends to result in massive migrations, to lead to war for control of the area. It often also decreases the proportion of property income in the total income flow, because, almost by definition, there is a good deal of land to be converted to the new technology, and because labor has to be paid a "migration premium." This equalization effect of frontiers depends, of course, on the concrete parameters of the productive process used there. Such situations obviously create distinct types of ecological movements and produce a spatial distribution of distinct types of social structures, but the concept itself is more properly the property of geography. It takes geographical and technological variables to explain why any particular area is a frontier in land.

Hence most sociological concepts having to do with the structure of activities in space have either the form of statements about external economies (or diseconomies) or statements about access.

The central consideration in constructing conceptual apparatus of the kind involved in external effects is to concentrate on causal interrelations among activities which decline with distance. Some of these are suggested in a general way above, but they reflect my particular interests rather than a general survey of the kinds of causal interrelations among activities. Undoubtedly exchanges of information are less important, relative to physical interrelations of production processes, than is implicit above. Because optimal behavior is so simply related to a monotonic relationship between efficiency and distance, such causal interrelations will provide powerful predictors of the clumping of behavior in space.

The central considerations in constructing concepts of nodes and nodal behavior, in the analysis of networks, consist in maintaining a relatively concrete notion of exactly what activity at nodes one is interested in. Occasionally one may be interested in the shortest path between two points, and "passing through" is the only relevant activity at nodes. This is typically the case in the linear programming of transportation problems. When decision activity, or mixing activity, or some other characteristic of nodal behavior is maintained in the center of attention, it becomes clear that significant properties of nodes do not in general derive from the fact that they are very often to be found on the shortest path between any two points. Then the segments that end in the nodes need to be conceived in terms of how much of the relevant nodal activity they generate (as with the concept of mixing demand above), rather than in terms of how long they are. In general, activity at one node will be related to activity at other nodes, because generally nodal activity, once done, need not be done again.

Envoy

This note is to indicate that this is a conclusion to the book and not to the work. Empirical problems will continue to appear which cannot be formulated precisely by any combinations of the conceptions formulated here. A book has to end, for technical reasons of book publishing and for flexibility in the intellectual lives of readers. Only very great genius can justify a book as long as *War and Peace,* let alone all the social theorizing a man could write.

This book in particular has to end because I am tired of theorizing, and of trying to teach theorizing. It is time for me, and you, to go back to the concrete and particular, and to try to wrestle it into sufficiently general form that it can be conveyed economically to our colleagues and descendants. That may help them, in their turn, to wrestle their concrete and particular into general form.

Edna St. Vincent Millay has formulated the joy of theorizing:

> Euclid alone
> Has looked on Beauty bare. Fortunate they
> Who, though once only and then but far away,
> Have heard her massive sandal set on stone.

But the beauty for me in Euclid is that the general form can be extracted from a raggedly drawn real triangle.

Index

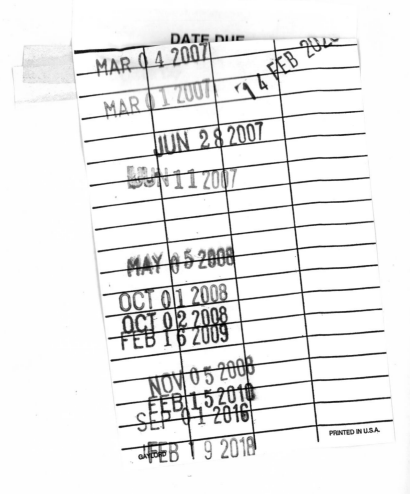